NARRATIVE

Narrative begins with an examination of such standard topics as plot structure, manipulation of time sequence, point of view and narration. Toolan then moves on to consider oral narratives such as stories told to and by children, and in a final chapter explores how narratives in newspapers, law courts and elsewhere carry ideological assumptions with political consequences.

Descriptive linguistic methods are introduced at various stages, explained, and clearly applied, and thought-provoking exercises at the end of each chapter foster increased understanding of the extent to which linguistics can illuminate the study of narrative.

The Author
Michael J. Toolan is Assistant Professor in the Department of English at the University of Washington, Seattle. Previously he taught for six years at the National University of Singapore.

The INTERFACE Series

The Series Editor

Ronald Carter is Professor of Modern English Language at the University of Nottingham and was National Co-ordinator of the 'Language in the National Curriculum' Project (LINC) from 1989 to 1992.

NARRATIVE

A Critical
Linguistic
Introduction

MICHAEL J. TOOLAN

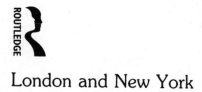

London and New York

First published in 1988 by
Routledge
11 New Fetter Lane, London EC4P 4EE

Simultaneously published in the USA and Canada by
Routledge
29 West 35th Street, New York, NY 10001

Reprinted 1991, 1992, 1994, 1995, 1997

Phototypeset in Linotron Souvenir Light 10/11pt
by Intype, London
Printed in Great Britain by
TJ Press (Padstow) Ltd., Padstow, Cornwall

British Library Cataloguing in Publication Data
A catalogue record for this book is available from the British
Library

Library of Congress Cataloguing in Publication Data
Toolan, Michael J.
    Narrative: a critical linguistic introduction/Michael J. Toolan.
    p. cm.—(Interface)
    Bibliography: p.
    Includes index.
    1. Discourse analysis, Narrative. I. Title. II. Series:
Interface (London, England)
P302.7.T66   1988
401.41—dc19   88–4407

ISBN 0–415–00869–7

Contents

In loving memory of
Margaret 'Mac' McAloren,
who told such stories,
and never told on us.

Series editor's introduction to the Interface series

There have been many books published this century which have been devoted to the interface of language and literary studies. This is the first *series* of books devoted to this area commissioned by a major international publisher; it is the first time a *group* of writers have addressed themselves to issues at the interface of language and literature; and it is the first time an international professional association has worked closely with a publisher to establish such a venture. It is the purpose of this general introduction to the series to outline some of the main guiding principles underlying the books in the series.

The first principle adopted is one of not foreclosing on the many possibilities for the integration of language and literature studies. There are many ways in which the study of language and literature can be combined and many different theoretical, practical and curricular objectives to be realized. Obviously, a close relationship with the aims and methods of descriptive linguistics will play a prominent part, so readers will encounter some detailed analysis of language in places. In keeping with a goal of much work in this field, writers will try to make their analysis sufficiently replicable for other analysts to see how they have arrived at the interpretive decisions they have reached and to allow others to reproduce their methods on the same or on other texts. But linguistic science does not have a monopoly in methodology and description any more than linguists can have sole possession of insights into language and its workings. Some contributors to this series adopt quite rigorous linguistic procedures; others proceed less rigorously but no less revealingly. All are, however, united by a belief that detailed scrutiny of the role of language in literary texts can be mutually enriching to language and literary studies.

Series of books are usually written to an overall formula or design. In the case of the Interface series this was considered to be not entirely appropriate. This is for the reasons given above, but also because, as the first series of its kind, it would be wrong to suggest that there are formulaic modes by which integration can be achieved. The fact that all the books address themselves to the integration of language and literature in any case imparts a natural and organic unity to the series. Thus, some of the books in this series will provide descriptive overviews, others will offer detailed case studies of a particular topic, others will involve single author studies, and some will be more pedagogically oriented.

This variety of design and procedure means that a wide variety of audiences is envisaged for the series as a whole, though, of course, individual books are necessarily quite specifically targeted. The general level of exposition presumes quite advanced students of language and literature. Approximately, this level covers students of English language and literature (though not exclusively English) at senior high-school/upper sixth form level to university students in their first or second year of study. Many of the books in the series are designed to be *used* by students. Some may serve as course books – these will normally contain exercises and suggestions for further work as well as glossaries and graded bibliographies which point the student towards further reading. Some books are also designed to be used by teachers for their own reading and updating, and to supplement courses; in some cases, specific questions of pedagogic theory, teaching procedure and methodology at the interface of language and literature are addressed.

From a pedagogic point of view it is the case in many parts of the world that students focus on literary texts, especially in the mother tongue, before undertaking any formal study of the language. With this fact in mind, contributors to the series have attempted to gloss all new technical terms and to assume on the part of their readers little or no previous knowledge of linguistics or formal language studies. They see no merit in not being detailed and explicit about what they describe in the linguistic properties of texts; but they recognize that formal language study can seem forbidding if it is not properly introduced.

A further characteristic of the series is that the authors engage in a direct relationship with their readers. The overall style of writing is informal and there is above all an attempt to lighten the usual style of academic discourse. In some cases this extends to the way in which notes and guidance for further work are presented. In all cases, the style adopted by authors is judged to be that most appropriate to the mediation of their chosen subject matter.

We now come to two major points of principle which underlie the conceptual scheme for the series. One is that the term 'literature' cannot be defined in isolation from an expression of ideology. In fact, no academic study, and certainly no description of the language of texts, can be neutral and objective, for the sociocultural positioning of the analyst will mean that the description is unavoidably political. Contributors to the series recognize and, in so far as this accords with the aims of each book, attempt to explore the role of ideology at the interface of language and literature. Secondly, most writers also prefer the term 'literatures' to a singular notion of literature. Some replace 'literature' altogether with the neutral term 'text'. It is for this reason that readers will not find exclusive discussions of the literary language of canonical literary texts; instead the linguistic heterogeneity of literature and the permeation of many discourses with what is conventionally thought of as poetic or literary language will be a focus. This means that in places as much space can be devoted to examples of word play in jokes, newspaper editorials, advertisements, historical writing or a popular thriller as to a sonnet by Shakespeare or a passage from Jane Austen. It is also important to stress how the term 'literature' itself is historically variable and how different social and cultural assumptions can condition what is regarded as literature. In this respect the role of linguistic and literary theory is vital. It is an aim of the series to be constantly alert to new developments in the description and theory of texts.

Finally, as series editor, I have to underline the partnership and cooperation of the whole enterprise of the Interface series and acknowledge the advice and assistance received at many stages from the PALA Committee and from Wendy Morris at Routledge. In turn, we are all fortunate to have the benefit of three associate editors with considerable collective depth of experience in this field in different parts of the world: Professor Roger Fowler, Professor Mary Louise Pratt, Professor Michael Halliday. In spite of their own individual orientations, I am sure that all concerned with the series would want to endorse the statement by Roman Jakobson made over twenty-five years ago but which is no less relevant today:

> A linguist deaf to the poetic function of language and a literary scholar indifferent to linguistic problems and unconversant with linguistic methods, are equally flagrant anachronisms.

Michael Toolan's *Narrative: A Critical Linguistic Introduction* is an excellent book with which to launch the Interface series. Narra-

tive is a topic of sustaining interest to linguists and literary critics
which has generated an extensive literature, especially in the
course of the last ten years. Michael Toolan's timely intervention
in this field serves to synthesize the various trends and developments, and to evaluate them critically. His lucid exposition of
issues in narrative theory is matched by a concern for clear
practical analysis and demonstration; the perspective he brings to
the field benefits from his not seeing narrative as an exclusively
'literary' phenomenon but as something integral to many
discourses. Particularly impressive is the breadth and range of his
survey which covers narratives by and for children alongside
canonical narrative texts. His chapter on the politics of narrative
is ground-breaking and illustrates most effectively that structural
description of narrative organization *cannot* be neutral and objective. All those associated with the Interface series hope that
readers find this a useful and insightful book and that they will
feel, as we do, that it gives a substantial impetus to the series.

Preface

Narratives are everywhere, performing countless different functions in human interaction, therefore the area of inquiry of this book must be delimited rather strictly. As the subtitle indicates, this study is intended as a critical introduction, and I hope to be both genuinely critical and genuinely introductory. More narrowly still, this critical introduction is specifically concerned with language-oriented or linguistically-minded perspectives on narrative: ways of looking at narrative that attend systematically to the language of stories, and models of narrative-analysis that focus on the linguistic form of narratives or their linguistically-describable structure. The basic rationale for such an emphasis, in this book as in all the others in the Interface series, is a conviction implicit in the work of all the scholars and theorists and models discussed herein: that systematic analytical attention to the logic and dynamics of language behaviour – an attention that lays stress on coherence, empirical testability, and descriptive and explanatory insight – can and should shed light on any sub-domain or mode of language behaviour. The mode spotlighted here is narrative.

What is it about narrative that makes it such a pervasive and fascinating phenomenon? And how can one begin to answer such a question without entering into a narrative of one's own? The fact is, as my opening sentence announces, narratives are everywhere. Or are potentially so. Everything we do, from making breakfast to making the bed to making love (and notice how those – in any order – make a multi-episode narrative) can be seen, cast, and recounted as a narrative – a narrative with a beginning, middle and end, characters, setting, drama (difficulties or conflicts resolved), suspense, enigma, 'human interest', and a moral. (The moral of the story of my making breakfast this morning could be summarized as 'Don't clean the toaster while cooking porridge.') From such narratives, major and minor, we learn more about ourselves and the world around us. Making, apprehending, and storing a narrative is a making-sense of things which may also help make sense of other things.

Just how pervasive and important oral and written narratives are to our lives becomes startlingly clear if we stop to think of the forms of narrative we depend on as props and inspirations: biographies and autobiographies; historical texts; news stories and features in whatever medium; personal letters and diaries; novels, thrillers and romances; medical case histories; school records; curricula vitae; police reports of 'incidents'; annual performance reviews.

These all seem to me examples of materials that are palpably narrative in form and function. But we might also consider many other preoccupations of our lives which, as a means of assisting comprehension, we 'narrativize'. Law students struggling to grasp and retain the ramifications of the law concerning theft may well, as a sense-making procedure, cast the law(s) as a developing story shaped by attendances to and departures from precedent, and by statutory revisions. And the law in its entirety can be seen as a revisable story: the story is about socially impermissible conduct and the means of redress available when such conduct is exposed. This all-embracing 'story of the law' subsumes an infinite number of more specific episodes (actual and hypothetical), with probable but contestable outcomes: if you do this, in those circumstances, then you may be liable to such and such punishment.

Science, too, may at first glance look very different from narrative. We often think of it as an expanding storehouse of incontestable facts, the hallowed repository of objective knowledge of how things in the world work: a rich but static description, quite remote from 'storytelling'. But that turns out to be mistaken in both theory and practice. In theory, the emphasis on scientific enquiry as an ongoing revisable narrative (with revisions made on the rational grounds that the revised account brings enhanced descriptive or explanatory power, and greater generalizability) is now commonplace. And in practice, too, one has only to think of how science is taught in schools to see the centrality of narrative to understanding.

For instance, the concepts of fuel, energy and work might be taught in the primary school by telling stories about eating breakfast before running around, and putting fuel in the car before going on a long trip. If the child doesn't get the point of these stories, and see the logical connections between the stages within each story as well as the analogical parallels across the stories, she won't begin to understand the concepts involved. At secondary school the presentation may be less informal and more theorized, but narrative methods persist. Any laboratory exercise in Physics, Chemistry or Biology, for example, is a planned and guided story in which the child is an essential participant. Testing for the hydrogen that is released when copper filings are added to sulphuric acid is, for teacher and lab assistant, an old, old story (ah, they don't make them like that any more!). But it's a new story, a narrative of enforced personal experience if you like, for the child, the moral of which is to be learned. And afterwards, in the passive voice style that tries to keep human interest out of the picture, she or he must 'write up' the experiment.

If the above is a reminder that narrative is a mode that, directly or more indirectly, may inform almost every aspect of human activity, I must now stress that the following chapters are concerned almost entirely with narratives in a narrower sense – literary narratives, folktales, stories by and for children, spoken narratives arising out of interviews and conversations with adults and teenagers, and stories in the media. There are linguistic similarities between these types of stories which I hope, rather than leading to a boring sameness, will be thought-provoking, and linguistic differences, too, which are yet not so great as to make for unmanageable heterogeneity.

The best way to read this book is to set it aside now – temporarily, that is, until you have read (some of) the narratives around which the discussion and application of theories in the early chapters will revolve. The reader is urged to make (or refresh) his or her acquaintance with Joyce's stories entitled 'Eveline' and 'The Dead', from his *Dubliners* collection; Faulkner's 'That Evening Sun' and 'Barn Burning'; Katherine Mansfield's 'Bliss'; and Nabokov's novel, *Pnin*. Many other narratives, short and long, oral and written, literary and nonliterary, will be discussed in the course of the book. But I have developed many of the presentations, in the earlier and more directly literary-oriented chapters, in relation to those few celebrated stories cited above.

A linguistic introduction can hardly avoid the occasional use of more technical terms that may at first seem off-putting to those who have taken no linguistics courses. I have tried to keep specialist jargon to a minimum, usually explaining terms as the discussion proceeds. On other occasions I have tagged the first use of strange linguistic terms with '(see glossary)', to indicate that more information on what, for example, 'paradigmatic' means is presented in the glossary at the back of the book.

Acknowledgments

Nearly all the work on this book was done while I was a member of the Department of English Language and Literature of the National University of Singapore, and much of the material presented here was first used in courses I taught there on Stylistics and Narrative Structures. I owe a great deal to very many of my former colleagues and students, who in one way or another made me think (or urged me to). From a longer list I must mention David Birch, David Butt, Tony Hung, Thiru Kandiah, Anneliese Kramer-Dahl, Victor Li, K. P. Mohanan, Brian Ridge, and Betty Samraj. I should especially mention the stimulating influence of Rukmini Bhaya Nair, with whom I had the pleasure of team-teaching the Narrative Structures course: many of the better ideas in this book have come from her. I should also like to thank James Thorne and Norman Macleod, of the University of Edinburgh, who first sparked my interest in stylistics; Talbot Taylor, now of the College of William and Mary, Williamsburg, respected analyst of stylisticians' more woolly and wishful thinking; and Roy Harris, who supervised my doctoral thesis at Oxford and, more than anyone else, has encouraged me to develop a properly critical approach to linguistic theorizing. I am most grateful to Ms Gouri Uppal for permitting me to reproduce conversational data from her National University of Singapore MA thesis (1984) on 'Narratives in Conversation'.

But my greatest debt of all is to Ronald Carter, of the University of Nottingham, Editor of the Interface series: not only for entrusting this project to me and for making many invaluable suggestions that have improved the book, but also more broadly for his continued interest in my work. I know I am only one of many working in the field of literary linguistics for whom Ron's active and generous support has made all the difference, personally and intellectually.

Finally, I owe an immense debt, particularly for their tolerance of the absenteeism and tetchiness that the writing deadline engendered, to Julianne Statham and our children, Roisin and Patrick. Julianne's suggestions as to the rewriting of those passages I had managed to make impenetrable to ordinary intelligent readers were immensely useful. And but for Roisin, Chapter 6 probably would not have been written.

1 Preliminary orientations

What is narrative? What do we mean by 'narrative structure'? What are the intentions and emphases behind using this term 'structure' in relation to narrative study? Where does a linguistic approach come in, and how helpful can it really be? And why are such topics worth pursuing in an academic course? The following are working notes on these and other basic issues, which should at least indicate the terrain to be covered, and why it is felt to be significant.

Commentators sometimes begin by stating the truism that any tale involves a teller, and that therefore narrative study must analyse two basic components: the tale and the teller. But as much could be said of any speech event – there is always inherently a speaker, separate from what is spoken. What makes narrative different here, especially if it is a literary or extended spoken one, is that the teller is often particularly *noticeable*. Tellers of long narratives are often surprisingly present and perceptible even as they unfold a tale that ostensibly draws all our attention to some *other* individual or individuals. We often feel our attention divided between two objects of interest: the individuals and events in the story itself, and the individual telling all this. Thus when we read Coleridge's 'Rime of the Ancient Mariner' or Brontë's *Wuthering Heights* or listen to the rambling yarns of some 'character' in the local pub, part of the experience is our 'reading' of the character of the teller: the returned mariner himself, Lockwood, old Charlie. Already the literary examples involve an enriching complication. In both texts mentioned, there is more than one teller: besides the mariner, for instance, is a 'higher' teller who writes 'It is an ancient Mariner/And he stoppeth one of three' and so on. But I will postpone handling such complications until later, and want to concentrate here on narrative's dual foci, teller and tale.

The possibility of achieving this effect of divided attention exploits a basic characteristic of narrative. Narrative typically is a recounting of things spatiotemporally distant: here's the present teller, there's the distant topic – hence the sense of gap. This can be represented diagrammatically thus:

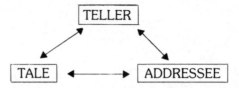

But since the present teller is the access to the distant topic, there is a sense, too, in which narrative entails making what is distant and absent uncommonly present: a merging rather than a division. Diagrammatically this merging-cum-immediacy might look like this:

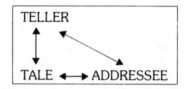

However, since tellers can become intensely absorbed in their self-generated sense of the distant topic they are relating, addressees sometimes have the impression that the teller has withdrawn from them, has taken leave, so as to be more fully involved in the removed scene. This third type of relation between tale, teller, and addressee (a merging-cum-withdrawal) might be cast thus:

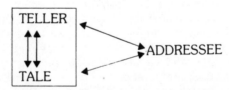

We will find that these different abstract representations are the bases of quite distinct ways of telling narratives.

Hawthorn (1985) broaches these same issues, taking a painting by Millais, *The Boyhood of Raleigh*, as capturing something central to narrative. In the painting an old seaman, with his back to the viewer, appears to be addressing two young boys who are evidently fascinated and absorbed by what he tells them. The old man is pointing with his arm out to sea, but the boys' eyes are on the *man*, not the gesturing arm or any distant scene it may be designating.

> Narrative focuses our attention on to a story, a sequence of events, through the direct mediation of a 'telling' which we both stare at and through, which is at once central and peripheral to the experience of the story, both absent and present in the consciousness of those being told the story. Like the two young boys we stare at the 'telling' while our minds are fixed upon what that telling points towards. We look at the pointing arm but our minds are fixed upon what is pointed at. (Hawthorn, 1985: vii)

One of the distinctive characteristics of narrative concerns its necessary source, the narrator. We stare at the narrator rather than interacting with him as we would if we were in conversation with him; and, in literary narratives especially, that narrator is often 'dehumanized', attended to merely as a disembodied voice.

Hawthorn also observes that contemporary interest in narrative is far from purely literary critical:

> We live in a world increasingly dominated – and characterized – by the telling of stories; by anonymous communication, by messages notable for what has been termed 'agency deletion', and by disseminated but disguised authorities and authoritarianism. (Hawthorn, 1985: x)

This brings us to another important asset of narrators: narrators are typically *trusted* by their addresses. In seeking and being granted rights to a lengthy verbal contribution ('OK, go ahead, let's hear it'/'OK, I'll give this story/novel a try') narrators assert their authority to tell, to take up the role of knower, or entertainer, or producer, in relation to the addressees' adopted role of learner or consumer. To narrate is to make a bid for a kind of power. Sometimes the narratives told crucially affect our lives: those told by journalists, politicians, employers assessing our performance in annual reviews, as well as those of friends, enemies, parents, siblings, children – in short, all which originate from those who have power, authority or influence over us.

If the authority of the narrator and his narrative is one area of controversy, a related one concerns the *interpretation* or interpretability of narratives. Even before we attempt a working definition of narratives, it's clear that these are typically 'cut off' from surrounding **context** and **co-text** [see glossary] in some ways. They often do stand alone, not embedded in larger frames, without any accompanying information about the author or the intended audience: they're just 'there', it seems, like a pot someone has made, and you can take them or leave them. So some of the normal constraints or controls over how we interpret discourse, or make sense of it, seem to be removed. We don't seem always to *have* to relate narratives to their authors, or socio-historical backgrounds.

We can begin to define narrative by noting and inspecting some of its typical characteristics:

1 A degree of artificial fabrication or constructedness not usually apparent in spontaneous conversation. Narrative is 'worked upon'. Sequence, emphasis and pace are usually planned (even in oral narrative, when there has been some rehearsal – previous performance – of it). But then as much could be said of, for example, elaborate descriptions of things, prayers, scholarly articles.

2 A degree of *pre*fabrication. In other words, narratives often seem to have bits we have seen or heard, or think we have seen or heard, before (recurrent chunks far larger than the recurrent chunks we call words). One Mills and Boon heroine or hero seems much like another – and some degree of typicality seems to apply to heroes and heroines in more elevated fictions too, such as nineteenth-century British novels. Major characters in the novels of Dickens, Eliot, Hardy, etc., seem to be thwarted (for a time at least) in roughly comparable ways. And the kinds of things people do in narratives (not just being born, and dying, but falling in love, going on long quests, coming to discover more about themselves or those around them) seem to repeat themselves over and over again – with important variations, of course. Again, prefabrication seems common in various types of writing and visual spectacle besides narrative, although the kinds of things mentioned above seem particularly to be prefabricated units of narrative.

3 Narratives typically seem to have a 'trajectory'. They usually go somewhere, and are expected to go somewhere, with some sort of development and even a resolution, or conclusion, provided. We expect them to have beginnings, middles, and

ends (as Aristotle stipulated in his *Art of Poetry*). Consider the concluding words of children's stories:

And they all lived happily *ever* after;
since then, the dragon has never been seen again . . .

and notice the finality and permanence conveyed by the *ever/never* pair. Or consider the common story-reader's exit-line

And that is the end of the story.

which has near-identical counterparts in the closing sequences of radio and television news bulletins. All these examples mark this attention to the expectation of closure and finality, itself just one aspect of the broader underlying expectation of **narrative trajectory**.

4 Narratives have to have a teller, and that teller, no matter how backgrounded or remote or 'invisible', is always important. In this respect, despite its special characteristics, narrative is language communication like any other, requiring a speaker and some sort of addressee.

5 Narratives are richly exploitative of that design feature of language called **displacement** (the ability of human language to be used to refer to things or events that are removed, in space or time, from either speaker or addressee). In this respect they contrast sharply with such modes as commentary or description. Narratives involve the recall of happenings that may be not merely spatially, but, more crucially, *temporally* remote from the teller and his audience. Compare our practices with those of the honeybee, whose tail-wagging dance overcomes spatial displacement, in that it communicates about distant sources of nectar, but cannot encompass temporal displacement. Accordingly, the honeybee's tail-wagging is no proper narrative in our sense, but merely a kind of reflex observation. As Roy Harris has remarked

Bees do not regale one another with reminiscences of the nectar they found last week, nor discuss together the nectar they might find tomorrow. (Harris, 1981: 158)

If the above are some characteristics of narrative, they still do not get us much further in the task of *defining* narrative. But the idea that narratives are texts with both a story and a storyteller may be a start. We must beware of problems when we attempt to elaborate this idea, however. Thus when Scholes and Kellogg define narrative as

> all those literary works which are distinguished by two charac-teristics: the presence of a story and a storyteller. (Scholes and Kellogg, 1966: 4)

they introduce (besides the exclusionary term 'literary') the diffi-cult and controversial idea of 'presence'. They do so in order to make a distinction between narrative and drama (story *without* a storyteller). But we shall find storyteller presence, in narratives, to be a significantly variable feature: some tellers are very present and quite intrusive; others are fleetingly so, enigmatic, removed. Furthermore, we might argue that behind any drama stands an invisible implied teller. We need to keep in mind that any tale, like any stretch of language or text, implies and requires a speaker, however removed.

In keeping with this broader view is Traugott and Pratt's defi-nition of *narration* as

> essentially a way of linguistically representing past experience, whether real or imagined. (Traugott and Pratt, 1980: 248)

The emphasis on 'representation of past experience' is important, and is one reason for our sense of the detachment, 'cut-offness', of narratives (which some theorists insist upon to the extent of denying the groundedness of narrative in an external world and author). And here, 'past experience' needs to be interpreted broadly: even if the narrative is futuristic science fiction, or a novel with future reference, or a novel in the present tense, the reader encounters and grasps it as 'events that have already happened'.

If the above reflections seem too arid, then Roland Barthes' memorable celebration of the impact of narratives on our lives may be an appropriate corrective:

> Able to be carried by articulated language, spoken or written, fixed or moving images, gestures, and the ordered mixture of all these substances; narrative is present in myth, legend, fable, tale, novella, epic, history, tragedy, drama, comedy, mime, painting, stained glass windows, cinema, comics, news items, conversation . . . [and] narrative is present in every age, in every place, in every society . . . Caring nothing for the division between good and bad literature, narrative is international,

transhistorical, transcultural: it is simply there, like life itself. (Barthes, 1977: 79)

Barthes goes on to say that although all-pervasive, narrative is still analyzable, and can be understood in a systematic way. It is with this emphasis on systematicity that we will proceed.

A first attempt at a minimalist definition of narrative might be:

1 a perceived sequence of non-randomly connected events.

Note that this definition recognizes that a narrative is a *sequence* of events. But **event** itself is really a complex term, presupposing that there is some recognized state or set of conditions, and that *something happens*, causing a change to that state. Note also that my emphasis on 'non-random connectedness' means that a pure *collage* of described events, even given in sequence, doesn't count as a narrative. For example, if each of us in turn supplies a one-paragraph description of something or other, and we then paste these paragraphs together, they won't count as a narrative unless we come to *perceive* a non-random connection. And by 'non-random connection' I mean a connectedness that is taken to be motivated and significant. This curious transitional area between sequential description and *consequential* description is one of the bases for the fun of a familiar party game in which people around a table take turns to write a line of a 'story', the other lines of which are supplied, in secret, by the other participants.

The important role of 'change of state' has been celebrated in the more linguistic term **transformation** by the French structuralist Tzvetan Todorov (1977: 233):

The simple relation of successive facts does not constitute a narrative: these facts must be organized, which is to say, ultimately, that they must have elements in common. But if all the elements are in common, there is no longer a narrative, for there is no longer anything to recount. Now, transformation represents precisely a synthesis of differences and resemblance, it links two facts without their being able to be identified.

Notice also that my definition suggests that consequence is not so much 'given' as 'perceived': narrative depends on the addressee *seeing it* as narrative – the circularity here seems inescapable. While most of us would agree that the traditional novel is a narrative, there can be legitimate disagreement as to the status, as narrative, of less familiar and complex structures. For example, imagine you enter a cartoonist's studio and find three frames, on separate pieces of paper, on his desk. They have quite different characters, settings, furniture, etc., and seem to be about quite unrelated topics. They seem to be rough drafts, because on the corner of one is a coffee-ring, where the cartoonist has carelessly left a cup, and on the second one there's a chilli stain in the top corner, while the third has some cigarette ash *and* a coffee ring on it! You think you see a narrative before you – though the cartoonist hotly denies this!

That example, however whimsical, tries to touch on a fundamental but problematic feature of narrative study. Perceiving nonrandom connectedness in a sequence of events is the prerogative of the addressee: it is idle for anyone else (e.g., a teller) to insist that here is a narrative if the addressee just doesn't see it as one. In this respect at least, the ultimate authority for ratifying a text as a narrative rests not with the teller but with the perceiver/ addressee.

But in practice we expect and demand much more complex connectedness, non-randomness, and sequentiality in the events of narratives. In the terms first highlighted by Aristotle, we expect **ends** as well as **beginnings** and **middles** (something not commented upon in the quotation from Todorov above). In more twentieth-century terminology, we expect complex **motivations** and **resolutions** – even in quite 'simple' tales such as folk tales. Thus Benjamin Colby has written:

> Folk narrative in its simplest form is the verbal description of one or more concern-causing events and of the way in which the concern is eliminated or diminished. (Colby, 1970: 177)

As we shall see in the next chapter, this definition is similar to that of the pathbreaking Russian narratologist Vladimir Propp. Propp studied the overarching structure of the Russian fairytale, identifying it as one in which an initial state of equilibrium is disturbed by various forces of turbulence. This turbulence brings disequilibrium and upheaval before some sort of action (perhaps an intervention) leads to the restoration of a modified version of the original equilibrium.

Note also that in my skeletal definition, I have emphasized the role of the perceiver, but not that of an independent teller. This is because the two roles are not entirely separate. I have already suggested that the activity of perceiving consequential relatedness of states is the enabling condition for narrative: now we might in addition speculate that it is an activity necessarily to be performed by all tellers and addressees, at least if they *intend* to be tellers or addressees.

In the next three chapters we shall look at some of the most influential linguistically-informed discussions of narrative as verbal art: written or oral, traditional and collective or innovative and individual. These chapters thus review what has been suggested about the **poetics** of narrative. By this I mean the relatively abstract and theoretical commentary on the more systematic and recurrent aspects of stories and storytelling. The poetics of any type of verbal performance (narratives, sonnets, whatever) is the study of the ground rules that shape all the productions within that type. And most of these ground rules are not logical require-ments at all, but conventional norms of narrative or sonnet production.

Some warnings are in order concerning the way students of narrative poetics have split the subject of study into two – and more recently *three!* – major domains or levels of inquiry. Thus the early Russian formalists (Propp, Tomashevsky, etc.) spoke of **fabula** and **sjuzhet**, roughly equivalent to the more recent French (Benveniste, Barthes) terms **histoire** and **discours**. These are roughly equivalent in turn to Chatman's English terms, **story** and **discourse**. By the first term of each of these pairs is meant a basic description of the fundamental events of a story, in their natural chronological order, with an accompanying and equally skeletal inventory of the roles of the characters in that story.

A *fabula* [story] is a series of logically and chronologically related events that are caused or experienced by actors. (Bal, 1985: 5)

This is the level at which we may expect the possibility of 'total transfer' from one medium to another: everything at the level of story in, say, *Great Expectations*, can and perhaps should appear as easily in a film or cartoon version, or a ballet, as in the original written version. It may be worth applying the linguistic terms **syntagmatic** and **paradigmatic** here (see glossary). In a story outline all the events and characters are presented synoptically, with the minimum attention to, for example, complexities of sequence, as if we're getting the paradigmatic raw materials or ingredients; the syntagmatic dimension – the linear distribution of event and character presentation, disclosure, elaboration, and so on – is severely attenuated.

Above I used the term 'version' to refer to actual cinematic or dance **realizations** of the core story of *Great Expectations*. And 'version' is as good a word as any to refer to the business of distinctive and creative *working on* a story to produce the discourse we actually encounter. In other words, *sjuzhet* or *discours* roughly denotes all the techniques that authors bring to bear in their varying manner of presentation of the basic story. As far as literary-minded people are concerned, *discourse* is much the more interesting area of narrative poetics. *Story* seems to focus on the pre-artistic, genre- and convention-bound basic event-and-character patterns of narrative, with scarcely any room for evaluative contrasts or discriminations – a level at which authorship seems an irrelevant concern. *Discourse* looks at the artistic and individualized working with and around the genres, the conventions, the basic story patterns, in the distinctive styles, voices, or manners of different authors.

For good or ill – as will become clear, I have my doubts! – the above binary picture (of *histoire* v. *discours*, or story *v.* discourse) has in recent discussions been complicated by the argument that we need to posit three levels, not two. As I understand it, this rearrangement does not involve adjustment of both the binary categories outlined above, but rather is simply a bifurcation of the second one, discourse. In the accounts of poetics of Genette (1980), and in the two books I will recommend as supporting textbooks in this area (Bal, 1985 and Rimmon-Kenan, 1983), the business of technical manipulation and presentation of the basic story is said to involve two levels. That is to say, if we think of *histoire*/story as level 1 of analysis, then within discourse we have

2 the level of text, at which decisions about the sequencing of events, the time/space spent presenting them, the sense of (changing) rhythm and pace in the discourse, together with choices as to just how (with what detail, and in what order) the particularity of the various characters is to be presented, together also with choices as to whose perspective or viewpoint will be adopted as the lens through which particular events or descriptions or characters are seen and reported (the business of **focalization**), are all made, and

3 the level of narration, at which the relations between the

posited narrator and the narrative she tells are probed (an obvious contrast is that between a stretch of narrative embedded within a novel and told by a character, on the one hand, and a narrative told as if by a detached, external and omniscient onlooker, on the other); this is also the level at which speech presentation (the mimetic effects of pure dialogue, the deliberate ambiguities of free indirect discourse) is analyzed.

This distinction between what we will call text and narration comes principally from Bal. It amounts to an attempt to separate a layer at which a narrative agent *relates* the text from other aspects of text (the level at which choices are made over how the story is *presented*). So text presents story in a certain manner, and in the narration an agent relates that presentation. However, this latter separation is still a source of controversy, and we may well want to question this confident separation of narration from presentation. Two-level analysts, who find the story/discourse bifurcation complicated enough, will always counter with the claim that types of narration, and strategies of speech and thought-presentation *are* aspects of the manner of presentation, part of a single domain of *discourse*.

These complex arguments will be returned to, but for now the chief thing to keep in mind is the disparity in terminology used. Latterly, in place of:

STORY   –   DISCOURSE

we have:

STORY   –   TEXT   –   NARRATION (as in Rimmon-
                                                    Kenan, 1983)

with the added complication that these three terms are translated in Bal (1985) as, respectively:

FABULA – STORY – TEXT

I shall try to stick to the Rimmon-Kenan terms wherever possible, even though I will also make frequent reference to the Bal book.

② Basic story structure

2.1 Story/*Fabula*/*Histoire*

As indicated at the close of the previous chapter, narrative poeticians have long worked with a theoretical division of their subject-matter into the domains of story (or *fabula*, or *histoire*) and discourse (or *sjuzhet*, or *discours*). Story is the basic unshaped story material, and (with qualifications) comprises events, characters and settings. The relations between these three are remarkably variable, but examples of all three are nearly always present in narrative, although it is possible to dispense with any explicit establishing of setting. Simply within the novel canon, compare the relative emphasis on event in an adventure novel with the relative emphasis on character in a Henry James novel, and (frequently) the relative emphasis on setting in an historical novel. If events, characters and settings are all important elements of story, the first of these has nevertheless always been treated as pre-eminent and foundational by theorists of plot. For many theorists, the expressions 'basic story structure' and 'event structure' seem virtually synonymous. And a similar preoccupation with events and event structure, especially to the neglect of character, will be apparent throughout this chapter. Character and setting will be examined, however (not too belatedly, I hope), in Chapter 4.

In order to discuss and describe story we have to adopt a medium of communication such as language. But it should be clear that the notion of unshaped, uncrafted, 'unaestheticized' story, underlying every organized, shaped narrative we encounter, is one that tends to treat the basic stuff of narrative as medium-independent. Terminology introduced by Chomsky (1957; 1965) to explain syntactic relations between simple sentences and more complex ones, and how the latter are derived from the former, may be of some use here. Story is a chronologically-ordered **deep structure** (see glossary) representation of all the primary and essential information concerning characters, events and settings, without which the narrative would not be well formed. The important point here is that this representation, or 'bald version', is *abstract but structured*. We may then think of the teller of a narrative (the creative artist, the eye-witness, or whoever) as generating the 'finished product', the presented discourse.

Here the Chomskyan analogy is weakest, since clearly most narrative transformations are not so much transformations as elaborations and enrichments, a fleshing-out of the basic story stuff. Reordering transformations, however, in which events which would happen in the real world in a particular sequence ABCD are reordered so that they are encountered in the discourse in the order BACD, are very widespread. An extreme form of reordering transformation, in which crucial explanatory information is withheld until the very end of a narrative, is common in crime and detective fiction, where significant information and clues, known to the author and sometimes even the fictional detective whose enquiries are portrayed, are withheld from the reader. Such withheld information is common in 'high' fiction, too: consider the withheld information as to who Pip's benefactor is in *Great Expectations*, or as to who Esther's parents are in *Bleak House*.

There is another linguistic analogy besides the Chomskyan one cited above that is often invoked in the discussion of relations between story as an abstract level, and particular narratives as actual and distinct texts. The analogy is with the broad division of linguistic analysis of the sounds of a language into two domains or levels, the phonological and the phonetic. **Phonology** is the study of the sound-system of a language at a relatively abstract level, as a system with its own internal logic, characterized by rules and principles governing what kinds of sounds are produced, and recognized, in what sequences, at the level of actual speech. **Phonetics**, by contrast, is the study of actual speech sounds, in all their slight acoustic or auditory variation. Sustaining this division of the study of speech sounds is the thesis that phonology identifies the abstract system of 'ideal' sounds of a language while phonetics scrutinizes the actually-produced tokens of each ideal type.

The flourishing of phonology as a coherent analytical enterprise, together with the very notion of 'basic story' itself, have given rise to claims to the effect that there is an abstract level of story from which all concrete narratives, embellished by variations of content, are derived. But this is untenable. We can begin with the banal bedrock observation that all narratives involve the report of some state and some change or changes to that state. But even as we attempt to specify the allegedly core events and characters of stories (the core 'types' of which events and characters in particular narratives are 'tokens') we find that *content* still remains. It has not and cannot be wholly removed. If we look at what Vladimir Propp (the pioneer Russian analyst of story structure) and others actually did we will find that, in search of basic story structure, they started – inevitably – with the rich performed narrative, and tried to 'sift through' that material, discarding all but the most basic patterns. And yet even those patterns – as we shall see with Propp – are quite clearly at best (as he conceded) *genre-specific*, but at worst corpus-specific. We need to see the implications of saying that certain identified patterns in fact hold only for a particular genre, or, more limitedly, hold only for the small collection of narratives actually analyzed. But let us turn now to the detail of Propp's theory of story structure.

2.2   Propp's morphology of the Russian fairytale

The starting point of Propp's famous study (Propp, 1968; originally published in Russian in 1928) would seem to be very much the sort of minimalist definition of narrative introduced in Chapter 1 – a text in which there is recounted a change from one state to a modified state. As noted earlier, we can label the actual change of state an 'event'. Thus 'event', or 'change of state', is the key and fundamental of narrative. And Propp's **morphology** of the Russian fairytale is basically an inventory of all and only the fundamental events (which he calls **functions**) that he identifies in his corpus, which comprises 115 Russian fairytales.

In other words, Propp analyzed his collection of fairytales, looking particularly for recurring elements or features (**constants**), and random or unpredictable ones (**variables**). He concluded that while the characters or personages of the tales might superficially be quite variable, yet their functions in the tales, the significance of their actions as viewed from the point of view of the story's development, were relatively constant and predictable. Both the number *and sequence* of the functions are asserted to be fixed: there are just 31 functions, and they always appear in the same sequence.

> Functions of characters serve as stable, constant elements in a tale, independent of how and by whom they are fulfilled. They constitute the fundamental components of a tale. (Propp, 1968; 21)

Here, for convenience in subsequent analytical tasks, is a full list of Propp's set of 31 key, fairytale-developing actions (functions), which bring sequential changes to a specified initial situation:

1 One of the members of a family absents himself from home. (An extreme exponent of this function of 'absenting' is where the parents have died!)
2 An interdiction is addressed to the hero.
3 The interdiction is violated.
4 The villain makes an attempt at reconnaissance.
5 The villain receives information about his victim.
6 The villain attempts to deceive his victim in order to take possession of him or of his belongings.
7 The victim submits to deception and thereby unwittingly helps his enemy.
8 The villain causes harm or injury to a member of a family (defined as 'villainy').
8a One member of a family either lacks something or desires to have something (defined as 'lack').
9 Misfortune or lack is made known; the hero is approached with a request or command; he is allowed to go or he is despatched.
10 The seeker agrees to or decides upon counteraction.
11 The hero leaves home.
12 The hero is tested, interrogated, attacked, etc., which prepares the way for his receiving either a magical agent or helper.
13 The hero reacts to the actions of the future donor.
14 The hero acquires the use of a magical agent.
15 The hero is transferred, delivered, or led to the whereabouts of an object of search.
16 The hero and the villain join in direct combat.
17 The hero is branded.
18 The villain is defeated.
19 The initial misfortune or lack is liquidated.
20 The hero returns.

21 The hero is pursued.
22 The rescue of the hero from pursuit.
23 The hero, unrecognized, arrives home or in another country.
24 A false hero presents unfounded claims.
25 A difficult task is proposed to the hero.
26 The task is resolved.
27 The hero is recognized.
28 The false hero or villain is exposed.
29 The hero is given a new appearance.
30 The villain is punished.
31 The hero is married and ascends the throne.

Propp notes some internal patterning within this sequence. Certain functions, for example, clearly go together as pairs, such as prohibition and violation (2 and 3), struggle and victory (16 and 18), and pursuit and deliverance (21 and 22). And clusters of functions are grouped under general headings. Thus functions 1–7 are potential realizations of the **preparation**, 8–10 are the **complication**, and later general groups include transference, struggle, return, and recognition.

In addition to the 31 functions, Propp identifies 7 basic character types or roles:

villain	dispatcher
donor/provider	helper
hero (seeker	princess (+ father)
or victim)	false hero

Note that an actual character may fill more than one character role (for example, some individual in the tale may be both villain and false hero) and of course one role might be filled by several individuals (there could be several people functioning as helper or villain). Demonstrating the application of this descriptive apparatus to his corpus of stories in meticulous detail, Propp concludes:

> Morphologically, a tale . . . may be termed any development proceeding from villainy . . . or a lack . . ., through intermediary functions to marriage . . . or to other functions employed as a denouement. Terminal functions are at times a reward . . . a gain or in general the liquidation of misfortune . . . an escape from pursuit . . . etc. Each new act of villainy, each new lack creates a new move. One tale may have several moves, and when analyzing a text, one must first of all determine the number of moves of which it consists.

One move may directly follow another, but they may also interweave; a development which has begun pauses, and a new move is inserted. (Propp, 1968: 92)

I will not spend time summarizing just how Propp applies this morphology to the particular tales in his corpus. The main purpose here is to outline what Propp means by 'function', 'role', 'move', and so on, so that we can identify similar elements in other stories. And the striking thing is that certain fictions rather remote from the Russian fairytale do seem to lend themselves to Proppian analysis without too much strain (see the 'notes and exercises' section at the end of this chapter).

The following story written by a 7-year-old child, with Proppian functions appended on the left may serve to demonstrate how easily and appropriately Propp's grammar can fit simple tales.

Initial situation	1 Once upon a time there was a bunny named Benjie
+ magical agent	2 and she had magic powers.
	3 One day she was walking in the woods and a
Departure	
	4 bunny boy appeared
Translation	5 and they went together for a walk
Reconnaissance	6 and a man appeared with a big net
	7 and he got the two bunnies and went in a big ship.
Villainy	8 Poor bunnies.
	9 They were caught now.
Struggle	10 But right then the girl bunny tripped the man
Villainy nullified	11 and they got free once again.
Reward	12 So the boy bunny thanked the girl bunny for saving him.
	13 The boy bunny asked the girl bunny to marry him
?Equilibrium (Wedding)	14 and she said yes.
	15 So they had six bunny babies
	16 and they lived happily ever after. (text and analysis from King and Rentel, 1982. See Christie et al, 1984)

If Propp's schema fits the above story with eloquent ease, we might now put it to work on a far more complex tale, that of

'Eveline', from Joyce's *Dubliners* collection. (I will be discussing this story in future chapters in relation to a number of issues.) Propp's very first function seems almost uncannily relevant:

One of the members of a family absents [himself] from home.

Relevant, but not applicable mechanically. We might say, for instance, that the 'action' of 'Eveline' is a dramatization (chiefly a mental dramatization) of a stage *within* that first function:

One of the members of a family reconsiders a decision to absent herself from home.

Where Propp's fairytales proceed through developmental actions, 'Eveline' is very largely a mental projection, both forward to possible future events and backward to actual past ones: remembered before-events and imagined after-events. Notice how her opening revery, up to sentence 24, is a conspectual review of past circumstances as they impinge on Eveline's present situation. As Propp notes, a story has to begin with an initial situation, one into which an element of disequilibrium is introduced by the function of absentiation or another of the seven preparatory functions. But in 'Eveline', it is the situation itself that is extensively dwelt upon, and none of the first 23 sentences appears to constitute a narrative-propelling function. Nor does this tendency lapse with sentence 24. It is just that with sentence 24 comes confirmation that introspective indirect discourse – the processes of thinking *about* living out a narrative of functional departure from the current and continuing situation – is the chief narrative mode adopted in this story (a mode I will discuss further in Chapter 4). But the emphasis on elaboration of the multiple habitual circumstances that comprise the initial situation, mere prologue to a story, remains.

However, we can do some reconstruction of a simple developmental story when Eveline's thoughts turn to Frank. She meets him, is taken out by him, at first finds this 'an excitement' but later begins to like him. All of that, one imagines, would count as simply one function in Proppian terms – 'The heroine meets with a (benevolent?) stranger.' Eveline's 'liking' for Frank seems related, not wholly ironically perhaps, to the latter's implied story-tellings, which themselves form a skeletal story: He had started as a deck boy, had sailed through the Straits of Magellan, had fallen on his feet in Buenos Aires, and had come to the old country for a holiday.

If the heroine's association with Frank is a first function, the second and third must be her father's discovery of that association and interdiction of its continuance: '[he] had forbidden her to have anything to say to him'. But subsequently (function 4?) 'she had to meet her lover secretly', so that now (function 5?) she was to go away with him to Buenos Aires to be his wife.

At this point in the text it seems that the gap between the story outlined in the two paragraphs above and the character's current reflections closes, for the next series of thoughts that are reported, incidents of family life (centred on her mother) both happy and grim, are the direct trigger of the 'sudden impulse of terror' she feels – a psychological impulse to act ('Escape! She must escape!') quite as real and compelling as an encounter with any forest-dwelling villain. Of course in this psychological story impulses are not pure and simple, but complex and clashing – a counter-impulse is to stay, keep her promise to her mother, and submit to a 'life of commonplace sacrifices'. The final paragraphs are all about that clash of impulses, the 'maze of distress' that renders her helpless and inert, unable to respond in any way to Frank's summons.

But while in one light Eveline's refusal to leave at the story's close can be designated as helpless failure, as an abortive move or episode or, worse, a succumbing to the villainy of oppression at home and at work, in another light, with Frank as the villain, her rejection of him may be viewed as 'manipulation resisted', as a positive act of sisterhood uniting Eveline with her mother. We shall find the pattern of these contrary readings neatly highlighted by Greimas' typology of character roles (which he calls *actants*), to be discussed in Chapter 4.

But now, and not for the last time, we may want to raise the question of reductivism. Is not Propp's bold anatomy of fairytales a procedure which hopelessly distorts, since it sets aside the important and necessary cultural context in which these tales occur, and also ignores the varying details of stories? Propp might retort to this that a structuralist/morphological approach *has* to 'reduce', and quite explicitly sets out to shear off the detail, the non-essential. Essential (and non-essential) with regard to what?, we might ask. Essential to the meaning, or rather, to meaning, would come the reply! For just as the phonologist, in positing all the core and distinct sound units of a language, the phonemes, deliberately discounts all the phonetic variation which does not constitute a meaning-bearing, word-changing variation, so the story structuralist will argue that he is identifying the basic narrative units of a mini-language, here the language of Russian fairytales, and in so doing is identifying the essential conditions within which story meanings can arise.

How tenable is the analogy? The strength of the phoneme case is that language use is something it's hard to stand outside of: we have strong intuitive judgments about what are and are not English sounds, English words, and so on. It's less easy to see, or insist upon, a sharp boundary to any set of stories supposedly covered by a Proppian analysis – although the boundary was sharp enough as far as Propp himself was concerned, since his corpus was quite specific: just those 115 stories. And, relatedly, we might ask why *31* functions? Why not 30 or 32? Because, Propp implicitly answers, just 31 functions are needed – for the given corpus. But what, we might still ask, are the grounds of this 'need'?

We may often encounter appeals to intuition at this point (while with simple-minded theorists, the reasoning is quite openly circular). The 31 functions identified (with neither needless duplication nor unjustified merging of types) are the only functions necessary to specify the essential action structure of the stories in the corpus. The question to consider is whether such intuitionism is defensible, or whether the whole descriptive apparatus is invalidated. But such questions cannot be addressed properly unless we also keep in mind just what the goals and expectations of a Propp- or Barthes-based analysis are. The business of really getting at our intuitive judgments (rather than our public and conditioned ways of talking about plots and plot structures) will always present difficulties. But we do readily find groups of readers (even whole communities) disclosing substantial agreement over what is essential and non-essential in plot, characterization and so on – disclosing, in short, a common grasp of structure. This generality of agreement and commonality of grasp are the essential justification for the inductive speculations of Propp, Barthes, and others.

2.3 Barthes on narrative

Entirely appropriately, Barthes' famous 'Introduction' (1977; first published in French in 1966) begins with an argument about inductive versus deductive methods (in linguistics and narrative study), and defends the latter, despite the inevitable provisionality entailed in moving from the particular observations to the general hypothesis. (Similar issues of goals, methodology and falsification are intelligently if controversially explored in a study that will figure in Chapter 4: see Banfield, 1982: 1–8). Barthes writes:

> Narrative analysis is condemned to a deductive procedure, obliged first to devise a hypothetical model of description (what American linguists call a 'theory') and then gradually to work down from this model towards the different narrative species which at once conform to and depart from the model. (1977: 81)

He suggests that linguistics 'seems reasonable' as a founding model for narrative analysis, but notes that discourse study will require a 'second linguistics' going beyond the sentence. But he does posit a homological relation between sentence and discourse, at least as far as **semiosis** – 'message-bearingness' – is concerned:

> A discourse is a long 'sentence' . . . just as a sentence . . . is a short 'discourse'. (Barthes, 1977: 83)

More particularly Barthes emphasizes the need to separate different levels of analysis, and the need for a hierarchical typology of units, in this early essay. He proposes three major levels of narrative structure:

1 functions (as in Propp, Bremond)
2 actions (by which he refers to 'characters', rather as Greimas – discussed below – refers to them as *actants*)
3 narration (equivalent to what we have termed discourse, *discours*, or *sjuzhet*)

What follows is almost entirely to do with the first level, that of function, that by which narrative is 'driven'. The essence of a function is 'the seed that it sows in the narrative, planting an element that will come to fruition later – either on the same level or elsewhere, on another level' (1977: 89). Thus function is **teleological** (see glossary), by which we mean it is concerned with the long-term goals of a narrative. Function is the means of achieving the overarching coherence of a narrative, rather than any merely local or adjacent cause-and-effect logic.

Barthes proceeds to distinguish two types of functions: (a) **functions proper** (which we might call 'Propp-type functions'); and (b) **indices**, which are a unit referring not to a complementary and consequential act but to a more or less diffuse concept which is nevertheless necessary to the meaning of the story. (Barthes, 1977: 92)

They include indices to characters' psychological states, notations of 'atmosphere', and so on. While functions proper are distributional, sequential, 'completed' further on in the story – and so have a kind of **syntagmatic ratification**, indices are said to be integrational, hierarchically-oriented, realized by relating them to some higher, integrated level, a **paradigmatic ratification**. On a broad continuum, Barthes suggests, there are heavily functional narratives such as folktales, rather sharply contrasted with heavily indicial ones such as psychological novels.

A further cut is now introduced. Functions proper are of two types:

1 **Cardinal functions** or **nuclei** or, to use Chatman's attractive label, 'kernels' (in Chatman, 1969): these are real hinge-points of narratives, moments of *risk* (when things can go 'either way'); they occur consecutively and *with consequences*.

2 **Catalysers** (not the best of terms): these fill in the narrative space between nuclei, and are described as parasitic and unilateral by Barthes, areas of safety and rest. For example, a ringing telephone or a delivered letter may herald a real nucleus in a story – and a preliminary 'hinge' would be whether the summons is answered or not, the letter opened – but all sorts of 'business', prevarications and accompaniments may surround that action as catalysers.

Indices, too, can be sub-classified as

1 indices proper (charged with implicit relevance)
2 informants (depthless, transparent, identificatory data).

Indices involve an act of deciphering, the reader is to learn to know a character or an atmosphere; informants bring ready-made knowledge . . . their functionality is weak. (Barthes, 1977: 96)

Finally Barthes notes that a unit can be a member of more than one class at a time: one could be both a catalyser and an index, for example. And he notes that in a sense nuclei (kernels) are the special group, with the other three unit types being expansions of nuclei. Nuclei provide the necessary framework, the other three fill it out.

Barthes goes on to appeal for descriptive study not merely of the 'major articulations of narrative' but of the organization of the smallest segments, which he sees as combining into coherent **sequences**:

> a sequence is a logical succession of nuclei bound together by a relation of solidarity: the sequence opens when one of its terms has no solidary antecedent and closes when another of its terms has no consequent. (1977: 101)

For example, 'having a drink' is suggested as a closed sequence with the following nuclei: order a drink, obtain it, drink it, pay for it. (But is paying as obligatory and integrated as the other three nuclei?) Now the business of seeing a sequence in such a string of reported events, and labelling it as 'having a drink' (rather than, say, 'quenching one's thirst' or 'making oneself socially available') is for Barthes the kind of projective interpretive activity readers are always doing in their narrative processing. It's what he later subsumes under his **proaieretic code** (Barthes, 1970). Naming is a key act of mental processing, under the assumption that the reader can't remember everything she reads, and instead registers, and may even verbalize, the broad scenario, the main threads, in a narrative – a kind of incremental and revisable précis-making and paraphrasing. It does not appear that Barthes drew on psycholinguistic evidence in his assumptions and theorizing of 'sequence naming', but there are some interesting parallels between his proposals here and more recent psycholinguistic research on narrative which I will refer to in Chapter 7.

Barthes' scheme can be set out as follows:

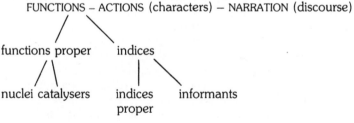

FUNCTIONS – ACTIONS (characters) – NARRATION (discourse)

functions proper   indices

nuclei catalysers   indices   informants
                      proper

and

named sequence: [nucleus . . . nucleus . . . nucleus] (logically bound together)

An   invaluable   critical   demonstration   of   the   Barthesian machinery applied to a text is Chatman (1969), which sets it to work on the same story, 'Eveline', that I discuss extensively in this chapter. Chatman identifies just 8 core narrative functions or kernels in the story; I list these below, with Chatman's interpretive labellings appended:

1 She sat at the window watching the evening invade the avenue. (SITTING AND LOOKING)
2 One time there used to be a field there in which they used to play . . . (REMINISCING)
3 Now she was going to go away . . . to leave her home. (REHEARSING THE DECISION TO GO)
4 Was that wise? (QUESTIONING)
5 She stood among the swaying crowd in the station at the North Wall. (PREPARING TO EMBARK)
6 Out of a maze of distress, she prayed to God to direct her, to show her what was her duty. (INDECISION CHANGING TO ANXIETY)
7 She felt [Frank] seize her hand. (FRANK'S URGING HER TO GO)
8 No! No! No! (REFUSAL)

This skeletal structure certainly tells a story, with the required connectedness of stages or moves. And Chatman's capitalized glosses of the kernels or functions proper reflect the story's attention to mental activity rather than physical change: the story is structured around reflection, reminiscence, thinking about doing something, and getting ready to do something, rather than on actions themselves. Even Eveline's turning away at the end is less emphatic than Chatman's gloss, 'refusal', would suggest: it's more a beginning-to-reject than a definitive rejection. And, as we might expect in such a crafted story, Chatman provides ample evidence that indices and informants of the character Eveline, and catalysers accompanying the narrative development that is principally 'driven' by the functions proper, all contribute to an integrated presentation. Even the smallest textual details, we might argue, play a role. Notice, for example, the words *swaying* and *maze* that are used in the course of functions 5 and 6 above. Besides their specific application in these sentences, they are also indexical, with reference to the entire story, of indeterminacy and vacillation, and encircling confusion, respectively. Many readers, casting the interpretive net wider, will proceed to extract dominating indices, informants, and so on, as they build up a sense of the basic structure of the *Dubliners* narrative as a whole.

Among the indices that many generalize from 'Eveline' are qualities of dependence, submission to duty, and ineffectuality.

Despite the attractions of Barthes' basic four-way categorization of narrative material, problems remain concerning the replicability of Barthes' model, and in particular over how (by what criteria) we can confidently judge what is and is not a nucleus, a catalyser, an index proper and an informant. Some of these problems can be outlined by examining Chatman's explanation of the difference between kernels (i.e., nuclei) and catalysers. Kernels are said to be hinges, alternative path openings, and so on, while catalysers (better, 'satellites') are non-essential actions ('business') accompanying the kernels, but of no larger prospective consequence. In the extract below, Chatman italicizes the alleged kernels:

> *One of the telephones rang in the dark room.* Bond turned and moved quickly to the central desk and the pool of light cast by the green shaded reading lamp. *He picked up the* black *telephone* from the rank of four.

What we might question here is the assumption that the phone-ringing and answering are *inherently* nuclei, that Bond's moving across the room is inherently secondary. Such decisions can only be made retrospectively, in the light of a fuller scanning and assessment of extended text. Chatman writes (1969: 13):

> The telephone rings: now, James Bond can either answer it or not, the choice sets off two different plot trains . . .

Not, the sceptic might be inclined to say, if it's a wrong number. The criteria for kernelhood here are just too vague: certainly a telephone ringing is an initiation, a summons, an opening move, as analysts of conversation remind us. But then, on the 'to answer or not to answer' test, are we to treat every direct speech turn in a novel as a kernel, on the grounds that on each occasion the addressee 'can either answer it or not'?

Similarly (as Culler, 1975b, also notes), Chatman begs many questions when he asserts

> The first sentence in 'Eveline' must be interpreted as a kernel – 'She sat at the window watching the evening invade the avenue' – because it raises the question 'Why? Why is she sitting and watching the evening?' (Chatman, 1969: 13)

Any utterance can prompt, in the listener/addressee, the question 'Why?'

I will presently propose that we can initially work 'longitudinally', like a reader, through the grammar (in a broad sense of the term) of the text, in pursuit of more local and grammatically-cued marks of the core narrative events. Ultimately, however, when we offer a determination of what the kernel narrative utterances are, we have to operate holistically and teleologically. And this assumption is necessary in order to apply any criterion of well-formedness.

An analogous truism is that you can't parse a sentence until you've read it. Notice, however, that you can *start* to parse it before you have finished reading it – I think we typically do. But we know that the analysis is provisional, may not 'go through' if we find a configuration of relations that is out of the ordinary, the unmarked form. We know, then, not to put too much trust in our parsing until the reading is complete, and we've seen all the structure there is to see. Thus as we read

It was John who

we expect that John is the 'underlying subject', the 'doer', made the focus through a clefting device. But if we read on and find John is in fact the underlying object, the 'done to' –

It was John who the boys attacked.

– we're not at all troubled by the need for revision. To revise the truism, then:

You *can* begin to parse a sentence or text before you've finished reading it, but you know you may need to revise your analysis.

The well-formedness test mentioned above is related to the grammatical distinction between obligatory and deletable material. In narrative 'grammar', there is a similar assumption: while catalyser and indexical material on character and setting are deletable, the functional kernels are obligatory material which, on their own, constitute a coherent 'bare' narrative (and recognizably related to the full version) – the discarded bits would constitute no sort of coherent narrative at all.

The upshot of these qualifications and reservations should be that we see more clearly that kernels and catalysers and so on are not so much textual 'givens' as analytical constructions; and that, as Culler explains, using a Saussurean phrase, they are 'relational terms only':

> What is a kernel in one plot or at one level of description will be a satellite at another. For the hero to lie in wait for the villain is, at one level, a kernel, since it logically requires a temporal consequence: the villain arrives and is shot down. But at another level these functions are satellites which expand the kernel 'revenge', a consequence of an initial kernel such as 'suffering harm'. In 'Eveline', for example, the actions of the past which the heroine recalls could be organized into kernels and satellites, but within the story they become satellites or expansions of a kernel such as 'weighing the evidence' . . . We must accept that we recognize kernels only when we identify the role of an action in the plot or, to put it another way, promote an action to a constituent of plot . . . One cannot determine the role or function of an action without considering its consequences and its place in the story as a whole. (Culler, 1975b: 135–6)

In this retrospective process of sense-making and plot-determination, Barthes' notion of 'sequence-naming', or something similar, must be crucially involved. That is to say, as we read through 'Eveline' we must be constructing a model or scheme into which the disparate propositions (sitting at the window, leaning her head, listening to the man's footsteps, thinking about childhood days) can somehow fit. Much of this model-building will be heavily guided by our cultural background, by what we think – and what we think the writer thinks – is important in life, about what is 'normal' behaviour, and so on. When we do any text-interpreting, it is not done *in vacuo*, a lonely and private interrogation of the text. Both texts and readers are inescapably shaped or framed by prior (but not fixed or eternal) cultural assumptions as to what is significant, salient. It is because there is always this context of cultural significances and saliences 'around' all our involvements with narratives that Barthes says we have 'a language of plot' within us even before we approach any particular story.

An outward sign of having made sense of the textual data is the production of reasonable paraphrase, i.e., a paraphrase that neither we nor other readers find incongruous or absurd. The paraphrase could be very long, many times the length of the original (as most literary critical articles on 'Eveline' are), or it could be single-proposition length, or just a single word. The opening paragraphs of 'Eveline' could be phraphrased as:

A young woman reflects on her past life

or as:

Reflection

But (and here the analyst's dilemma begins to look remarkably like that of those who attempt to identify the structure of spoken discourse) does it make sense to work 'from the bottom up', as Barthes and Chatman claim to be doing? Don't we have to work 'from the top down', i.e., first setting up some broad hypothesis as to what happens in the story as a whole, thus specifying the top-level constituents of story, then trying to move down the hierarchy, analysing so as to separate out the bits that have been complexly bound together? Or is this dramatic opposition of top-down *v.* bottom-up itself a misdirection? Culler's objection to Barthes' model is quite simple but fundamental:

> [It] remains strangely atomistic, through the lack of any specification of what one is moving towards as one collects kernels and satellites and groups them into sequences . . . [And] Chatman is able to pick out [the sentence 'One time there used to be a field there'] as a kernel only because he has some sense of an abstract structure towards which he is moving. (Culler, 1975b: 138)

And along the lines of the 'broad hypothesis' I have suggested above, he argues:

> What the reader is looking for in a plot is a passage from one state to another – a passage to which he can assign thematic value. (Culler: 139)

Again, we are back to a linked before and after. The before and the after can be labelled, if we like, oppositionally as problem and solution, or more logically as cause and effect. More neutrally, we might simply label them as situation 1 and situation 2, linked by one or multiple experiences.

2.4 Plot-summarizing: modelling intuitions

Jonathan Culler's 'Defining narrative units' (Culler, 1975b), focussing on problems of generalizability, and of adequacy, of certain proposed models of plot analysis, concludes:

Competing theories of plot structure can only be evaluated by their success in serving as models of a particular aspect of literary competence: readers' abilities to recognize and summarize plots, to group together similar plots, etc. This intuitive knowledge constitutes the facts to be explained. (127)

To this characterization we should add a couple of caveats. The first is that, even more immediately apparent than in relation to the notion of linguistic competence on which it is loosely based, literary competence seems to be very largely learned rather than innate, and markedly culture-specific. Thus when we talk of 'readers' abilities' we have to keep clearly in mind that we are talking only of the acquired and developed ability of a group of readers, rather than some universal mental ability, comparable to the near-universal ability to walk or subtract.

The second related point is that what it means to call these culture-specific abilities 'intuitive knowledge' remains unclear. People can be better or worse at plot-summarizing, and can *get* better at it: does this suggest an intuitive faculty? I would be inclined to take a far more behavioural approach and argue that we get good at plot-summarizing largely because, in our kind of world, constructing and communicating summarized plots is a valued skill. By 'our kind of world' I mean a world in which children and adults frequently face examinations; in which we often have our recall of events put to various kinds of test; in which it is common to share 'at second hand' a narrative whose performance one's addressee has missed; and in which there is particularly sharp awareness of the universal constraint that influences the shape of so much of our behaviour, namely, limitation of time. Would plot-summarizing be such a valued skill in a settled, integrated oral community, where a set time and social space was reserved for storytelling? There, to précis a plot might be regarded as either incomprehensible or, worse, proof that one was a very poor storyteller.

In modification of Culler's 'intuitive competence' approach, then, we need to understand what we mean when we acknowledge – as we surely should – that people in general, given various non-universal cultural predispositions, do become adept at producing and understanding plot summaries. What is meant, I would suggest, is that people develop community-validated skills in specifying the more important characters and events in narratives. Most crucially of all, they get good at identifying what, relative to their own frameworks of world knowledge and cultural assumptions, is the 'main point' of a story. One of the questions we need to try to answer is how on earth they do this. That they should do it is surely no great surprise: it is merely an instance of the process of ranking or ordering things that we do all the time in all sorts of activities, making rational decisions about what things most need our attention – again, given our limited resources of time, money, energy.

Some such emphasis is attended to when Culler goes on to examine 'Eveline', first noting that we can construct and agree on hierarchies of appropriate plot summaries, from very succinct to rather detailed ones. If we set a culturally homogeneous group of people the task of summarizing, say, a short story, in 20, 40 and 100 words, the degree of agreement over what to mention and what to discard is often gratifying (sharp disagreement may be due either to weak skills of summarizing or some covert subcultural clash).

Culler notes how various potentially important plot incidents are eventually rejected by us as not central to plot, more an indirect description of Eveline's consciousness: for example, the man out of the last house going home, Eveline watching from her window. But 'She had consented to go away. . . . Was that wise?'

> is immediately recognized as an important structuring element which enables us [to re-interpret preceding material] . . . and to structure the material. (Culler, 1975b: 130)

And he adds:

> As we move through 'Eveline' we must decide which actions serve only to characterize her and the situation in which she has placed herself, which of these are crucial attributes involved in the change compassed by the plot, and which actions are in fact crucial as actions. (134)

Well, perhaps. But most readers reading 'Eveline' know that it was written by Joyce, that it is therefore 'Literature', and that failure to nominate a clear developmental plot, in such fiction, has its own cultural warrant. In other words, perhaps 'Eveline' is too category-marginal, too de-automatizing of plot logic, to be a suitable exemplification of our standard ability to summarize. (A rather more straightforward story, also about leaving home and the familiar, is supplied in the first exercise appended to this chapter.) When asked what happens in 'Eveline' it isn't absurd to reply 'I'm not entirely sure', although such a verdict on the plot of, say, a James Bond novel, would be felt to be defective. In the case of 'high fiction', perhaps more than elsewhere, the force of James's famous observation seems especially telling:

> What is character but the determination of incident? What is incident but the illustration of character? (1963: 80)

At any rate, Culler goes on to defend Propp's teleological conception of plot structure – rightly, I think – in which evaluation of acts is held in abeyance until their significance within the encompassing sequence is perceived. He also notes that such retrospective definition of units relies very much on internalized cultural models shared by readers (e.g., sitting by a window and recollecting the past need to be recognized as a cultural index – cliché even – signalling introspection and serious reflection). And on another level, leaving home (as Eveline contemplates doing) is deeply culturally significant (with a special resonance for Joyce and readers of Joyce).

On comparing, evaluating, and falsifying theories of story   2.5

In his celebrated 'Introduction to the structural analysis of narrative', Roland Barthes asserts that 'it is impossible to combine (to produce) a narrative without reference to an implicit system of units and rules' (1977: 81). Propp's system was just the first of very many 'grammars' aimed at describing that system of units and rules. As Culler (1975a: 206) notes, the diversity of proposals becomes baffling, but the real problem remains 'the lack of explicit procedures for evaluating competing approaches'. Relatedly, Rimmon-Kenan (1983: 14) has observed that in story descriptions (whether these are in the form of one-word labels or clause-size propositions – Propp supplies both) persistent problems concern consistency and uniformity in the description. And without consistency in description, comparison and generalization would seem to be very difficult to achieve. As Culler later added (Culler, 1975b: 125), reliability and replicability of the procedures of analysis-cum-description depend on the explicitness and coherence of the governing criteria:

> Each theory, constrained to define for itself the basic units of

narrative, becomes a coherent and self-contained system in terms of which practically any plot can be described, and consequently they are difficult to compare. If any progress is to be made it will not be by erecting yet another system but by thinking seriously about the *criteria* to be used in evaluating competing approaches and hence about the *goals* of an analysis of plot structure.

Propp is thus the first of many to be structuralist in certain of his procedures of analysis but quite intuitive in his grounds for asserting particular similarities or differences. He is intuitive, for example, in asserting that various characters in various stories are mere variant concrete realizations of a single abstract role (no replication test using informants was ever used by him to support his judgments); and he seeks our intuitive assent to those claims. He is structuralist in a variety of ways: his roles and functions, for example, are limited paradigms with various members, 'just as the phoneme is a functional unit which can be manifested in various ways in actual utterances' (Culler, 1975a: 208). In fact Propp's functions have a syntagmatic significance as well as a paradigmatic one, in that they always occur in the same order, and in that contextually the same action (e.g., the hero is given a sum of money) can be the realization of two quite distinct narrative functions, and is so distinguished. It could be an early complication in the story, or a conclusion to the tale (cf. the 'same' noun phrase variously performing the function of subject or object). The search is for a set of interrelated elements that constitute the essential terms in a system – terms that are only definable and only have meaning when considered in relation to the other terms within the system. (The vocabulary and sounds of a language are complex systems of this sort; traffic lights are a simple one. What does an amber light 'mean'? Not much, on its own. But when it is illuminated, between green and red lights that are off, suitably sited at a road junction, and so on, it is a meaningful part of a finite and meaning-bearing system.)

But to search for something in no way guarantees you will find it, nor does it establish that the thing is there to be found. We should keep in mind the speculative strain in all theorizing about story, and the relativism of remarks grounded in the nexus of the interests and habitual preferences (i.e., the culture) of a particular analyst from a particular society. All theory, like all science, is necessarily speculative, speculation with the intent of advancing our understanding of some phenomenon. Bal (1985: 23) places just the right emphasis on systematicity's interdependence with personal intuitions of relevance when she writes, at the close of a lengthy presentation of one theory of semantic content,

> [The] model can be used as a basis [of structural analysis], but it can also be left out of consideration, not because it would be invalid but because we can foresee that the results would not be very relevant to the fabula in question.

These remarks are by way of the first mention of the issues of model-evaluation and theory-falsifiability that frequently arise in both linguistics and literary theory – issues that I will touch upon again at various points in the book.

We should see Propp, then, as a fascinating pioneer exploration of the narrative 'competence' that readers seem to share: we do have quite definite ideas about the basic plots of the narratives we read or hear; we do have an ability to summarize plots; we can often agree in identifying what is not essential to plot; and we can identify 'transformationally-related' plots.

In search of the grammaticization of plot structure　　2.6

To restate the complication that 'Eveline' presents: as we read this story we're not entirely sure whether we *should* – as normally – be looking for incidents, or, instead, attend to character. But let us proceed by trying to see why, as many readers claim,

> She had consented to go away, to leave her home. (sentence 24)

is one of the more important disclosures of plot structure in the story. In doing so, we should always remember that 'importance to plot' is a co-text-relative criterion: in some sorts of stories, the fact that an individual had consented to leave home might be very small beer given an array of more dramatic and immediate events: cf.:

> She had consented to go away, to leave her home, while the place was being redecorated.

This example is a reminder of the importance, already emphasized, of the teleological status of events in narratives. On the other hand it is only fair to say that 'permanently leaving home' seems a significant and 'tellable' event in most cultures.

In probing the high plot-structuring status of sentence 24, we should first compare it to the 23 text sentences that precede it. When we come to look at things more holistically or teleologically, we must relate sentence 24 to all that follows it as well as all that precedes it, but it should be worth first approaching the sentence the way a first-time reader would, 'from the left', seen in the textual light only of those sentences that precede it. And what we find, in those preceding sentences, are various grammatical cues that deflect or argue against treatment of the content of many of those sentences as crucial narrative events. We may begin by looking at the finite verbs of the opening sentences (my emphasis of the finite verbs):

> She *sat* at the window watching the evening invade the avenue. (1) Her head *was leaned* against the window curtains and in her nostrils *was* the odour of dusty cretonne. (2) She *was* tired. (3)

All are distinguished by being **stative verbs** (see glossary), or at least verbs of static description, with no intrinsic implication of change. Now one immediately questionable assumption I seem to have made is that if we are looking for the reporting of narrative events we should look particularly and only at the finite verbs. In response to such a complaint I should stick by the 'particularly' but not the 'only'. Almost any major part of the clause can express change-of-state, including non-finite verbs:

> (a) Chick watched the men confront McAndrew, shoot him, carry his body on the back of a pack-mule out to the bottom piece, and bury him.

And narratives can be expressed through **nominalizations** (see glossary):

> (b) Chick saw a confrontation between the men and McAndrew, the latter's death by shooting, the transportation of the body by mule to the bottom piece, and its burial.

But I think nearly all of us would agree that (a) works and feels better than (b) as a narrative, and that an alternative version which reported the confrontation and shooting and so on through finite main verbs would probably be preferable to either. In making those judgments we are justifying the argument for looking for narrative events 'particularly' in finite verbs. The finite verb, in short, is the unmarked, preferred and unexceptional vehicle for expression of plot events, while the other forms I have mentioned are marked and noticeable alternatives. Accordingly, and while mindful that our assessment is probabilistic and corrigible in the light of later text, we calculate that, for example, the embedded clause 'the evening invade the avenue' (embedded under the verb of static condition *sat*) does *not* express a crucial plot event.

The text continues:

> Few people passed. (4) The man out of the last house passed on his way home; she heard his footsteps clacking along the concrete pavement and afterwards crunching on the cinder before the new red houses. (5) One time there used to be a field there in which they used to play every evening with other people's children. (6)

What of sentence 4? Are there any intrinsic grounds for doubting this clause's plot-structuring importance? Perhaps only if we compare it with the nearly synonymous

> A few people passed.

The latter could be used to describe the passage of a particular group of pedestrians (e.g., 'A few nuns passed'), where we respond by wondering 'What sort of people?'. This is not true of the textual alternative without the indefinite article, which lacks the required sense of **deictic** (see glossary) or spatiotemporal specificity; it is, rather, a summative, retrospective and hence descriptive, rather than narrative, comment. And the term denoting the participants here, *people*, is one of a group of noticeably general, all-purpose items (others are *thing, person, stuff*) noted in Halliday and Hasan (1976). While lacking the deictic delimitedness that would render it suitable to be followed by a punctual temporal phrase, the clause readily accepts qualification by a durative phrase:

> ?Few people passed at 6.30.
> Few people passed between 6 and 7.

Cf.:

> A few people passed at 6.30.
> A few people passed between 6 and 7.

By contrast the next sentence does exhibit the kind of identificatory specificity I am positing as a preferred characteristic of narrative clauses, particularly in its definite description of a particular individual:

The man out of the last house passed on his way home

Again, one has to say that it would be possible for this incident to be crucial in the plot, even in the face of the following counter-signals:

1 Neither in sentence 6 nor in those that follow is the man named, though he is apparently known. Characters crucial to plots are *usually* denoted (by name, profession, distinguishing characteristics) rather more specifically than as 'the man'.

2 Important characters and their important denoted actions are not usually mentioned and immediately discarded as discourse topics. There is *usually* a 'follow-up principle', such that one or more following clauses maintain either the prominent character or his/her action as *some* inner clausal element (subject, predicate, object), with the preferred option being to maintain the character as **subject** and **theme** (see glossary). Here, to the contrary, there is an immediate switch ('she heard his footsteps'), itself discarded as an extendable topic in the following sentences' reflective reversion to the distant past:

One time there used to be a field there in which they used to play every evening with other people's children. (6) Then a man from Belfast bought the field and built houses in it – not like their little brown houses but bright brick houses with shining roofs. (7) The children of the avenue used to play together in that field – the Devines, the Waters, the Dunns, little Keogh the cripple, she and her brothers and sisters. (8)

There are basically two grounds for discounting most of this material as crucial to story development: one is the frequent emphasis on the events reported as habitual and repeated, an emphasis that becomes almost excessive in the following sentence:

Her father *used often* to hunt them in out of the field . . . but *usually* little Keogh *used* to keep *nix* (apart from *nix*, my emphases)

The second ground suggesting plot non-salience is the pervasive use of distancing deictic or spatiotemporal markers, reinforcing the relative remoteness of the events and situation from the speaker's (or, in this case, the thinker's) present. Distal deictics (*one time, there, then, that,* and so on) are remarkably prominent:

Still they seemed to have been rather happy then. (11) Her father was not so bad then; and besides, her mother was alive. (12)

The above sentences are of course inherently non-event-implicating anyway since their main verbs are stative and **intensive** (see glossary), but the observation that follows recapitulates the 'extradiegetic' nature of these reflections: 'That was a long time ago'. (The term 'extradiegetic' will be properly introduced in the next chapter.) The text continues:

she and her brothers and sisters were all grown up; her mother was dead. (13) Tizzle Dunn was dead, too, and the Waters had gone back to England. (14) Everything changes. (15) Now she was going to go away like the others, to leave her home. (16)

Again, we have a series of stative relational descriptions in sentences 13 and 14, closing with a distant, past perfect tense verb; and a timeless (i.e., deictically unanchored) generic sentence in 15.

Only with sentence 16 do we encounter an utterance grammatically quite distinct from all those preceding. Introduced by the proximal deictic 'Now', in striking contrast to all the previous instances of 'then', it is oriented to the speaker/thinker's narrative present, with an explicitly dynamic verb (the very test of dynamic status is progressivizability) in progressive aspect. Not only is the utterance oriented to the thinker's present, it also has futuritive force, expressing an intended future course of action. The links between sentence 16 and the surrounding text are plentiful: the 'go away' is lexically related to the 'gone back' of sentence 14; the 'others' in 'like the others' is indeterminately anaphorically tied to the previously-mentioned brothers and sisters, or the Waters, or possibly her dead mother and Tizzle Dunn, or any combination of these; and the mention of 'home' is echoed in the exclamatory 'Home!' that follows. All such cohesive ties do nothing to detract from the narrative distinctness of sentence 16 in terms of its deixis, aspect, futuritive force, its dynamic verb expressing a clear change of state, and its use of an already textually-prominent participant ('she', Eveline) as sentential subject and theme.

What I have done, perhaps a little laboriously, for these first two paragraphs could be done for the third, leading up to sentence 24, which Culler and others have identified as important to plot. Briefly, paragraph 3 displays many of the same non-narrative characteristics as the previous two, particularly either stative main verbs or at least ones implying no change of state

> She looked round the room . . . Perhaps she would never see again those familiar objects . . . He had been a school friend . . . 'He is in Melbourne now'

habitual or iterative processes

> which she had dusted once a week for so many years . . . Whenever he showed the photograph . . . her father used to pass it . . .

or both

> from which she had never dreamed of being divided . . . during all those years she had never found out the name of the priest.

Again, by sharp contrast with all these, and now with the additional impact of being a near-repetition of sentence 16, comes sentence 24:

> She had consented to go away, to leave her home.

But it is, note, an iteration with some differences which make it all the more salient to plot. For while sentence 16 can be read as the expression of the subject's own purely personal decision to act, it now emerges that another party is involved, has proposed a specified course of action to which Eveline has agreed. And if we compare sentence 24 with:

> She had decided to go away.
> She had agreed to go away.

the subtle semiotic overtones of the verb *consent* – so prominently used in quasi-legal discussion of sexual matters – should be quite evident.

In this final section of the chapter I have tried to offer some simple principles which may guide a reader's 'real time' processing of text in the search for plot. In this way I have tried to uncover links between grammar and plot-structure, in the conviction that such links quite typically do exist. But notice that I repeatedly argue in terms of preferences, expectations, and tendencies (we expect main events to come in main verbs, we expect main characters to be designated – and designated recurringly – in individualizing ways, and so on). The procedure is thus necessarily fuzzy and provisional, but not, I would argue, haphazard. There is little that is arbitrary or haphazard about the grammar of a language or the grammar of stories. And as conceded earlier, this whole exercise of provisional plot-assessment may need radical recasting after the fact and act of reading, when a synoptic and teleological perspective is adopted.

Further reading

Clearly the place to begin further reading on basic story structure is with the seminal works to which I have referred: Propp (1968), and Barthes (1977). In addition, Chatman (1969) is both a sympathetic overview of the early story-structuralist work of Barthes and Todorov, and a source of numerous narratological insights into the story 'Eveline', while Culler's book *Structuralist Poetics* (1975a) and his article (1975b) contain lucid critical commentaries on theories of plot. Chapter 2 of Rimmon-Kenan (1983) covers some of the same ground as this chapter, and students might like the 'bivocal' effect of having two introductions to the same topic; Rimmon-Kenan also includes many apposite literary examples. I particularly admire and recommend Chapter 1 ('Fabula: Elements') of Bal (1985) – an advanced and authoritative introduction to both theory and practice. This text (a translation) requires attentive reading, but is a rigorous treatment rich in intelligent insight. Also well worth reading are the opening chapters of Chatman (1978). Several more specialized contributions are referred to in the course of the notes and exercises below.

Notes and exercises

1 Below is part of the written text of a text-and-pictures story for children by Nigel Snell entitled *Julie Stays the Night* (London: Hamish Hamilton, 1982):

> One morning the telephone started to ring.
> Mummy answered it. She said, 'It's Sally's Mummy. She has invited you to go and stay. Would you like to go?'

'Oh yes' said Julie. 'I'd love to.' And she ran to tell Alexander, her pet beetle.
The days went by and soon it was time to pack. Julie began to feel scared.
She was going away from her Mummy and Daddy and her toys, her bed and her home.
Julie started to cry. 'Don't be sad,' said Mummy. 'You will love it when you get there.'
Julie wasn't so sure.
She decided to take Alexander along in a matchbox, just in case.
Mummy took her to Sally's house by train. Julie felt very homesick. But when they got to Sally's, her mother was very kind. They had a big tea and played with lots of toys. That night Julie and Sally were both allowed to stay up an extra half hour.
When they went to bed Julie showed Sally her beetle, Alexander, but he crawled out of the matchbox and went down a crack. 'He seems quite at home here,' thought Julie.

Attempt an analysis of this story, labelling events and states in terms of Propp's functions, and/or Barthes' functions and indices, and/or my proposal about the grammaticization of core narrative clauses. Which method or combination of methods seems to you to highlight basic story structure most effectively?

Now turn to Katherine Mansfield's story 'Bliss' and analyze it according to one or more of the three methodologies just mentioned. With particular reference to my grammaticization thesis, consider such psychological/evaluative sentences in 'Bliss' as the following, in which Nanny indicates her reluctance to hand over the baby while the latter is eating:

She oughtn't to be changed hands.

In the light of such sentences, where modal verbs accompany finite dynamic verbs such as *change*, should we qualify my previous assumption that all finite dynamic-verb clauses are potentially core narrative ones?

2 As indicated in section 2.1, I believe there are a number of problems in treating the distinct but related linguistic disciplines of phonology and phonetics as not merely an instructive analogy with, but a model of, the relations between story and particular narratives. The reason why the parallel is misleading has to do

with the insights into language most influentially introduced by Saussure – in particular, his insistence that a language as an analyzable economy of signs is a form imposed upon substance Thus as a study of the logic of the sound system of a language, phonology is the study of linguistic form. That system of forms is like a grid through which we channel our speech activity: we learn to school our production of sounds so that these conform to the types ordained in the phonological system of the language. But it is hard to see how anything similar goes on in narrative, for the simple reason that, unlike a sound-system, narrative does not entail moulding or shaping itself upon formless substance but already-organized, signifying, representational form – whether the form is words, or pictures, or the gestures of mime.

Read Chapter 4 in Part II of Saussure's *Course*, entitled 'Linguistic value'. This encapsulates the essence of Saussure's position on the role of form and substance in a language (the recent English translation by Harris [Saussure, 1983] is particularly to be recommended). Can narratives be treated as a system of forms in the way that Saussure treats a language as a system of forms?

3 In Chapter 1 I described story as strongly paradigmatic and weakly syntagmatic in orientation, by contrast with the diverse syntagmatic exploitations of actual narrative versions. But note that story is not *purely* paradigmatic: there are more abstract, 'deep structure' accounts of the logic of stories which go even further in pursuit of what they take to be the fundamental paradigmatic essence of the syntagmatic behaviour we call narrative. Two of these accounts (Levi-Strauss, 1968; and Greimas, 1966) are briefly discussed in Rimmon-Kenan (1983: 11–13); for fuller treatment of Levi-Strauss, see Culler (1975a) and Hawkes (1977). Such accounts strive to identify the alleged mythical or quasi-mythical roots (typically, tangled roots where, for example, disorders in kin-relations interact in complex ways with disordered responses to the facts of human mortality) of stories. But in doing so they move far away from the *language*-based phenomena that are my special concern.

4 Some of the ways we can use Propp, or a Proppian approach, are noted in Dundes's introduction to the *Morphology*. If structural analysis is not to be an end in itself, it seems vital to relate the forms Propp found to the culture (Russian, Indo-European) out of which they emerged. Dundes speculates pertinently:

Does not the fact that Propp's last function is a wedding indicate that Russian fairy-tale structure has something to do with marriage? Is the fairy tale a model, a model of fantasy to be sure, in which one begins with an old nuclear family . . . and ends finally with the formation of a new family? . . . Propp's analysis should be useful in analyzing the structure of literary forms (such as novels and plays), comic strips, motion-picture and television plots, and the like . . . . Do children become familiar enough with the general nature of fairy-tale morphology to object to or question a deviation from it by a storyteller? . . . Finally, Propp's scheme could also be used to generate new tales. (Dundes, 1968: xiv–xv)

Apply Dundes's questions to the next awful episode of a television series that you watch (*The A-Team* or *Knightrider* or *Love Boat*). How predictable is the villainy or lack that is grappled with, and what form does the resolving 'marriage' typically take? Compare these predictabilities with the functions (villainy, 'marriage', etc.) of a rather less formulaic series, such as *Miami Vice*.

5 One of the most influential objectors to Propp was Levi-Strauss, who complained that the approach was too oriented to the logic of formal structure and was neglectful of content – especially, for Levi-Strauss, of the underlying logic of that content (Levi-Strauss' own work really offers a structuralist approach to anthropological content, in terms of myth):

Before Formalism we certainly did not know what these tales had in common. After it we are deprived of all means of knowing how they differ. We have passed from concrete to abstract and cannot get back . . . Propp discovered (magnificently) that the content of tales is permutable. He came to the odd conclusion that the permutations were arbitrary and had no laws of their own. (Levi-Strauss, 1960:124; quoted in translation in O'Toole, 1975: 146)

As Levi-Strauss argues (see also O'Toole, 1975), Propp was insufficiently attentive to the possible **transformational interrelatedness** of functions, roles and plots; he should have moved beyond his relatively modest enterprise of abstraction and considered the general structural conditions which a story must fulfil, and have treated his functions as realizations or transformations of more fundamental structures. Such developments are evident in the work of Todorov (Todorov, 1977), which seems to have won few adherents. In fairness to Propp, however, and indicative of the breadth of this seminal study, it should be noted that he does recognize that 'inverted sequences' occur (Propp, 1968: 107). An inverted sequence is a marked variant of the unmarked order, e.g., where the hero meets a helper *before* the misfortune that the helper is to assist him in overcoming has actually taken place.

What might be one's grounds for siding either with Propp or with Todorov in this dispute?

6 One of the best critiques of the whole formalist orientation is F. Jameson's *The Prison-House of Language* (1972), though this is not a book for the beginning student. In a slightly earlier article he concluded, only a little unfairly:

> Formalism is . . . the basic mode of interpretation of those who refuse interpretation: at the same time it is important to stress the fact that this method finds its privileged objects in the smaller forms, in short stories or folk tales, poems, anecdotes, in the decorative detail of larger works . . . . The Formalistic model is essentially synchronic, and cannot adequately deal with diachrony, either in literary history or in the form of the individual work, which is to say that Formalism as a method stops short at the point where the novel as a problem begins. (Jameson, 1970: 12)

This pregnant summary is almost prophetic in its references to **diachronic reception** (the way a community's assessment of a literary text changes and develops as the years go by), which is now so central a critical concern. But it also advertises its (Jameson's) own preferences: its interests are in a world where 'the novel as a problem' is an important problem, rather than in the world of so many people today, whose narrative consumption/ reception is almost never in novel form, but rather in that of the newspaper story, the television series and commercials, personal anecdotes, and so on – those that he appears to dismiss as the 'smaller forms'. What arguments could we develop either for or against devoting our attentions to those smaller forms, such as the television commercial?

7 Taking Propp's 31 functions and 7 roles, attempt to apply them to one or two narratives you know well. Determine how much adjustment of the scheme is needed for it to capture the basic story of one of the following: a medieval morality play; one

of Chaucer's Canterbury Tales, – e.g., 'The Wife of Bath's Tale'; one of Shakespeare's comedies or one of his problem plays; any Dickens novel, though *Oliver Twist* and *Bleak House* seem particularly manageable candidates; Pope's 'The Rape of the Lock'; Melville's *Moby Dick*.

In fact the narratives you choose to analyze could be of any type. It might be your grandmother's oft-rehearsed story of her pursuit and courtship by your grandfather (perhaps there's no villain here, but presumably it concludes with marriage!), or you could look at any simple children's story you might have to hand.

But if even these narratives look at first glance unmanageably different from Propp's stories and morphology, you could certainly begin with a story which, intuitively, you feel is not too unlike those examined by Propp, e.g., a Grimm or Hans Andersen folktale.

How well does the Propp 'grammar' fit your chosen target text? Where do the problems and difficulties lie? As you move away from traditional oral-based folktales, you should expect that the kinds of functions and roles involved in the basic story structure will be rather removed from those of Propp – removed, but not unrelated. And that's the point: in looking for the kinds of functions and roles from which multifarious stories are generated, we are indeed committed to identifying relatedness of structure.

8 Are the blurbs that accompany books of fiction – the brief filers or advertisements for books that appear somewhere on their jackets – plot summaries? If not, what are they? Analyze the blurbs of three books of fiction, thinking about this question in particular. Whatever differences of detail you find, it will become newly apparent to you just how structured, carefully-worded and important such blurbs are. In a bookshop, taking a quick glance at the merchandise, the blurb may be the only part of the text that the critical potential purchaser has time to read. You might move on to compare your fiction blurbs with the blurbs that accompany popular non-fiction, academic literary criticism, linguistics textbooks, science textbooks, biographies, etc.

9 Do press reviews of books of fiction contain plot summaries? Not necessarily, it seems. Can you see any pattern to this variation, where certain types of fiction get fairly full summaries, others almost none at all? Why might it be that certain reviews *start* a story summary (often identifying the characters, the setting(s) but only the first few events – to use the three categories

noted at the opening of the chapter) but do not complete it? Compare and contrast the reviews, in a range of publications, of a current notable fiction. Where in the review does the plot summary come, if it appears at all? Does it come all in one chunk, or intermittently? How much agreement does there seem to be over what to put into the summary, and where do there seem to be differences of emphasis? What possible grounds might there be for those differences? How might all this relate to the idea raised in this chapter that plot perception may be culturally relative?

10 Bal (1985: 24) lists a number of alternative principles of 'structuring' to those we have focussed on in this chapter. Thus she suggests that events can often be grouped into sequences on the basis of the identity of the actors (characters) involved, and the kind of role (seeker, victim, villain, helper, and so on) they are playing. Or classification can be done on the basis of the nature of the confrontation:

Is there verbal (spoken), mental (via thoughts, feelings, observations), or bodily contact? Are these contacts successful, do they fail, or is this impossible to determine?

Similarly, classificatory grouping can sometimes be effected on the basis of the *temporal* connectedness, contiguity or overlap of events, by comparison with apparent temporal unrelatedness; or on the basis of the types of *location* in which events take place.

Use just one of these principles on a narrative of your choice (again, any of the stories in *Dubliners* might repay such treatment), and consider what – if anything – the groupings thus devised suggest about the dynamics of that narrative. Clearly, if you apply several of these principles of classification in turn to a single story, you will arrive at a 'multi-layered' analysis which may be rather more revealing.

11 A final and sceptical orientation on theory of plot structure can be gained from a lengthy critique of the book (Fowler, ed., 1975) in which Culler (1975b) appears: see Smith (1978). Although many of Smith's criticisms of Culler's paper seem to me unfair, she does raise interesting questions when she challenges the assumption of 'substantial agreement' (as if this were worldwide) over plot summaries:

The extent to which we produce comparable plot summaries

may have a good deal to do with who 'we' are and how we learned both what 'plots' are and also what it means to 'summarize' them. It is doubtful, for example, that a South American tribesman would produce the same plot summary of one of his myths as would Claude Levi-Strauss. Or to put it another way, wouldn't our explaining to the tribesman (or, of course, to a child) what we wanted when we asked for a 'plot summary' be the same as telling him how to 'process' the story the way 'we' have learned to? (Smith, 1978: 183)

Take a narrative familiar to you and your friends (it doesn't have to be highly literary, it could be, for example, *ET* or *Raiders of the Lost Ark*), and attempt a summary of the story which is *not* a *plot* summary – but still feels to you a fair summary in some respects (e.g., of the mood or tone). Now present your summary to one or more of those friends and ask them their opinion of it as a summary of the story. Your problems in producing a non-plot summary, and their reactions to it, should be instructive.

12   There are other approaches to the 'basic grammar' of stories than those discussed in this chapter, perhaps most notably the work of Prince (1973; 1982); and a vast body of psycholinguistic research into our mental modelling of story format. This research hypothesizes that we construct schemas, or frameworks, of archetypal stories, which we hold in our minds, and that we use these frameworks as a mental aid when we attempt to comprehend or recall particular stories. Although space-limitations forbid full review of the theory and assumptions, some applications of this psycholinguistic approach will be discussed in Chapter 7.

The articulation of narrative text I: time, focalization, narration

Narrative text: a single level of analysis

In this and the following chapter we turn from characterization of the 'elementary particles' of narratives, grouped under the label 'story', to the various expansions and individualizations of those elements that go on in the production of text. We can think of the move from the abstract level of story components to the concrete level of textual realizations as both a process and an articulation. The main processes or articulations involved are listed by Bal as the following (I have replaced her terms 'fabula' and 'story' by 'story' and 'text' respectively, to avoid confusion):

1 The events are arranged in a sequence which can differ from the chronological sequence.
2 The amount of time which is allotted in the text to the various elements of the story is determined with respect to the amount of time which these elements take up in the story. [That is to say, our experience-based judgment of how long various events or states would take or last in the story is the baseline or yardstick for our sense of the relative abundance or scarcity of time allocated to presentation of that event or state in the text.]
3 The actors are provided with distinct traits. In this manner, they are individualized and transformed into characters.
4 The locations [settings] where events occur are also given distinct characteristics and are thus transformed into specific places.
5 In addition to the necessary relationships among actors, events, locations, and time, all of which were already describable in the layer of the story, other relationships (symbolic, allusive, etc.) may exist among the various elements.
6 A choice is made from among the various 'points of view' from which the elements can be presented. (Bal, 1985: 7)

This chapter concentrates on items 1, 2 and 6 on this list (i.e., time and focalization), before concluding with a discussion of narration – the complex different ways of narrating or being a narrator. The next chapter will focus on items 3 and 4 (character and setting), and the subtle technique for disclosing characters' words or thoughts known as **free indirect discourse**. Notice that in separating the areas for analysis in this way, while retaining an umbrella title that applies to both chapters (The articulation of narrative text), I am in effect reverting to a kind of *two*-level model of narrative production, rather than the three-level one favoured by Bal and Rimmon-Kenan. I will defend this decision in passing at various points in the chapters, but do not wish to make too much of this difference. Notice also that item 5 on Bal's list will not be addressed adequately here: this reflects the inadequacy (in my view) of its treatment to date by narrative theorists and grammarians.

3.2   Text and time

Turning to time in the text, some general observations are perhaps first in order. Notice that time itself, in the sense of the systematic measurement of the distance between, for example, particular past states and our present one, is itself a structuring and structuralist notion. Structuring, because it asserts and articulates *relations* between particular states or changes of state, and structuralist, in so far as it relies on our recognition of particular similarities and particular differences between specified states. What we call 'a year' must have been first perceived as a single full cycle of the warmer and colder seasons and of the natural world, matching a full cycle of the sun's movements towards and away from one's earthly location. Similarly, the perceived recurring succession of day and night gives rise to the introduction of temporal measurement in just those terms. As Rimmon-Kenan puts it (1983: 44):

Time 'is', paradoxically, repetition within irreversible change.

although we might want to modify this slightly and say:

Time is perceived repetition within perceived irreversible change.

But in addition we need to remember that there is something unreal and heavily convention-laden about so-called story time and text time, for in both cases we are not referring to actual temporal progression, but the linear verbal *representation* of temporality. A kind of artifice is at work, in which we look for a match between the 'real-world' intervals and sub-intervals of time that the narrative implies, and our sense of time passing during our experience of reading that narrative. Whether we regard a particular match as appropriate or not is a judgment largely guided by our prior reading experience, our familiarity with the particular genre that the text belongs to, and the seriousness of the events depicted.

Because text time is inescapably linear, there is an obvious and immediate disruption of any neat correlation of real time to text time as soon as the narrative involves more than one story-line: that is to say, as soon as there is more than one set of developing circumstances affecting different sets of characters. But even when we compare text time to what Rimmon-Kenan calls 'an ideal "natural" chronology' (1983: 45), we rarely find that the standard of steady correspondence is maintained. Even, say, when a story is purely direct speech (monologue or dialogue), it's likely that we spend considerably longer reading that written 'transcript' than would be spent in any actual speaking.

The most influential theorist of text time is Gerard Genette, who isolates three major aspects of temporal manipulation or articulation in the movement from story to text:

1 Order: this refers to the relations between the assumed sequence of events in the story and their actual order of presentation in the text.
2 Duration: for Genette this chiefly concerns the relations between the extent of time that events are supposed to have actually taken up, and the amount of text devoted to presenting those same events.
3 Frequency: how often something happens in story compared with how often it is narrated in text.

As may be apparent from the foregoing discussion, the most potentially problematic of these aspects is that of duration, and I shall devote rather greater space to this aspect.

ORDER   3.2.1

Any departures in the order of presentation in the text from the order in which events evidently occurred in the story are termed by Genette **anachronies**. An anachrony is any chunk of text that is told at a point which is earlier or later than its natural or logical position in the event sequence. Strictly speaking, we can find anachrony even within a single sentence. In

The king died of grief because the queen had died.

the subordinate clause of reason is an anachrony, presented after the report of the king's death even though it contains the report of an event which logically and naturally – in the story – preceded his death.

But anachronies in extended narratives are more complex than that example. They naturally divide into flashbacks and flashforwards, or what Genette calls **analepses** and **prolepses**. An analepsis is an achronological movement back in time, so that a chronologically earlier incident is related later in the text; a prolepsis is an achronological movement forward in time, so that a future event is related textually 'before its time', before the presentation of chronologically intermediate events. Any delayed disclosure (the reader expected, on the basis of chronological sequence, to be told this earlier) is thus analeptic, while any premature disclosure (the reader did not expect, if strict chronology were observed, to be told this until later) is proleptic. Incidentally, Bal's useful terms for the two types of anachrony are **retroversions** and **anticipations**.

An analepsis may be either **homodiegetic** or **heterodiegetic**, depending on whether it carries information about the same character/event/storyline as has been presented in the immediately-preceding text, or about some different character or event. Examples of homodiegetic analepsis are easy to find. We could cite the second paragraph of 'Eveline', with its movement back in time to the games of Eveline's childhood days; actually the analepses in 'Eveline' are more complex than this suggests, and will be returned to later. But if we turn instead to Nabokov's *Pnin* (1957), we find many clear cases of homodiegetic analepsis dotted throughout its opening pages. The following is the novel's second paragraph, describing the middle-aged Pnin's appearance as he travels by train to an engagement as a guest lecturer:

His sloppy socks were of scarlet wool with lilac lozenges; his conservative black Oxfords had cost him about as much as all the rest of his clothing (flamboyant goon tie included). Prior to the 1940s, during the staid European era of his life, he had always worn long underwear, its terminals tucked into the tops of neat silk socks, which were clocked, soberly coloured, and held up on his cotton-clad calves by garters. In those days, to reveal a glimpse of that white underwear by pulling up a trouser leg too high would have seemed to Pnin as indecent as showing himself to ladies minus collar and tie; for even when decayed Mme Roux, the concierge of the squalid apartment house in the Sixteenth Arrondissement of Paris where Pnin, after escaping from Leninized Russia and completing his college education in Prague, had spent fifteen years – happened to come up for the rent while he was without his *faux col*, prim Pnin would cover his front stud with a chaste hand. All this underwent a change in the heady atmosphere of the New World. Nowadays, at fifty-two, he was crazy about sunbathing, wore sport shirts and slacks, and when crossing his legs would carefully, deliberately, brazenly display a tremendous stretch of bare shin. Thus he might have appeared to a fellow passenger; but except for a soldier asleep at one end and two women absorbed in a baby at the other, Pnin had the carriage to himself.

Here is analepsis within analepsis. From the story's present time, the text jumps back to a description of Pnin's 'staid European era' and his relations with Mme Roux. But then during the description of those relations with Mme Roux, there is a further jump back, in the text, to youthful Pnin's escape from Russia. Thus we see a simple demonstration of how complex transformations of temporal order, in the articulation of story as narrative text, make that text more entertaining, engrossing, and polished.

Nowhere in *Pnin* do we get a plodding, blow-by-chronological-blow account of Pnin's youth in revolutionary Russia, his escape to Prague, his fifteen years there, and so on. That important background only emerges 'naturally', as it were, when, as part of Pnin's ongoing narrative present, his past briefly ceases to be distant background and becomes currently experienced foreground, as in Pnin's grieving recollection of a girl he had loved in pre-revolutionary Russia who was subsequently murdered at Buchenwald (see p. 110ff.). In fact the recollection is remarkably intense, more like a living-through. Middle-aged Pnin is taking a vacation, along with assorted other Russian emigrés and their children, in an upstate country retreat. But when the name of Mira Belochkin crops up in conversation, Pnin withdraws into an

intense memory of his youth, of country house summers at a
Baltic resort, of his father and Mira's father engrossed in their
chess game in a corner of the verandah.

> Timofey Pnin was again the clumsy, shy, obstinate, eighteen-
> year-old boy, waiting in the dark for Mira – and despite the
> fact that logical thought put electric bulbs into the kerosene
> lamps and reshuffled the people, turning them into ageing
> *emigrés*... my poor Pnin, with hallucinatory sharpness,
> imagined Mira slipping out of there into the garden and coming
> toward him among tall tobacco flowers whose dull white
> mingled in the dark with that of her frock. (111)

Later in the same revery it is disclosed that

> In order to exist rationally, Pnin had taught himself, during the
> last ten years, never to remember Mira Belochkin . . . One had
> to forget – because one could not live with the thought that
> this graceful, fragile, tender young woman with those eyes, that
> smile, those gardens and snows in the background, had been
> brought in a cattle car to an extermination camp and
> killed . . . . And since the exact form of her death had not
> been recorded, Mira kept dying a great number of deaths in
> one's mind, and undergoing a great number of resurrections,
> only to die again and again, led away by a trained nurse,
> inoculated with filth, tetanus bacilli, broken glass, gassed in a
> sham shower-bath with prussic acid, burned alive in a pit on
> a gasoline-soaked pile of beechwood. (112–13)

As such passages show, grief is a powerful trigger (perhaps the
most powerful) of character-based analepsis, while the willed 'not-
remembering' that is Pnin's means of coping with grief amounts to
a powerful suppression of analeptic tendencies in a character,
reflected in our clichéd injunctions to the grief-stricken to 'live in
the present' and 'look to the future'.

An example of *hetero*diegetic analepsis, offered by Genette, is
the focus on Swann as protagonist of certain events in section 2
of Proust's *A la recherche du temps perdu*: events that clearly
occurred long before the quite different focus of section 1,
Marcel's boyhood. To return to *Pnin*, consider the extraordinary
final chapter of that novel, in which the narrator himself, whom
we gradually realize is the 'old friend' and academic rival whose
appointment at Waindell College causes Pnin's departure, steps
forward to give his own account of events. That account begins

with heterodiegetic analepsis: a reversion to the narrator's own youth in Russia in 1911.

All these examples are also *external* analepses, moving back to a time prior to the opening of the text. *Internal* analepses are a textual moving-back in the story, but not such a radical moving-back as to involve crossing the text's opening, and notably include any repetitions of incidents previously narrated in their proper chronological place. Of course an analepsis could straddle or overlap the previously-established start of the narrative, in which case Genette labels the analepsis 'mixed'. We will need to reflect further on the function of analepses, but a first observation might be that they seem to be designed to 'fill gaps' in stories, though these gaps may themselves be the contrivance of the writer, and may not be perceived as gaps until after the analepsis has appeared.

A little more may be said of the function of analepses, in particular those which cover events previously reported. On such repetitive analepsis, Bal makes some valuable observations:

> The repetition of a previously described event usually serves to change, or add to, the emphasis on the meaning of that event. The same event is presented as more, or less, pleasant, innocent, or important than we had previously believed it to be. It is thus both *identical* and *different*: the facts are the same, but their meaning has changed. In Proust, such internal retroversions form a part of the famous and specifically Proustian interruption of the linearity in searching for, and recovering of, the elusive past. But in much simpler literature too, frequent use is made of possibilities such as these. Detective novels and all kinds of texts which are constructed around mysteries, masquerades, and puzzles adopt this technique as an important structural device. (Bal, 1985: 61)

Prolepses – much rarer – undercut or remove suspense, since they reveal future circumstances to you long before any chronological imperative dictates that they be told. On the other hand, a different kind of engaged puzzlement is fostered by prolepses: the reader is frequently made aware of her own bafflement as to how characters and events get from their current situation to the distant future one prematurely revealed, and is all the more intrigued to learn of the intervening happenings. It is probable that prolepsis is commonest in first-person narratives, possibly because it may seem more natural for such a narrator to jump forward occasionally to subsequent events which are closer to that narrator's own present. Like analepses, prolepses can be homo- or heterodiegetic, depending on whether they entail a switch of focus to a different character, event or storyline; and internal, external or mixed, depending on their chronological relation to the endpoint of the basic narrative.

One qualification one might make concerning certain examples of prolepsis, such as this one from *The Prime of Miss Jean Brodie*:

> 'Speech is silver but silence is golden. Mary, are you listening? What was I saying?'
> Mary Macgregor, lumpy, with merely two eyes, a nose and a mouth like a snowman, who was later famous for being stupid and always to blame and who, at the age of twenty-three, lost her life in a hotel fire, ventured, 'Golden'.

is that they are typically examples of proleptic 'traces' inscribed in a narrative, rather than the full-fledged shift of temporal orientation where an extended stretch of text – a chapter, or a section – reports distantly future events. Similarly, my first example of homodiegetic analepsis in *Pnin* might be regarded as fleeting tracery rather than structural temporal reordering (in Barthesian terms, more an index than a function). Thus there seem to be two strikingly different kinds of anachrony with different functions. The former is a contribution to dense narrative texture, but is often more a local insight into a character, or the narrator, than a manipulation of the event line; the latter is more substantially a contribution to narrative structure, sometimes requiring the reader to revise his or her assumptions as to just what the story is that is being told.

In characterizing anachronies Genette also suggests we can distinguish their chronological distance from the present moment in the story (which I will call their 'reach', and Bal calls 'distance'), and their chronological duration (which I will call their 'extent', and Bal calls 'span').

Before leaving the topic of 'order' it perhaps needs stressing that in discriminating the types of anachronistic deviations that a narrative text makes from the underlying story, all our observations are relational. That is, we proceed not with the goal of simply unravelling the sequential jumble of a Faulkner or Joyce novel, restoring the wholesome chronology that might satisfy a scientist. Certainly unravelling is involved and is important, but equally so is a sense of the *relations* between the various chunks of the text, where chunks in the order A B C D E in fact denote events that occurred in the order B C D A E, with considerable gaps or ellipses between the first three of these, temporal contiguity of the last three, and so on: a potentially quite elaborate network of temporal relations. (The picture becomes considerably more complex if we determine that any two or more of these chunks are at a single point in time in the story.) And in emphasizing relation one is also emphasizing *scale*. An external analepsis that reaches back twenty years with an extent of one month, embedded in a story whose extent otherwise is just twenty-four hours, should and can be distinguished from an analepsis identical in extent and reach but embedded in a story of year-long extent.

DURATION   3.2.2

What is text duration? Can it be reduced simply to the reading time of a narrative? Even if we do so view it, it is clear that any posited reading time will be a source of controversy: readers read at different speeds, decide to break off from reading at different places (or not at all), so that every reader will have a different reading time for a narrative. On the other hand, granted absolute differences of reading pace, we might still want to argue that there are relative similarities of reading time, for fluent native speakers, for particular types of text. The application of such posited norms of reading duration, against which one would then compare the likely temporal duration of the events, etc., that the text relates, are pretty much limited to scenic passages reporting monologues, dialogues, sequences of physical actions which are punctual or of short duration, and short journeys. So many light-weight novels seem to be aimed at the travelling reader these days – the person travelling alone by train or plane, on a journey lasting four or five hours – that one imagines some powerful effects might be achieved by contriving that both the reading time and the text duration of such a book be just four or five hours.

Some such pan-textual norms of reading time are sometimes invoked in stylistic commentaries on effects of (variation of) pace, but this is not the approach adopted by Genette. Genette opts for an intra-textual strategy, where textual pace at any particular place in a narrative is assessed relative to pace elsewhere in that same narrative, and that pace is then expressed as a ratio between the indicated duration of the story (in minutes, hours, days) and the extent of text (in pages) devoted to its telling. This leads to identifying a *norm* of pace for a particular narrative, against which accelerations and decelerations can be perceived. The norm is thus text-bound, and a constancy of pace would emerge if the ratio between story-duration and extent of textual presentation were invariable – e.g., a page for every month of a character's life.

Genette's ratio is very often far more mechanical than actual texts are. For example, suppose there were a chapter for every year of a character's life, but those chapters were of rather different lengths: is this constancy of pace or variation of pace? And how should we reformulate this ratio for application to *oral* narratives? Presumably we would be back to hypothesizing a norm for the 'duration of delivery' – although we could alternatively take an intra-performance perspective, and make judgments about pace relative to just a particular performance of a narrative. Rather simplistic, too, is the assumption that event or story time is easy to deduce or infer from the narrative, as if the heading of each page of the text carried a digital read-out of the time elapsed. For example, just how long, in story time, is Eveline's revery? It could be anything from a few minutes to several hours: it takes place between early and late evening (when the mail-boat goes). Since we can't be sure about the pace of the revery presentation, neither can we be sure as to whether the later scene at the quayside is a presentational acceleration or deceleration.

Maximum speed is said to constitute **ellipsis**, where no text space is spent on a piece of story duration; the opposite situation is **descriptive pause**: text without story duration (for example, the descriptive openings of *A Passage to India*, Ellison's *Invisible Man*, Hardy's *The Return of the Native*, and many more). An example of ellipsis cited by Chatman is that between the close of Chapter 5 of *The Sun Also Rises*, where Jake has finished lunch and sets off for his office, and the opening of Chapter 6, when he is waiting for Brett at five o'clock. Such ellipses, Chatman argues, are widespread in modernist fiction, where a series of detailed scenic presentations are linked by abrupt spatio-temporal jumps. However, it seems worth distinguishing this sort of ellipsis, which is simply an exploitation of the temporal discontinuity we not only tolerate but probably prefer in our narratives (so we don't have to read about every dull thing a character does), from the accelerations of presentation to the sharply abbreviated summary, which *are* perceived as involving change of pace. For we surely do not feel any change of pace, any acceleration, at the junction of Chapters 5 and 6 of *The Sun Also Rises*. I would suggest, then, that ellipsis, in the form of a spatiotemporal gap or **aporia**, is a minor or major narrational strategy (depending on just what gets left out) but is not really a type of narrative pace, if we conceive of the latter as dependent on our judgments about the rapidity *of the telling* of story events. In other words I am arguing for a view of pace as the rapidity of the telling of what does get told.

SUMMARY AND SCENE   3.2.3

But more common and interesting than these are the relatively accelerated and the relatively decelerated presentation, known since Lubbock's interpretive account of Jamesian poetics as **summary** and **scene** respectively. In summary, the pace is accelerated through a textual compression of a given story period into a relatively short statement of its main features. Rimmon-Kenan (1983: 53) cites an amusing example of Nabokovian summary, a foregrounded and conscious play with our conventional expectations both of novel duration and of what Barthes calls **catalysers** (satellites), **indices** and **informants**:

> Once upon a time there lived in Berlin, Germany, a man called Albinus. He was rich, respectable, happy; one day he abandoned his wife for the sake of a youthful mistress; he loved, was not loved; and his life ended in disaster.
>
> This is the whole story and we might have left it at that had there not been profit and pleasure in the telling, and although there is plenty of space on a gravestone to contain, bound in moss, the abridged version of a man's life, detail is always welcome. (Nabokov, *Laughter in the Dark*)

In scene, story and text duration are conventionally considered identical (e.g., purely dialogue passages, as in Hemingway, Ivy Compton-Burnett, among a number). But note that we can posit a sharper counterpart to summary, one that is slower even than scene: the situation in which text is more extended than story, which Chatman terms 'stretch'. Notice, too, how in discussing scenic pace, naturalistic assumptions and a covert comparison with the pace of real, natural interaction, creep back in. Hitherto I have been stressing that the pace of any portion of a text (the rapidity of presentation of time and events passing) is relative to the pace in *other* portions of that text, or relative to the pace of the text as a whole, or relative to the pace of other texts. But when we start thinking about scene, and especially the representation of direct speech exchanges between characters, something revealing happens. We tend not to assess the pace of a scene in relation to co-textual standards, but rather in relation to real-world standards.

This is a telling reminder of how our usual unquestioning view of fictional dialogue is that it is the most complete and mimetic representation of real dialogue, that reading direct speech dialogue 'amounts to the same thing' as being a witness to actual spoken interaction, so that to talk of the 'pace' of such written-up scenes – as if they could go faster or slower – barely makes sense to us: obviously, scenes go at just the pace of the actual interaction. Well of course the point is that what has become obvious to us is not an inescapable feature of fictional dialogue, but a convention and an *effect*. The fictional direct speech representation of any dialogue *can* go faster or slower, and we neglect the artifice in fictional dialogue, the ways in which it is non-naturalistic, is not a full transcription, at our peril. We will return to the natural and the conventional in speech represen-tation when examining free indirect discourse in the next chapter.

When the reader encounters relative acceleration or deceler-ation of presentation, she will often interpret the shift in pace as an authorial or narratorial indication of the marginality (on the one hand) or the centrality and importance (on the other) of what is being presented. More important events and conversations are usually given in scenic detail, less important or background ones in summary précis. But again, these are norms from which writers often depart with strong motivation. A writer may play with our conventional expectations, a narrator–character may attempt to suppress or retreat from certain important but distasteful events, and so on. Shock and irony can be created by disclosing a central event briefly, following detailed presentation of trivial events.

Chatman (1978: 76–8) also notes the contrast between narratorial summary common in the traditional novel, and what goes on in many modern novels, where *characters* provide summaries in their own recollections of past events (as in *Mrs Dalloway* and many others). Hence we are really witnessing *scenes* here, if the duration of character-derived remembered events, and the extent of text devoted to their presentation, are commensurate with ratios for reflection-cum-presentation else-where in the narrative. The puzzle hinges on what counts as a story event, the presentational duration of which is to be compared with comparable events elsewhere in the novel. Is the story event 'Clarissa reminisces one day, from morning shopping to evening party'; or is there here a *series* of story events, the various incidents from her past that Clarissa reviews in memory? Perhaps the best answer to give is 'both'; we *see* the framing narrative, a day in the life of Clarissa Dalloway (and some others), a narrative within which the reminiscence is just a single event among others. We also *see*, as the reminiscence unfolds, that an embedded story is being disclosed, spanning a much greater period of time than the framing one ('a life in the day of Clarissa Dalloway').

In saying this we can maintain a dual characterization, just as, in sentence grammar, we can say that an embedded nominal clause counts simply as an object relative to the clause in which it is embedded, but has its own internal structural logic when viewed independently of the embedding clause. Thus we can now say that as a unit within the framing narrative the reminiscence maintains normal order, text-normal duration (allegedly), and singulative frequency. But as a separate narrative embedded *within* the framing narrative, we encounter the text of a story (of thirty years of Clarissa's earlier life) which involves various anachronies (many of the events are analeptically recollected, and their normal order of occurrence is departed from), variations of duration (some material is sharply summarized), and some instances of repetitive frequency.

But even this dual characterization, we might argue, leaves unremarked certain effects that merit comment. A dual perspective seems all that is strictly required, distinguishing the embedded story of incidents-remembered-by-Clarissa-Dalloway from the superordinate story of incidents-on-the-day-of-Mrs Dalloway's-party – two stories at different levels: two distinct configurations of order, duration and frequency. But while our account of order can say things about that dimension in the two separate stories, it fails to identify the *reader's* experience of retroversion as she finds Mrs Dalloway's thoughts jumping back to moments in her youth. As readers processing the linear unfolding of the text, it seems we do not keep levels and stories quite as separate as the analytical approach outlined above does. In sophisticated ways that resist analytical unravelling, we unite the story of things-happening with that of things-remembered-as-having-happened, and understand Mrs Dalloway's recollected experience to be both timely and achronistic, utterly past in actuality, wholly present to consciousness. Nor are these the only stories that we unite or hold in view as we read this novel. There are the ongoing and remembered stories of Lucrezia Warren Smith, of her husband, of Peter Walsh, and many more. All these stories we hold in view, unable to integrate them into a single 'macro' story, but also unable to separate them out as distinct: the textual form denies us that solution. In the reading, our requirements of chronology and causal relation in narrative are subordinated to attention to the logic (in Clarissa Dalloway and all the rest) of human reaction, whether physical or mental.

My conclusion, then, is that in a many-storied novel like *Mrs Dalloway* our experience of the temporal order resists analysis – at least analysis in terms of chronology. We seem to recognize and overlook anachronies at the same time; we neither merge (in the sense of assimilate) nor unravel these separable story sequences, but hold them in a complex enigmatic suspension. I would urge the reader himself to hold these points in view when we come to examine free indirect discourse in the next chapter, for it seems that a very similar unmergeable duality, resistant to analytical dissection, operates there too. Hence the above paragraphs can be viewed as related both to the current topic and, proleptically, to that of speech and thought presentation – the embedding of voice within voice.

Note that above I describe Mrs Dalloway's reminiscence as *allegedly* of normal duration: the strict test, we know, is to find other cases of reminiscing in the novel, of apparently similar 'real time', and compare how much text is used up in the different cases – a fairly rough and ready reckoning! And perhaps an inappropriate one. There still seem to be several problems with Genette's notion of duration – it doesn't always seem to be addressing what readers are responding to when they say one passage is pacey, another passage is slow. And it seems that there is an underpinning of text-internal **vraisemblance** (see glossary) or verisimilitude in Genette's approach, ie., an unspoken reliance on what we recognize as realistic and reasonable lengths of text to spend on particular incidents, given some sense of the overall pace of the narrative. In linguistic terminology, we could complain that his simple calculation of duration leans too far towards assuming a natural fit, at least within the narrative, and too far away from acknowledging that the norms of text-extent in the presentation of various kinds of salient incidents may be quite arbitrary and conventionalized.

In analyzing pace, supratextual comparisons are one interesting area that calls for more study. That is to say, we might usefully assess the pace of Mrs Dalloway's reminiscences relative to similar reveries in other Woolf novels, other modernist novels of the period, and in other recent British novels (James, Hardy, Galsworthy and Bennett). In doing so we are proceeding intertextually, and sensitive to genre and period. For it does seem we become accustomed, as experienced readers, to certain kinds of duration linked with certain kinds of culturally-salient narrative incident. We get used to a certain kind of length of presentation of the details of a hero's early childhood in novels by Dickens and Thackeray, a certain degree of extendedness in their presentations of love scenes and death scenes and murders, so that our perceptions of duration must be partly intertextual as well as intratextual. And intratextually, as in the case of narrative discontinuity in *The Sun Also Rises* cited earlier, we accept all sorts of ellipses related to cultural taboo or tellability: no one has sex or goes to the bathroom in Austen or Dickens – or more precisely, such actions are not narrated, being taboo or felt to be uninteresting. This is no longer true when we get to Joyce and Lawrence. But, as I have argued earlier, by duration we should mean something more than the selectivity and discontinuity that can always be ascribed to a narrative (we can always think of things that must have happened but haven't been reported).

FREQUENCY   3.2.4

By the term 'frequency' we denote the business of repeated textual telling of a single story incident. If the norm is 'singulative' frequency (telling n times what happened n times), 'repetitive' frequency is exemplified in Faulkner's *Absalom, Absalom!*, in which the murder of Charles Bon by Henry Sutpen is told 39 times, by various tellers. Sometimes singulative presentation would strike us as strangely redundant and verbose: where there are multiple occurrences of an incident of a single type. An option in such cases is 'iterative' frequency – telling once what happened n times. Frequency is somewhat different in kind from order and duration. It is something finally determinable only retrospectively, upon completed reading of a text, though it is also encoded fairly straightforwardly by temporal phrases and the verb-phrase structure ('the children of the avenue used to play together in that field' in 'Eveline'). Order and duration are temporal features that the reader grapples with experientially in the ongoing processing of text, features about which we adopt revisable hypotheses as we work through a text: there is nothing so 'experiential' or tied to ongoing text-processing about frequency of telling.

3.3 Temporal refractions in text: Nabokov's *Pnin*

So much for theorizing. We now need to return to some text, of manageable length, and see just how insightful the Genettian model can be. And here it is important to remember that although it seemed best to present order, duration and frequency separately, in the practice of text-articulation they are dimensions that reinforce or interact with each other in significant ways. Deviations along one dimension may give rise to deviations along the others: an event or episode told with repetitive frequency will inevitably involve anachronisms in terms of order, and more complex oddities in duration. But we should also keep in view the possibility that other, non-Genettian methods – e.g., stylistic ones focussing on tense and aspect in the verb, adverbials of temporal qualification, and an appeal to readers' norms (rather than the textual norm) may be more in tune with our judgments of textual reorderings, pace and frequency. As attractive a text as any for these purposes of demonstration is the novel already mentioned several times in this chapter, Vladimir Nabokov's *Pnin*. In what follows I will focus on temporal processes in the first section of the first chapter of that novel.

Chapter 1, section 1, of *Pnin* recounts part of middle-aged Russian emigré, US-naturalized, university professor Pnin's mishap-ridden journey to a women's college where he is due to present a guest lecture. The first paragraph is almost purely descriptive (I will return to this 'almost'), with, therefore, no scope for temporal classifications. It consists of two sentences: the first locates and names Professor Timofey Pnin (and hence concerns character and setting, not event), the second supplies a brief evaluation of the prominent features of his appearance:

> The elderly passenger sitting on the north-window side of that inexorably moving railway coach, next to an empty seat and facing two empty ones, was none other than Professor Timofey Pnin. Ideally bald, sun-tanned, and clean-shaven, he began rather impressively with that great brown dome of his, tortoise-

shell glasses (masking an infantile absence of eyebrows), apish upper lip, thick neck, and strong-man torso in a tightish tweed coat, but ended, somewhat disappointingly, in a pair of spindly legs (now flannelled and crossed) and frail-looking, almost feminine feet.

Paragraph 2, which I have quoted in full in 3.2.1, has an early trivial anachrony:

His Oxfords *had cost* him as much as all the rest of his clothing . . . (my emphasis)

But, as we have seen, more significant homodiegetic analepses follow. Are these – the references to his European era, and its several stages (Russia, Prague, Paris) – internal or external to the basic story? That, of course, depends entirely on what we take to be the basic story and since the whole Genettian exercise is an uncovering of *relations* between parts, it is quite reasonable, in principle, for different analysts to adopt different – but congruent – solutions.

Thus if we adopt the implied time point of paragraph 1 (October 1950) as the opening of the story sequence as well as that of the text, then the European references are clearly analepses (of varying reach and extent), of sharply summarized duration and – at this stage at least – singulative frequency. Such a working hypothesis is, I think, supported by the content of the rest of the novel: I take the novel's basic story to be an account of Pnin's last few months as a professor at Waindell College, 1950–1 (an account interspersed with analepses providing retrospective glimpses of Pnin's earlier life).

But one could, alternatively, see the basic story as about and including Pnin at all the stages of his depiction. There are several reasons why such a solution, in this case at least, seems unattractive. Broadly, it casts the novel in its entirety as a very oddly formed narrative: some fairly full presentations of parts of Pnin's childhood and adolescent experiences, often of brief temporal extent and repeatedly interrupted by extremely lengthy 'prolepses' concerning Pnin in 1950–1, with – and this is oddest of all – very few references to developments during a huge chronological span from *c.* 1920 to *c.* 1950. And more specifically, tense and temporal qualification in the opening pages compel us to treat the Pnin of 1950, on the train, as the Pnin of the narrative present.

Nowadays, at fifty-two, he was crazy about sunbathing, wore sports shirts and slacks . . . .

– while the Pnin of earlier days is the pre-story Pnin.

The third paragraph confirms our preferred hypothesis of the temporal structure of the novel, with amusing retrospective explanations as to Pnin's current, unrecognized, error:

> Now a secret must be imparted. Professor Pnin was on the wrong train. He was unaware of it, and so was the conductor, already threading his way through the train to Pnin's coach. As a matter of fact, Pnin at the moment felt very well satisfied with himself. When inviting him to deliver a Friday-evening lecture at Cremona – some two hundred versts west of Waindell, Pnin's academic perch since 1945 – the vice-president of the Cremona Women's Club, a Miss Judith Clyde, had advised our friend that the most convenient train left Waindell at 1.52 p.m., reaching Cremona at 4.17.

But Pnin, we are told, consults his timetable and boards what he takes to be a more convenient train:

> Unfortunately for Pnin, his timetable was five years old and in part obsolete.

Now, and only now, do we see the point, in the first sentence of the novel, of the unexpected adverbial 'inexorably', and the occurrence of that word is the single indicator of story temporal sequence in the first paragraph. 'Inexorably' implies something already begun, continuing, and impossible to stop or cancel before its own predetermined and unwelcome conclusion: a proleptic announcement of misfortune.

There then follow several pages of description of Waindell College, of Pnin's handful of students (these briefly characterized with the aid of deadly analeptic commentary – e.g.:

> languid Eileen Lane, whom somebody had told that by the time one had mastered the Russian alphabet one could practically read 'Anna Karamazov' in the original.),

and of Pnin's bizarre teaching style. This latter is heavily dependent on digressions, personal anecdotes, and the reading of comic passages from books.

> But since to appreciate whatever fun those passages still retained one had to have not only a sound knowledge of the

vernacular but also a good deal of literary insight, and since his poor little class had neither, the performer would be alone in enjoying the associative subtleties of his text. The heaving we have already noted in another connexion would become here a veritable earthquake. Directing his memory, with all the lights on and all the masks of the mind a-miming, toward the days of his fervid and receptive youth . . . Pnin would get drunk on his private wines as he produced sample after sample of what his listeners politely surmised was Russian humour. Presently the fun would become too much for him; pear-shaped tears would trickle down his tanned cheeks. Not only his shocking teeth but also an astonishing amount of pink upper-gum tissue would suddenly pop out, as if a jack-in-the-box had been sprung, and his hand would fly to his mouth, while his big shoulders shook and rolled. And although the speech he smothered behind his dancing hand was now doubly unintelligible to the class, his complete surrender to his own merriment would prove irresistible. By the time he was helpless with it he would have his students in stitches . . .

Here, with a vengeance, we see the significance and impact of the two essential components of narrative noted in Chapter 1: the teller and the tale. For while Pnin himself is absorbed in the seemingly devastating humour of the texts, his student audience's amusement is entirely derived from the absorbing spectacle of the teller. And framing these two is the reader's amusement at the artful telling of the students' amusement at Pnin's amusement: a warming feeling of togetherness in humour, all the more poignant for our awareness of the different kinds of estrangement that separate Pnin from his students, and both of them from us. The practical irrelevance of *what* the passage-content is that sets Pnin off is underlined by the fact that we neither seek nor require any details about it whatsoever.

The other great attraction of this stylistic tour de force is its use of the modal of iterated or habitual activity (*would*). The stages of physical collapse in Pnin's performance, culminating with the sudden emergence of his false teeth, seem so detailed and specific as to make their recurrence all the more extraordinary and laughable. And such iterative-frequency narration, telling once what happened often, given the light-hearted nature of what is told, itself enhances the spirit of familiarity, recognizability and sympathy that such incidents promote.

But if such a spirit were to render the reader too relaxed, the terse one-sentence paragraph that follows ensures otherwise:

All of which does not alter the fact that Pnin was on the wrong train.

The point about Pnin's habitual performance, described above, is that while iterative in frequency, and of uncertain duration, it is, being habitual, both analeptic and proleptic, a potential event at numerous points in time. It cannot arise during this train journey of Pnin's, to be sure, since his students are not present with him: we may thus designate its textual position as an achrony. But being habitual events, these are not very firmly anchored to any particular point or points in time: the only delimitation is the obvious one that these hysterics can only arise during Pnin's classes. (The habit is rather less of a constant recurrence than, say, giving a little cough every time one begins to speak.)

The reminder that in 'our' present-time Pnin is 'still' on the wrong train is in turn followed by a long paragraph of characterization (again, a descriptive pause in terms of duration, not tied to any point in terms of order) concerning his fatal attraction to gadgetry. This too is followed by a terse reminder of the situation in the ongoing basic story:

And he still did not know that he was on the wrong train.

The running joke continues, with a lengthy account of his eccentric command of the English language followed by yet another resumption of the story proper:

The conductor . . . had now only three coaches to deal with before reaching the last one, where Pnin rode

before we are treated to the lovely ramifications of a 'Pninian quandary' as to where, on his person, he should store his lecture manuscript:

If he kept the Cremona manuscript . . . on his person, in the security of his body warmth, the chances were, theoretically, that he would forget to transfer it from the coat he was wearing to the one he would wear. On the other hand, if he placed the lecture in the pocket of the suit in the bag *now*, he would, he knew, be tortured by the possibility of his luggage being stolen. On the third hand (these mental states sprout additional forelimbs all the time), he carried in the inside pocket of his present coat a precious wallet . . .; and it was physically possible to pull out the wallet, if needed, in such a way as fatally to dislodge the folded lecture.

Pnin's quandary is an acute form of the kind of anxiety we all feel over unwelcome possible future consequences of our present actions, proleptic imaginings all the more ironical since we know Pnin is *already* in a mess. Incidentally, the detached conditional 'if needed', towards the close of the quoted extract, indicates how very skilled is Nabokov's use of the English language. On an unexceptional reading it qualifies 'the wallet'. But on a more bizarre – but appropriately bizarre – reading it would qualify 'pulling out the wallet so as fatally to dislodge the lecture'. That is, if the wallet needed to be pulled out in such a way as fatally to dislodge and lose the lecture, Pnin could be relied on to do the job!

The first section closes with more complex temporal reflections and projections, as Pnin learns he is on the wrong train and is redirected by the conductor. But I hope enough has been shown of just how widespread and complex the manipulations of time-lines can be even in quite short passages. To repeat, the point of such close analyses is not to unravel a text, to return to some underlying singulative, steady-paced, linear chronology, but rather to understand more fully how, in our narratives as in our lives, we constantly demand and draw upon potential complexities of pace, iteration, and reordering.

Focalization   3.4

The very presence in any discourse of features such as *I* and *you*, of tense choices, of discriminating adverbs and adjectives such as *here, there, this* and *that*, (all of which can be brought together under the label of **deixis** – see glossary), means that that discourse is consequently interpreted as grounded, or anchored, coming from a particular speaker at a particular place at a particular time. Any text, then, that contains deictic information is thereby understood as oriented from the spatiotemporal position that those deictics imply.

What applies to discourses in general applies particularly importantly to narratives. In the process of telling a narrative, with almost inevitable and copious specifications of time and place, some perspective or another has to be adopted as the vantage point from which the spatiotemporally determinate events are related. Even

> Once upon a time in a distant land there lived a beautiful princess

signals, through the emphasis on *once*, *distant* and past tense *lived*, that the perspective adopted in the telling assumes teller–listener proximity, and a spatiotemporal remoteness, in the past, of the events to be narrated.

> Perception depends on so many factors that striving for objectivity is pointless. To mention only a few factors: one's position with respect to the perceived object, the fall of the light, the distance, previous knowledge, psychological attitude towards the object; all this and more affects the picture one forms and passes on to others. (Bal, 1985: 100)

Genette's term for this inescapable adoption of *a* (limited) perspective in narrative, a viewpoint from which things are seen, felt, understood, assessed, is **focalization**. By this is meant the angle from which things are seen – where 'seen' is interpreted in a broad sense, not only (though often most centrally) in terms of visual perception. As Rimmon-Kenan comments (1983: 71), this term does not entirely shake off the optical-photographic connotations that have made its Anglo-American critical equivalent, **point of view**, problematic. I hesitate to offer another variant term to compete with those we already have, but I do think **orientation** is a usefully wider, less visual, term than 'focalization', and would help us to remember that 'cognitive, emotive and ideological' perspectives, in addition to the simply spatiotemporal one, may be articulated by a narrative's chosen focalization. Accordingly, though I will mostly retain Genette's term 'focalization' in what follows, the reader is welcome to substitute 'orientation' if this is any help.

The great and continuing nuisance perpetuated by the term 'point of view' is that it does nothing to discourage the conflation and confusion of two distinct aspects of narrative practice. Those two separable aspects are:

1 The orientation we infer to be that from which what gets told is told.
2 The individual we judge to be the immediate source and authority for whatever *words* are used in the telling.

Those two aspects have been summarized in the two distinct questions 'Who sees?' and 'Who speaks?'

Now of course in many narratives, orientation and discourse-authorship are sourced in a single individual. But speaking/ thinking and seeing need not come from the same agent. We need to allow for cases where a narrator 'undertake[s] to tell what another person sees or has seen' (Rimmon-Kenan, 1983: 72). This, in Rimmon-Kenan's view, is precisely what happens at the opening of Joyce's *Portrait of the Artist as a Young Man*, where Stephen as a child is argued to be the focalizer

His father looked at him through a glass: he had a hairy face.

but not the narrator. And in the early chapters of *Great Expectations*, Rimmon-Kenan points out, the narrator is Pip the adult, with an adult's extended vocabulary, while the focalizer is Pip the child, whose perspective of weakness, roughness and dependence is articulated. Relatedly, in 'third-person centre of consciousness' novels such as James's *The Ambassadors*, the reflector is the focalizer (the main character, Lambert Strether), while the source of the third-person pronouns used to denote Strether is a distinct narrator. An inevitable corollary of the notion of focalizer or subject-of-the-focalization is that there must also be someone or something that is the object of the process, i.e., the focalized. In the following section the different types of focalizer and focalized identified by Bal are outlined.

TYPES OF FOCALIZATION   3.4.1

Here the basic contrast is between external and internal focalization. External focalization occurs where the focalization is from an orientation outside the story (what this seems to mean is that the orientation is not associable with that of any character within the text). In any event, in such cases the narrator/focalizer separation tends to collapse, so that the focalization has no particular interest independent of that of the narration. Internal focalization occurs inside the represented events or, perhaps better, inside the *setting* of the events, and almost always involves a character-focalizer, though some unpersonified position or stance could be adopted. Thus in Faulkner's 'Barn Burning', the boy Sartoris is often the focalizer, since the story is told largely from his orientation, but he is not directly responsible for the words used, as this extract from the opening should show:

The store in which the Justice of the Peace's court was sitting smelled of cheese. (1) The boy, crouched on his nail keg at the back of the crowded room, knew he smelled cheese, and more: from where he sat he could see the ranked shelves close-packed with the solid, squat, dynamic shapes of tin cans whose labels his stomach read, not from the lettering which meant nothing to his mind but from the scarlet devils and the silver curve of fish . . . (2) He could not see the table where the Justice sat and before which his father and his father's enemy stood, but he could hear them . . . (3)

Here, sentence 2 expresses the boy's orientation; sentence 1 is not just his perspective, but that of anyone inside the store; and sentence 3 mixes the boy's focalization ('he could hear') with information about the relative positions of the Justice and his father and the table which cannot be through the boy's eyes since the text explicitly states he 'could not see'.

Compare the above with the opening of another story by Faulkner, 'Shingles for the Lord', where a boy is both (major) focalizer *and* narrator, (i.e., source and authority for the words used):

Pap got up a good hour before daylight and caught the mule and rid down to Killegrew's to borrow the froe and maul. He ought to been back with it in forty minutes. But the sun had rose and I had done milked and fed and was eating my break-fast when he got back. . . .
. . . 'Give me my breakfast,' he told maw. 'Whitfield is standing there right this minute, straddle of that board tree with his watch in his hand.'
And he was. . . . We tied the mule to a sapling and hung our dinner bucket on a limb, and . . . we went on to the board tree . . . and Whitfield was standing jest like pap said, in his boiled shirt and black hat and pants and necktie, holding his watch in his hand. It was gold and in the morning sunlight it looked big as a full-growed squash. (my ellipses)

Again, the boy is the major but not invariable focalizer, since his father's riding down to Killegrew's, for instance, was not some-thing he witnessed in its entirety.

Like the two types of focalizers, there are also two types of focalized, where the distinction is between viewing from outside or from within. In the former, only the external, literally visible phenomena are reported; in the latter, facts about the feelings, thoughts and reactions of a (or several) character(s) are reported, so that a penetrating intrusive portrayal is achieved. Molly Bloom in *Ulysses* is both internal focalizer and focalized from within, while in Hemingway what is focalized is very commonly viewed from without.

Focalization may remain fixed, tied to a single focalizer, throughout a novel, as in *What Maisie Knew*. Of this novel Bal writes:

> In Henry James' *What Maisie Knew* the focalization lies almost entirely with Maisie, a little girl who does not understand much about the problematic relations going on around her. Consequently, the reader is shown the events through the limited vision of the girl, and only gradually realizes what is going on. But the reader is not a little girl. S/he does more with the information s/he receives than Maisie does, s/he interprets it differently. Where Maisie sees only a strange gesture, the reader knows that s/he is dealing with an erotic one. The difference between the childish version of the events and the interpretation that the adult reader gives them determines the novel's special effect. (Bal, 1985: 104–5)

But the focalizing may vary between two or more positions (e.g., *The Sound and the Fury*). It might be more accurate to say that focalization very commonly (as in 'Barn Burning') varies between the orientation of a particular character and that of a rather neutral, detached position. And yet, at least from Dickens onwards, there has been a well-established tradition of using more than one focalizer as refracting lenses through which events are apprehended.

The great interest in focalization stems from the argument that, as Bal puts it,

> the way in which a subject is presented gives information about the object itself *and* about the focalizer. (Bal, 1985: 109, my emphasis)

Furthermore, such revelatory focalization can and does go on regardless of whether the object focalized really exists. In this respect we probably need to distinguish between focalizeds that we as readers accept actually exist in the world of the narrative from those we take to be dreams, fantasies or other figments of one character-focalizer's imagination. We might label this distinction actual v. imagined focalizeds (a distinction slightly different from and more difficult than Bal's 'perceptible'/'non-perceptible one). Some narratives trade heavily on our uncertainty as to whether what is focalized is actual and potentially 'public experience', or imagined and hence an index of psychosis (a magnificent example is *The Turn of the Screw*).

3.4.2   FACETS OF FOCALIZATION?

Mieke Bal, with whom the notion of focalization is now chiefly associated, has written:

> The subject of focalization, the *focalizor*, is the point from which the elements are viewed. That point can lie with a character (i.e. an element of the fabula), or outside it. If the focalizor coincides with the character, that character will have a technical advantage over the other characters. The reader watches with the character's eyes and will, in principle, be inclined to accept the vision presented by that character. (Bal, 1985: 104)

And she seems to prefer not to attempt a detailed discrimination of *types* of focalization, emphasizing rather the levels involved.

But Rimmon-Kenan (1983), evidently considerably influenced by Uspensky (1973) does attempt a typology of what she calls the facets of focalization, the major ones being perceptual, psychological and ideological. In relation to each of these facets, great variation is possible concerning the power or breadth of the focalizing. For example, with regard to the perceptual dimension of focalization, the focalizer may enjoy (and relay to us from) a panoramic perspective which allows holistic descriptions of large scenes, and even of several distinct but simultaneous scenes; this obviously entails an external focalizer. On the other hand, where the focalizer is a character within the narrative, the limited view of that spatiotemporally limited observer is to be expected.

A similar broad contrast between the constrained and unlimited perspectives (actually with many intermediate degrees of limitedness) applies also to time focalization. External focalization can range over different time periods if the focalizer is unpersonified, but is limited to retrospection if tied to a character. More narrow yet is the kind of self-imposed restraint observed, in the interests of a more suspenseful telling, by some character-narrators. In Faulkner's 'A Rose for Emily', as Rimmon-Kenan notes, the townsperson-narrator (who must, like any narrator, be assumed to know the end of his story before he begins telling it) very noticeably confines his presented material, as an internal focalizer viewing from within, to just what he saw, as and when he saw it, when he was a participant in the events related. There are no prolepses here!:

> That was when people had begun to feel sorry for her. People in our town, remembering how old lady Wyatt, her great-aunt, had gone completely crazy at last, believed that the Griersons held themselves a little too high for what they really were. None of the young men were quite good enough for Miss Emily and such.

In addition to variation in spatiotemporal orientation, there is psychological variation, which Rimmon-Kenan separates into the cognitive (e.g., the internal focalizer's limited knowledge *v.* the external focalizer's theoretical omniscience) and the emotive (neutrality *v.* involvement in presentation). And in involved emotive focalization, for example, scenes are represented in a noticeably idiosyncratic way, such as seems best attributed to the mood and personal evaluations of a character.

The *focalized*'s mind and emotions are also open to either external or penetrative/internal treatment, assuming that focalized is human. Hemingway's 'The Killers', for example, has an external treatment of the gangsters when they are the focalized, while many narratives opt for an internal treatment. As Rimmon-Kenan writes:

> When the focalized is seen from within, especially by an external focalizer, indicators such as 'he thought', 'he felt', 'it seemed to him', 'he knew', 'he recognized' often appear in the text. On the other hand, when the inner states of the focalized are left to be implied by external behaviour, modal expressions – suggesting the speculative status of such implication – often occur: 'apparently', 'evidently', 'as if', 'it seemed', etc.

A final facet of focalization variation is the ideological. We could say that all text containing either explicit or implicit evaluation of the major categories or classifications that inform our daily lives (*man, woman, husband, wife, child, work, poverty, justice, freedom, equality, discipline, duty,* etc.) and/or evaluation of known individuals or groups or positions that are regarded as ideological (Mao, Toryism, feminism, etc.) is disclosing significant ideological orientations or focalizations. This is not the place to go into the details of the differences between what I have termed above 'explicit or implicit evaluation' – but it seems to parallel Fowler's (1986:132) distinction between language which makes an explicit 'announcement of beliefs' and language which is 'symptomatic of world-view'.

Often, it seems, one ideology or world-view, of an external narrator-focalizer, is the dominating norm, and any characters' ideologies that deviate from this standard are at least implicitly (and sometimes explicitly) censured. On the other hand, there may be a juxtaposition of different ideological orientations without any overt adjudication between them, so that the reader is torn between different views of certain events in particular and (by extension) the world in general. On this topic, see Bakhtin (1981).

Notice also that in so far as both the psychological and the ideological facets of focalization are a matter of how things are evaluated, there seems to be plenty of room for overlap between these two. (Spatiotemporal perceptual focalizing, by contrast, is non-evaluative, a stating of *facts* about the when and where of what is witnessed.) In a typical situation, it may well be that as analysts we talk of some deviant main character as revealing weird psychology, this being highlighted and counteracted by the orthodox and 'reasonable' ideology of an external narrator: I wonder if we couldn't as properly talk of the character's ideology being 'corrected' by the narrator's ideology in such cases.

3.5 Perceptual focalization as primary

A considerable doubt remains in my mind as to whether there is a focalizer position distinct from the narratorial one in most texts, and whether we should typically work on the assumption that we can identify a focalizer's spatiotemporal, psychological and ideological orientations as distinct from those of the narrator. In particular very many of Rimmon-Kenan's examples of psychological or ideological focalization seem to me easily accommodated within more orthodox characterizations of jejune or childlike or self-conscious or paranoid, etc., narrators. Orientational limitation attributed to a particular character's perspective does seem to make the best sense in relation to spatiotemporal matters; in the areas of psychology and ideology it seems far less easy to resolve that a particular emphasis is not that of the narrator – except, of course, where we are faced with the speech or thought of a character, directly or indirectly rendered, but that is another matter.

We should bear in mind, in this respect, that in Bal's own discussion of focalization, attention is chiefly drawn to the spatio-temporal indices or signals as to whose perspective – an external narrator-focalizer or an identifiable character within the text – is being adopted. That is not to say she wants to deny the ideo-logical consequences of focalization, but rather that she proceeds (sensibly, I think) by first using spatiotemporal clues as justification for attributing a focalized passage to a particular character, and only then evaluating whatever of that character's mental and ideological preferences is revealed therein. Rimmon-Kenan and Fowler (1986) draw quite heavily on Uspensky (1973) in their treatments of the area of focalization or point of view. And in my view Rimmon-Kenan (like Uspensky) attempts too many sub-categorizations, as if these fitted uncontroversially into the Bal model. (Fowler is less confusing: his presentation is Uspensky-derived, not a merging of Uspensky and Bal.)

In the elaborate attempted discrimination of types of focalizer and focalized there is a danger of losing sight of our objective, that of identifying and describing the major options used by authors/speakers in their fashionings of bare stories (fabulas) into tellable, provocative, engaging narratives.

The essential issue that focalization theory attempts to address (and that I shall argue a theory of free indirect discourse attempts to address also) is that of **attribution**. As the simple question cited earlier indicates, in focalization we are asking 'Who sees?' Better, we could say that the question asked in spatiotemporal focalization is:

> Who is the immediate seer here, and whose is the 'zero-point' for time measurement here, to whom we attribute the spatio-temporal orientations we are given?

Similarly with psychological and ideological evidence, whether explicit or only implicit:

> To whom do we attribute these traces or revelations of psycho-logical or ideological orientation? Who is their immediate source?

The notion of 'immediate source' is important here, because I want to maintain the common sense principle that the *ultimate* source of everything in the narrative, including the focalizations and the free indirect discourse (henceforth, FID), is the narrator or teller. It's just that in more complex narratives which narrow down the angle of vision on a scene to that of a particular character, or which refract the telling of a scene through the distorting lens of a character's mental hang-ups or political preferences, or which let a character's words or thoughts occupy the (usually past tense, third person) narrative frame via FID, *it makes best sense* to posit a more immediate and direct source than the narrator for the viewpoint, or the preferences, or the words or thoughts: typically, one of the characters involved. In summary, the ultimate source of everything in the narrative is the narrator, and attributing the words and orientations in the narrative to her is always the 'default' option. In more complex narratives, orientation and FID are well-explored techniques for enabling us as readers more fully to inhabit the spatiotemporal, psychological and verbal words of the characters we encounter.

3.6 Narrators and narration

In section 3.3 I introduced a distinction between

1 The orientation we infer to be that from which what gets told is told, and
2 the individual or 'position' we judge to be the immediate source and authority for whatever words are used in the telling.

The former we distinguish as focalization, the latter as narration, and it is to this latter domain that I now turn.

The business of specifying just how many optional or obligatory roles are involved in the process of narration can soon get remarkably complex. Rimmon-Kenan reprints Chatman's (1978: 151) diagram, itself similar to Prince's models, in which six participants are identified:

$$\text{real author} \rightarrow \text{implied author} \rightarrow \text{(narrator)} \rightarrow \text{(narratee)} \rightarrow \text{implied author} \rightarrow \text{real reader}$$

In Chatman's discussion, the real author and reader are left out, on the grounds that their 'implied' counterparts are the functioning substitutes in the business of narrative transmission. Furthermore, Chatman makes the strange claim that the narrator-narratee pair are optional positions. What I will propose here will, I hope, simplify the above picture without making for an utterly impoverished distortion of the potential complexities involved.

Basically I want to argue for just three essential roles in narrative transmission, and an optional fourth:

author → narrator → (narratee) → real reader

To begin with the implied author, and why I dispense with it: first, what is an implied author? The answer – and here I will draw on the discussions of people who believe in such a construct – is not at all clear or convincing to me, and there begin my doubts about its status. Chatman (1978: 148) tells us

> Unlike the narrator, the implied author can *tell* us nothing. He, or better, *it* has no voice, no direct means of communicating. It instructs us silently, through the design of the whole, with all the voices, by all the means it has chosen to let us learn.

Curiouser and curiouser, one might remark. These muddy waters scarcely clear when, in a revisionary spirit that wants to dispel the impression that the implied author is a 'personified "consciousness" ', Rimmon-Kenan asserts:

> The implied author must be seen as a construct inferred and assembled by the reader from all the components of the text. . . . [It] is best considered as a set of implicit norms rather than as a speaker or a voice. (Rimmon-Kenan, 1983: 87,88).

When Wayne Booth introduced the term 'implied author' (Booth, 1961: 70ff.) he probably had little intention of this being taken up and posited as a distinct and separate role in narration. In his discussion the emphasis is on the (partial, value-laden) picture of the author that a reader gets in – or takes from – a text.

> As [the author] writes, he creates not simply an ideal, impersonal 'man in general' but an implied version of 'himself' that is different from the implied authors we meet in other men's works . . . the picture the reader gets of this presence is one of the author's most important effects. However impersonal he may try to be, his reader will inevitably construct a picture of the official scribe who writes in this manner. (Booth, 1961: 70–1)

In subsequent discussions of the implied author, the emphasis has tended to be on the word *implied*: in Booth the emphasis seems to me to be far more on the word *author*. There the claim is that we project or reconstruct back, from the text, some sort of version or picture of the author. Consequently (but I think this a trivially true observation) that version of the author is not the author herself; it may be a version that the actual author vigorously rejects, or that is unduly flattering or derogatory of her.

Booth goes on to suggest that each novel from an author projects a different 'official version' of that author and his or her norms. While this seems intuitively true, it doesn't necessarily warrant the introduction of the distinct role of an implied author as if this were a distinct level of narrative structuring. We can retain the term 'implied author' to refer to the picture of Faulkner we conjure up from *The Sound and the Fury* (a very different picture, surely, from that which we conjure up from *The Reivers*), but we might as happily simply distinguish the Faulkner of *The Sound and the Fury* and the Faulkner of *The Reivers*, the Joyce of *Dubliners v.* the Joyce of *Finnegan's Wake*. As far as these novels and narratives are concerned, these are the only versions of the author we know, and there is *no* 'real author', unitary, unchanging, standing behind these narrative-derived versions. If we've read Blotner's biography of Faulkner, or Ellmann on Joyce, we've read another narrative presenting (rather more fully and directly) another version of the author. Even if we know an author personally, we still perform the same process of forming a mental picture or representation (itself a kind of narrative) of that author to ourselves, as an integral part of the activity of knowing a person. In short, the pictures we have of authors are always constructions, so that all authors are, if you like, 'inferred authors'. But we can and should separate such pictures from the actuality of authorial narrative production: those pictures may be important in narrative reception and critical theory, but they are irrelevant to narrative production. The implied author is a real position in narrative processing, a receptor's construct, but it is not a real *role* in narrative transmission. It is a projection back from the decoding side, not a real projecting stage on the encoding side.

3.6.2 NARRATEES AND IMPLIED READERS

Having reduced the production side of narrative transmission from three participants to two, I seem to be far more drastic on the reception side, where I throw out two participants and treat only the real reader as central. Again, who are the narratee and the implied reader? To deal first with the narratee: a narratee is an individual, involved in or quite detached from the events of the story, who is *directly addressed* by the narrator. Very occasionally a narrator addresses her discourse to herself, but much more typically the specific narrative addressee is a character-receiver within the story, if rather marginal to the action (the psychiatrist Dr Spielvogel who is told all the young man's hang-ups in *Portnoy's Complaint*, the naval men who are told Marlow's story in *Heart of Darkness* and so on). Sometimes, as in Sterne's *Tristram Shandy*, a narratee is playfully conjured up and has her ears boxed for inattentiveness:

> How could you, Madam, be so inattentive in reading the last chapter? I told you in it, *that my father was not a papist!* You told me no such thing, Sir. Madam, I beg leave to repeat it over again, That I told you as plain, at least, as words, by direct inference, could tell you such a thing . . . . (1967: 82, quoted in Rimmon-Kenan, 1983: 105)

We readers enjoy the joke in which a fictional entity *as if in our position* gets ticked off in a way that we know we sometimes deserve. But we do also see that this is an 'as if' relation, that this is a strategy, a device, a fabrication (if the narrator were really ticking us off we would probably resent and resist that impertinence). Any residual nervousness on the part of any Madam-reader that she is being directly addressed is dispelled, of course, by the direct speech attributed to this other, fictional Madam.

In all these cases and others besides, I will argue that the narratee position is not properly part of the framework of the telling, but an integral device in narrational strategy. Notice that in all the cases cited, and almost always, in fact, the narratee is addressed by an intradiegetic narrator, i.e., not the narrator of the narrative in our foundational sense (the source or agent for *everything* that gets told). As Bal says of this 'foundational' narrator:

> We . . . do not mean a story-teller, a visible, fictive 'I' who interferes in his/her account as much as s/he likes, or even participates as a character in the action. Such a 'visible' narrator is a specific version of the narrator, one of the several different possibilities of manifestation. . . . We shall rigorously stick to

the definition of 'that agent which utters the linguistic signs that constitute the text'. (Bal, 1985: 120)

Typically, then, a narratee is a visible fictional character whom we witness being addressed by an even more visible second-order narrator, and behind their fake dialogue is some storyteller (the first-order or foundational narrator) whom we take to be the agent of all their words (both the visible narrator's and the narratee's), and any other material besides (e.g., the insertion of chapter breaks in the telling, chapter numbers, headings, etc.).

Narratees, then, are real enough textual entities, but they are not an extratextual participant in the way that narrator and reader are. But when we come to assess the status of the so-called 'implied reader' I rather doubt whether this animal is real even in a textual-strategic sense. Chatman insists

It is as necessary to distinguish among narratees, implied readers . . . and real readers . . . as it is among narrator, implied author, and real author.

But he doesn't really tell us why the distinctions are so necessary:

The 'you' or 'dear reader' who is addressed by the narrator of *Tom Jones* is no more Seymour Chatman than is the narrator Henry Fielding. (Chatman, 1978: 150)

Any reader knows that, surely, and hardly needs to posit a separate narratological role to explain the phenomenon. If we look in Chatman's book for more explicit definition of the implied reader we will not find any (just a few references on p. 150). Accordingly, I will dispense with the implied reader the way I dispensed with the implied author, regarding it, similarly, as the inescapable *version* of a reader that we can assume an author to have in mind. Besides avoiding the proliferation of roles that gives rise to barely-comprehensible sentences such as the following,

Just as the narrator may or may not ally himself with the implied author, the implied reader furnished by the real reader may or may not ally himself with a narratee. (Chatman, 150)

we also want to avoid making the whole business of storytelling seem too fixed and determinate in advance. As Walter Ong (1975) has insisted, the writer's audience is always a fiction, a convenient provisional target. Real readers, real audiences, can apprehend stories in quite unpredicted ways, seeing a different point to them, and picturing quite dissimilar authors of them.

Relations between story and narration 3.7

Possibly the foregoing discussion of roles in narration is overlong, but it should make what follows more coherent. One area of story-narration relations is again to do with time – as arose at the level of text, too. But while there we looked at order, duration and frequency, here we are simply concerned with how long after (or before) the putative occurrence of the events the narration actually takes place. Typically, as reflected in common sense and the use of past tense, events precede their narration – by anything from just a few minutes to many years. But we can also get 'anterior narration', a telling of what *will* happen (as in a famous future tense novel by Michael Frayn, *A Very Private Life*). A third type of narration, simultaneous with the action, reports events as if they are currently taking place (in the present tense). Of course the simultaneity is notional rather than real, with an effect of minimizing the story-narration distance – more like news footage, in which we see things as if they are just happening, even if the film is broadcast many hours after the incidents have taken place. Simultaneous narration is popular with many contemporary novelists (Updike, Bradbury, Coetzee, Gordimer, among others).

Rather more varied than the temporal relations between story and narration are the framing or embedding relations. For a single text can have several stories within it, and, like clauses, these can be coordinately chained together (like the stories in *The Canterbury Tales* or *One Thousand and One Nights*) or subordinately embedded one within the other. Whenever the story includes presentation of a character who herself tells a tale, we have a main story and an embedded one. Using the Genettian terms we have already come across, we can talk of the main story as the diegetic level, narrated by an extradiegetic narrator, while the embedded story is at a **hypodiegetic** level with an **intradiegetic** narrator. Such hypodiegetic narratives seem to have certain common functions: to advance the action of the first narrative, to explain the background of the first narrative (analepsis is often involved here), or, through its similarity of theme with that of the first narrative, to act as an analogical and resonant echoing of theme.

3.8 A typology of narrators

Here, too, we can follow Rimmon-Kenan (who follows Genette) in setting up different categories of narrator depending on whether that narrator is extradiegetic or intradiegetic, and whether she is a story participant or not (homodiegetic *v.* heterodiegetic). In addition to such a categorization, we can assess the visibility of a narrator by looking for the following kinds of textual material, which are indicative – in increasing order of intrusiveness – of narratorial presence:

1 descriptions of settings
2 identification of characters
3 temporal summaries
4 *definition* of characters
5 reports of what characters did not think or say
6 commentary – interpretation, judgment, generalization

The above six types of material reflect – in order – greater knowledge and understanding of whatever story is articulated. Material of types 5 and 6, in particular, indicate (or at least involve claiming) that a narrator has a deeper understanding of just what has happened in a story. We should also recognize degrees of intrusion and understanding at any stage: in the domain of setting-description, consider the different kinds of description we might get of a nuclear power plant, depending on the narrator's knowledge and articulateness. (See Rimmon-Kenan and Bal for demonstrations of incrementally intrusive narration, and also the notes and exercises for this chapter.)

But a simpler and yet equally effective typology is the sort outlined in Fowler (1986), who draws on Uspensky (1973). Fowler posits four basic types of narration, themselves grouped into pairs on the basis of whether the narration is internal and intrusive or rather external and limited:

'Internal' narration is, then, narration from a point of view within a character's consciousness, manifesting his or her feelings about and evaluations of the events and characters of the story (which I shall call type A); or from the point of view of someone who is not a participating character but who has knowledge of the feelings of the characters – the so-called 'omniscient' author (type B). 'External' point of view relates the events, and describes the characters, from a position outside of any of the protagonists' consciousnesses, with no privileged access to their private feelings and opinions (type C), and in some cases actually stressing the limitations of authorial knowledge, the inaccessibility of the characters' ideologies (type D).

We can summarize the differences between the four types of telling as follows:

A: intrusive, limited, character-based and hence mimetic
B: intrusive, unlimited, omniscient
C: detached, limited, impersonal, 'Hemingwayan'
D: detached, limited, estranged.

The particularly interesting business for us to chart is the subtle and significant modulation from one stance to another that takes place in much narrative. It is quite possible for type-A narrative to modulate into B or vice versa, or for A and D to alternate, and so on. Fowler notes that the interweaving of types A and B is what makes for the 'dual voice' feel of free indirect discourse where, typically, pockets of type-A narrative, with not merely a character's orientation but his or her words, crop up in a predominantly type B narrative. In fact FID can also emerge where type A narration is embedded within type C narrative – as we find in Hemingway himself sometimes. The other attraction of the Fowler scheme is that it makes plentiful reference to linguistic features that are said to be representative and consti-tutive of the different narrative modes. For the details, see Fowler, 1986: 135ff.

Finally, it should be noted that if the Fowler/Uspensky categ-ories are adopted we do away with focalization as a separate domain from narration. The business of 'which orientation?' becomes a question to be dealt with within our account of narration, though still, very often, a separate question from that of 'who tells?'

Further reading

As in the previous chapter, the best places to begin further reading on the topics discussed are Rimmon-Kenan (1983) Chapters 4, 6 and 7, and Bal (1985). Rimmon-Kenan's discussions of time and focalization, in particular, include numerous useful examples from the literary canon, while Bal's long chapters on text and narration explain her distinctions painstakingly, with much careful comparative analysis of simple constructed examples. Familiarity with either of these should be adequate preparation for an analeptic move back to their chief source, the work of Genette. Genette (1980) includes a lucid forward by Culler; it is essential to have some familiarity with Proust's *A la recherche du temps perdu*, on and around which the theory is elaborated, in order to appreciate Genette's analysis properly. Chatman (1978) contains extensive stimulating discussion of the issues, with copious exemplification from well known films and literary texts: see especially pp. 62–84, 146–8, and 209–37. Fowler's discrimination of four types of narrative perspective comes in Chapter 9 of Fowler (1986); that chapter concludes with an abridged but useful analysis of perspective switches – and their functions – in a crucial scene in Mervyn Peake's novel *Titus Groan*. Among the more advanced and technical discussions of narration and focalization, the following are important contributions: Prince (1982); Lanser (1981; Lodge (1977 and 1981: Chapters 2 and 4 of the latter are attractive applications by a critic and novelist interested in – but rightly not uncritical of – narrative theorizing); Berendson (1981, 1984); Ryan (1981); Fowler (1981); Uspensky (1973); Rifelj (1979); Nelles (1984); and, on narrators that 'engage' the reader as valued addressee, Warhol (1986).

Notes and exercises

1 William Faulkner's story 'That Evening Sun' opens thus:

  (a) Monday is no different from any other weekday in Jefferson now. The streets are paved now, and the telephone and electric companies are cutting down more and more of the shade trees . . . to make room for iron poles bearing clusters of bloated and ghostly and bloodless grapes, and we have a city laundry which makes the rounds on Monday morning, gathering the bundles of clothes into bright-colored, specially-made motor cars . . . and even the Negro women who still take in white people's washing after the old custom, fetch and deliver it in automobiles.

  (b) But fifteen years ago, on Monday morning the quiet, dusty, shady streets would be full of Negro women with, balanced on their steady, turbaned heads, bundles of clothes tied up in sheets, almost as large as cotton bales, carried so without touch of hand between the kitchen door of the white house and the blackened washpot beside a cabin door in Negro Hollow.

(c) Nancy would set her bundle on the top of her head, then upon the bundles in turn she would set the black straw sailor hat which she wore winter and summer. She was. tall, with a high, sad face sunken a little where her teeth were missing. Sometimes we would go a part of the way down the lane and across the pasture with her, to watch the balanced bundle and the hat that never bobbed nor wavered, even when she walked down into the ditch and up the other side and stooped through the fence. She would go down on her hands and knees and crawl through the gap, her head rigid, uptilted, the bundle steady as a rock or a balloon, and rise to her feet again and go on.

(d) Sometimes the husbands of the washing women would fetch and deliver the clothes, but Jesus never did that for Nancy, even before father told him to stay away from our house, even when Dilsey was sick and Nancy would come to cook for us.

(e) And then about half the time we'd have to go down the lane to Nancy's cabin and tell her to come on and cook breakfast. We would stop at the ditch, because father told us to not have anything to do with Jesus – he was a short black man, with a razor scar down his face – and we would throw rocks at Nancy's house until she came to the door, leaning her head around it without any clothes on.

(f) 'What yawl means, chunking my house?' Nancy said. 'What you little devils mean?'

(g) 'Father says for you to come on and get breakfast,' Caddy said. 'Father says it's over a half an hour now, and you've got to come this minute.' (my ellipses)

Working through these opening paragraphs in sequence, make notes on what is going on in each of them in terms of temporal order, duration and frequency; focalization; and narration. In doing so you will have to consider many issues:

(i) Is paragraph 2 analeptic or is paragraph 1 proleptic?

(ii) What are the temporal boundaries of the basic story?

(iii) At what point(s) do we move from iterative-frequency narration to singulative narration, and how is this shift achieved?

(iv) The description of Nancy in paragraph 3 invokes the image of her carrying a balloon, and in paragraph 6 she refers to the children as 'little devils': in relation to the story that unfolds, what unexpected significances may these two allusions have, in terms of proleptic force, character elucidation, or insight into the narrator-focalizer?

(v) What insights, however slight and inconclusive, into the psychological and ideological partialities of the narrator-focalizer might be felt to be revealed in paragraphs 1 and 2? Is the 'we' of paragraph 3 and onwards the same group as 'we' of paragraph 1 ('we have a city laundry')?

(vi) Most of this story seems focalized by the boy Quentin, aged nine. What is the evidence to support this view? However, paragraph 1 cannot have Quentin as a child as focalizer: it is a view of a scene that only comes into existence when that child is an adult of twenty-four. And who speaks, in the sense of 'narrates', in this story? Is it an adult narrator who writes (p. 292)

> Dilsey was still sick in her cabin. Father told Jesus to stay off our place. Dilsey was still sick. It was a long time. We were in the library after supper.

(vii) Among the focalizeds, can we point to any differences (e.g., in detail of description) between the way the other children, Caddy and Jason, are focalized, and the way Nancy is focalized? Why might such differences arise?

(viii) In terms of the six degrees of narratorial intrusion and interpretation ranked in 3.8, there seems scarcely any intrusive commentary here beyond rank 4, i.e., few claims to special knowledge of characters' motives and impulses. What kinds of extra interpretive burdens does this place on the reader? By contrast with the non-interpretive norm, consider these two cases of intrusive commentary:

> A. 'What is it?' I said. 'What is it?'
> 'I aint nothing but a nigger,' Nancy said. 'It aint none of my fault.'
>   She looked at me, sitting in the chair before the cold stove, the sailor hat on her head. I went back to the library. It was the cold stove and all, when you think of a kitchen being warm and busy and cheerful. And with a cold stove and the dishes all put away, and nobody wanting to eat at that hour.

B. 'Jason!' mother said. She was speaking to father.
You could tell that by the way she said the name. Like she believed that all day father had been trying to think of doing the thing she wouldn't like the most, and that she knew all the time that after a while he would think of it. I stayed quiet, because father and I both knew that mother would want him to make me stay with her if she just thought of it in time. So father didn't look at me.

Are either or both these departures from the general trend defensible, or are they blunders of 'inconsistency in telling'?

2. Guided by the kind of questions raised above in the discussion of 'That Evening Sun', attempt a similar analysis of time, focalization, and narration in one of the following short stories: Joyce's 'Counterparts', Flannery O'Connor's 'Revelation', Saul Bellow's 'Looking for Mr Green', or John Updike's 'A & P'.

3 In this chapter I have commented at some length on the complexities of time manipulation in *Mrs Dalloway*. But that novel is of exemplary complexity in other respects, too. Work through the opening paragraphs of the novel, and comment on any complications of focalization or narration you uncover.

4 Despite its uses, Genette's model of duration (or pace, or rhythm) may still leave us dissatisfied. Does it really address the topic that many analysts find interesting about textual 'pace' – viz., why it is that, in the reading, we have impressions of acceleration and deceleration at certain points? In the case of 'Eveline', I have argued, a Genettian relational assessment might conclude that there was no clearly determinable change of pace, since we cannot conclusively determine the real-time duration of events in either of the story's two sections.

And yet readers do feel a great shift in mood, an extraordinary tension between Eveline's frozen attitude and the urgency of departure in the quayside scene. What are the grounds for that impression? The answer may simply be that in the second and concluding section of the story, a number of events are actually happening, and Eveline's developing reflections respond to those developing events. In the first section of the story, by contrast, only one thing is happening at basic story level (she is reviewing her past and her plans), even though that one 'action' involves recalling, as embedded particulars, many events and incidents. In terms of perception of narrative pace, as in many other respects, it seems that there is all the difference in the world between (a report of) living a thing and simply recalling it. The second section may be short in time, but is packed with sequenced events. The crucial thing seems not to be a ratio of story time to textual extent, but of story time to story events.

5 Much of the discussion in the later stages of this chapter has been getting us to the point where we can begin to consider what happens when a narrator wilfully or unwittingly distorts, misleads, or suppresses. The topic of narrational unreliability is an extremely rich theme, and has been probed by critics and theorists extensively for a very long time (cf. Lawrence's warning: 'Never trust the teller, trust the tale'), especially vigorously in the last twenty-five years, since Booth's *Rhetoric of Fiction* appeared. And here, let it be stressed, we are particularly concerned with the (un)reliability of intradiegetic narrators, i.e., narrators visible – if only by way of the first-person pronoun – within the narrative. That is to say, the detection of 'corrupt' narration is especially commonly a challenge set for readers by intrusive/evaluative first-person narrators (Fowler's type A narration). Modern stories or novels where the reader can readily perceive the narrator's unreliability include Saul Bellow's *Dangling Man*, Flannery O'Connor's 'Everything that Rises Must Converge', J. M. Coetzee's *Waiting for the Barbarians*, and Nadine Gordimer's *The Conservationist*.

We attribute unreliability to any narrator the veracity of whose account we come to suspect. Some narrators are liars, or consciously flatter themselves and are clearly intended to be seen as attempting to deceive; other narrators mislead for less culpable reasons: e.g., they may have the limited knowledge of a young narrator, or be mentally retarded like Benjy in *The Sound and the Fury*. Personal involvement with events – especially when the narrator is a direct or indirect victim of those events – may often give rise to narratorial suppression, distortion, prevarication, and so on (as one example, consider Rosa's account of events in *Absalom! Absalom!*). In a more general way, abnormal values may give rise to a type of unreliability that makes it difficult to decide whether we have a normal narrator telling terrible things with much covert irony, or simply an awful narrator. In assessing veracity and reliability, we have to act rather like a juror, weighing the evidence, looking for internal contradictions in what a narrator says (especially when they serve that narrator's purposes) or a clash between a narrator's representations of things and those of (other) characters whom we have independent grounds for trusting and respecting. The great attraction and danger of unreliable narration is, as Booth (1961) rather regrets, that no clear moral or ideological stance is spelt out and held to, and we as readers are not *told* what to think.

4 The articulation of narrative text II: character, setting, free indirect discourse

4.1 Character

Virtually all the discussion of story in Chapter 2 focussed on one of the basic components of story, events, to the neglect of the others, setting and character. There was some sense in this, since, as we have argued, an event, bringing a change of state, is the most fundamental requirement in narrative. But character, in particular, does need a fuller treatment – if only we could see how this could best be done. It is a paradox within narrative study that the one dimension that attracts so many readers and listeners to novels and stories in the first place – a revelatory portraiture of character and personal motive, the refreshingly distinct views of their world of different individuals – is the single area apparently least amenable to systematic analysis. Or at least, until recently there was a noticeable neglect, among narratologists, of character.

To begin with, many narratologists were not quite convinced that here was a genuine topic to explore: what is called the **ontological status** (see glossary) of character, individuals, and the self, was widely questioned. There was an understandable reaction to, for example, A. C. Bradley's profoundly influential treatment of Shakespeare's tragedies as the case-histories of real people, and an equally heavy emphasis on character in both nineteenth-century British novels and the traditional criticism of them. *Nouveaux romanciers* such as Robbe-Grillet and Sarraute wrote their novels in a manner defiant of the cult of the individual, the over-valuing of the allegedly unique experience and response of particular personages whose psychologies were to be dramatized. On the contrary, in such experimental fiction at least, similarity of experience and personal behaviour, rather than difference, was asserted.

The structuralist approach to character is summarized very neatly by Culler (1975a: 230):

The notion of character, structuralists would say, is a myth.

Character is an illusion in which the reader is a creative accomplice: a variety of descriptions of some posited individual, together with descriptions – implicit or explicit – of that individual's actions and reactions, suffice to lead most readers to conceive of a *person* of whom these references and insights are just glimpses. An iceberg principle is at work in the way most people read characters: we operate on the assumption that the evidence we are shown is a necessarily limited selection of material, that much more lies beneath the surface of the novel, in the rest of that 'person's' life.

Structuralists, by contrast, have been strenuous in their reminders that the fraction of the iceberg we see is, in fact, all there is! And furthermore, they have argued, the idea that that body of material is a coherent, unified set of glimpses of a stable individual is a trickery we have chosen to fall for. Instead, we should treat all these references, linked by nothing more psychological than textual devices asserting co-reference (repetition of a name, of pronouns, and of definite descriptions), as a fabric of interwoven traces: message-bearing (semiotic) data on the status, goals, drives, consciousness, etc. of a person embedded in some particular culture, located in history, shot through with various (probably inconsistent) values and beliefs, defined by their gender and their role as nuclear family wife/mother, Victorian family eldest son, and so on. In short, the text of the person, in narratives, belies individuality and discloses at every turn their *typicality*.

Relatedly, many have sought to revalue a new literalism which reminds us that novel characters are really 'just words', are radically non-representational, and should not be unthinkingly 'recuperated' by means of any direct and unguarded application of amateur (or professional) psychological diagnosis. One of the complaints about such responses – common enough in literature classes – is that they ignore the art and textuality of novels, the degree to which character, event, and everything else is a literary production, a construction. The mere verbal surface of novels having been ignored, there is no clear limit to the arabesques of psychologizing: they can spiral on with precious little need for grounding in the text. Surface text can be dismissed as censored testimony, heavily repressed, *requiring* startlingly unexpected symbolic readings. (Here we may begin to see how the more radical psychological readers of character may even come to join hands with endlessly rereading deconstructionists, behind the backs, as it were, of plodding structuralists.)

At any rate, the 'purist' approach to character asserts the non-representational dimension in narrative art. As Joel Weinsheimer has starkly put it:

> Emma Woodhouse is not a woman nor need be described as if it were. (1979: 187)

The more one reads of this battle between the psychologist students of character and the structuralist analysts of *actant*, the more one wonders if the argument is silly and irresolvable. As the new American pragmatism might say, these readers are simply adopting quite different criteria for reading narrative, and for the identification of great narrative, in the first place. Repeated attacks on an allegedly innocent and unconsidered practice of mimetic interpretation tend to rebound rather badly on the attackers, who appear to be killing a straw man. I have a lot of sympathy for arguments in favour of a dual perspective, where we see characters in a different light according to the change of perspective:

> In the text characters are nodes in the verbal design; in the story they are – by definition – non (or pre-) verbal abstractions, constructs. Although these constructs are by no means human beings in the literal sense of the word, they are partly modelled on the reader's conception of people and in this they are person-like. (Rimmon-Kenan, 1983: 33)

The most telling part of that quotation, I believe, comes at its close, where there is both reference to 'the reader's conception' (strikingly rare in some of the earlier narrative theory), and judicious recognition that characters are '*partly* modelled' on real people.

The fact is, whatever theorists keep telling us, most readers do unshakeably continue to apprehend most novel characters as individuals (whether seen dimly or sharply, whether recognizable, comprehensible, **lisible** or impenetrable, alien, unfathomable), and as those apprehensions are built up, revised, and articulated, all sorts of extra-textual knowledge, including our knowledge of characters in the real world, is brought to bear. Profound mimesis as the truest and highest goal of fictional characterization is incoherent, let it be granted; but to say as much is to say very little, particularly if we also want to question whether there is a radical gulf between the 'fiction' of novels and the 'fact' of the real world for mimesis to traverse. If, rather, we think of the semiotic constructedness of people, things, and non-fictional texts as of the same order as the semiotic constructedness of novels, then we may come to see a middle way, where art is not a supplement to life, hence cannot be vulgarly mimetic of it, but where art and the rest of life are both seen as representational.

Greimas' *actant* model   4.2

If character analysis can proceed at all, it looks as if it will involve working with some notion of 'trait'. But before elaborating on this point, it may be useful to consider one simple model of character roles in narrative which, for all its reliance on intuitive schematization, remains a tellingly workable anatomy. Greimas (1966), working along the lines of Propp, who had earlier ident-ified seven broad narrative roles while insisting on their subordi-nation to the 31 functions, proposed that, as general categories underlying all narratives, there were just six roles, or *actants*, comprising three interrelated pairs:

giver/receiver
subject/object
helper/opponent

The six roles are usually diagrammatized as follows:

sender (superhelper) → object → receiver (beneficiary)
                          ↑
                          |
                          |
helper → subject ← opponent

Such a model fits many traditional folk and fairy tales remarkably well: the subject or hero, perhaps a young man of lowly origin, seeks marriage to a beautiful princess (object), in which case the man will also be beneficiary (possibly the princess and the country will too). In his quest he is helped generously but with limited success by a friend or relative (helper), but their combined efforts count for little in the struggle against some opponents (a wicked uncle of the princess, some other eligible but ignoble suitor), until a sender (better, a superhelper), such as the king, or God, or some individual with magical powers for good, intervenes.

Despite the model's simplicity, and despite the need to annotate it variously so as to fit different genres better, the scheme is worth applying to a range of texts. One thing to note is that two of the roles, sender and object, are typically not strictly characters at all in most modern stories. The sorts of things that count as object in our narratives, and the sorts of special help we may get in our quest of those objects, are far more typically abstract than concrete. Thus our highbrow modern narratives are likely to have life, liberty, the pursuit of happiness, greater self-knowledge, or mental peace, as their object. (There remain plenty of spy stories, Westerns, romances and detective stories, however, where a particular concrete object clearly is the target: a double-agent or secret document, a gun-toting baddie, a particular lover, the undeclared murderer.) And the role of higher help, outside of certain varieties of science fiction, television series such as *The A Team* and *Knightrider*, and comic strips of the Superman variety, seems to be becoming attenuated.

One recent application of Greimas' notion of six roles is offered by Vestergaard and Schroder (1985) in their book on the language of advertising. They demonstrate just how well the roles fit the dramatis personae in an advertisement for Sanatogen multivitamin tablets. The addressee ('you') is both subject and receiver, continued good health is the object, and your pursuit of this goal is ordinarily assisted by vitamins and minerals from meals (the helper), but made more difficult by some undesirable consequences of your assumed busy life: snack lunches, dieting, reheated food and skipped meals (the opponent). In steps Sanatogen as Superhelper: 'Sanatogen multivitamins give you essential vitamins and minerals.' As Vestergaard and Schroder observe:

> Of particular interest are the facts that the role of object is not filled by the product but by some quality or state associated with it, and that the consumer is both subject and receiver. Advertising, in other words, does not try to tell us that we need its products as such, but rather that the products can help us obtain something else which we do feel we need. (1985: 29)

And the pattern revealed by the Sanatogen ad does seem to apply to a variety of other products too: face lotions, tampons, beer, petrol, oil, toothpaste, shampoo, after-shave lotion. In all advertisements in which, then, there is a narrative-style emphasis on change of state, with a before ('How *can* I get rid of this dandruff?'/'Why *do* we need so many fillings at the dentist's?') and an after ('I've said goodbye to dandruff thanks to Glam'/ 'Now we've switched to Chopperbopper the dentist has nothing to do!'), the product fulfils the role of important aid or accessory in reaching or maintaining a general quality of life, the desirability of which is relatively uncontroversial. Conversely, notice how such a narrative format tends to fall away when it comes to promotion of truly luxury items such as perfumes, fur coats, very expensive cars, and so on. In these, a more **synecdochic** (see glossary) relation seems to obtain, where the product is presented as an intrinsic part (however small) of the chic and elegant lifestyle that the advertisement typically portrays. Instead of representing the sender, the product is part of the object. As a consequence, the roles of sender, helper and opponent (at least), and any marked sense of a before and an after, are usually absent. Such luxury product advertisements are very much more *description* than narrative.

If we turn to application of the Greimas model to a literary narrative, such as Joyce's 'Eveline', we can use it to highlight the degree to which the story is shot through with ambiguity, uncertainty, and the paralyzing effect of uncertainty, such that this may be said to become the story's theme. Eveline herself is fairly clearly the subject and receiver, and her object would appear to be freedom (especially from verbal and physical abuse) and happiness (at one point she reflects 'she wanted to live. . . . She had a right to happiness'). In pursuit of this object it first appears that Frank is her helper, while her potentially violent father is the opponent. But at the close of this very short story it is fairly (not incontrovertibly) clear that Eveline does *not* join Frank on the steamer that would take her away to Buenos Aires. Why? Is it due to the failure of a superhelper to appear?:

> Out of a maze of distress, she prayed to God to direct her, to show her what was her duty.

Not simply, surely. For notice that her prayer is not merely for assistance with her escape, but for assistance with identifying 'what was her duty', i.e., with deciding what *should* be her object, her first consideration. The neat, five-role scenario sketched above is suddenly revealed as susceptible to a rewriting, in which her current hard-working life ('now that she was about to leave it she did not find it a wholly undesirable life'), looking after her father ('Sometimes he could be very nice'), according to her promise to her mother 'to keep the home together as long as she could' supplants previous assumptions as to which is the better object. In pursuit of this reinstated object of familial care and duty, there seem to be two helpers: her father, on occasion at least, and her brother Harry, who 'always sent up what he could'. The opponent is now Frank, of course, and whether his intentions are honorable or not becomes newly suspect.

But again, we seem to lack a powerful superhelper who might intervene to arbitrate and resolve the choice between going and staying, choosing Frank or the family. No doubt some will see Eveline's 'set[ting] her white face to [Frank]' as a clear choice, where the subject – as in so many modern stories – has looked to resources within herself for the required extra help. But the text does go on to describe her as 'passive, like a helpless animal', which hardly fits an interpretation of Eveline as powerful arbiter.

Ironically, a couple of textual clues may prompt us to consider a physiological dysfunction, a weakness of the heart in the face of acute anxiety, as the superhelper. For in the midst of her anguished uncertainty at the quayside, a distress which 'awoke nausea in her body',

All the seas of the world tumbled about her heart.

This may be sufficient textual warrant, perhaps, to recall an earlier and somewhat cryptic (because unelaborated) allusion to heart trouble:

Even now . . . she sometimes felt herself in danger of her father's violence. She knew it was that that had given her the palpitations.

(In their notes on revisions of 'Eveline' between its first magazine appearance and subsequent publication in the *Dubliners* collection, Scholes and Litz remark on 'the interesting addition of the palpitations' [Scholes and Litz, 1969: 239].) As we read those earlier sentences we are entitled to question this analeptic allusion: '*What* palpitations?' Here at the close, possibly, we see their effect.

Character traits and attributes   4.3

In many modern narratives of the more complex kind, the basic role or function of a character as explored in the previous section turns out to be far less interesting to the reader than what the character is *like*. This is something of a paradox: what a character *does* in a story may be essential for the text to count as a well-formed narrative ('He gets the girl in the end'/'She detects and traps the killer', etc.), but what interests us is what *kind* of super-helper Sherlock Holmes is shown to be, and just *how* he conducts himself in the course of particular scenes and episodes. Details of characterization, the kind of material that we have seen Barthes label as **indices** or (mere) **informants**, often irrelevant to story, are equally often just what the reader finds engrossing in a text. In deciding these judgments of type and manner of character conduct we are inevitably very much guided – as Bal (1985: 80f.) notes – by data from reality or extratextual situations. We carry to our reading of a Sherlock Holmes tale plentiful knowledge gleaned from various sources about doctors, detectives, crimes and human entanglements. We may have ideas about more marginal aspects too, such as housekeepers, the non-inspirational style of traditional policework, about Victorian beggars and urchins (and social stratification in general). We may have even stood in London's Baker Street, looking – at least metaphorically – for 221b, Holmes's fabled residence.

What this amounts to saying is that, in our making sense of any particular text, we have extensive resources of knowledge (we can call this extratextual knowledge, or knowledge of the world, if that helps), which we can bring to bear on our intepretation of the text under scrutiny. Now that 'bringing to bear' will vary from reader to reader in at least two broad ways, to do with the accuracy of one's knowledge, and the interpretive evaluation one makes of that knowledge. We might summarize these two components of adducible background knowledge as **facts** and **ideology**.

To take a simple example: suppose I am reading a text which runs

It is August 1880, and the prosperous streets of London's West End are busy with the carriages of ladies on leisurely shopping expeditions. The afternoon is warm and sunny, but in the shaded doorway of a house off Regent Street can be discerned the crouching form of a beggar.

In the final words here an individual has been specified and, potentially at least, we have encountered the first introduction of an important character. But even without reading on, a certain fleshing out of that single descriptive phrase, 'a beggar', takes place. I have some ideas about what 'a beggar' is or means, but I additionally have ideas about what a London beggar *circa* 1880 would be like, based on my own knowledge of late Victorian social history, from whatever sources.

That knowledge is partial – in two senses, the factual and the ideological. The partial factual knowledge means that I cannot bring to mind a depth of knowledge, and perhaps understanding, of the beggar that is available to someone familiar with the details of the economic, social, spiritual, etc. life of Victorian beggars. The ideological partiality means that I take a certain *view* of Victorian beggars in general; in particular I think of them as the victims of callous and inhuman neglect, a living index of a moral degeneracy in the larger society. Ideologically, of course, that is just one way of looking at beggars, and other readers may alternatively assume that the degeneracy lies principally within the beggars themselves. Notice, furthermore, that in these ideological fleshings-out of the simple textual denomination, I have been treating the beggar as some sort of problem to be solved. That kind of emphasis seems triggered by the very term 'beggar'. What happens if the text instead ends in this way:

> . . . can be discerned the crouching form of a Buddhist monk?

Now a rather different body of extratextual knowledge is brought to bear in our probabilistic characterization; we might note greater incongruity here, on the assumption that Buddhist monks were rare in the London of 1880. But, despite the fact that Buddhist monks rely on begged donations of food to live, the text has not called this individual a beggar nor is the reader likely, ideologically, to take the monk's begging as the primary issue to have a view on.

Before proceeding it is perhaps worth stressing that our limitations of knowledge and partiality of view are not inherently disqualificatory. Some readers will have fuller extratextual knowledge than others, or ideologies more congruent with the narrator's than other readers have, but we cannot predetermine the relevance of those facts and views. The knowledgeable reader may read too much into a marginal reference or character. Background facts and views are to do with actual Victorian beggars in general: this particular beggar may be a very special one – Sherlock Holmes in disguise, or one with mystical powers – so that the general type is of limited help in our grasp of this particular character. But the essential fact, despite the need for revision and amendment of our probabilistic assessments, is that we *do* undertake this inference-based fleshing-out of seemingly slight textual data, in character-comprehension as in other matters. (The role of inference in relation to children's narratives will be examined in Chapter 6.)

Distinctive feature characterology   4.4

The interactive matching of textual facts and ideology with extra-textual facts and ideology that I have outlined above is, like the method of event identification sketched at the close of Chapter 2, a 'bottom-up' type of processing: it is, I would submit, an important feature of the experiential real-time activity of reading, something we do as we read a text, not something postponed, or really postponable, until the text has been read, when a holistic overview may be attempted. In principle, the 'semantic feature' approach to character that I am about to discuss *could* be undertaken developmentally and incrementally *or* holistically, although it tends to be presented in the latter way and may therefore appear overly static. But if applied non-statically this resolutely structural approach can be of value too.

A semantic feature analysis of the characters of a text involves specifying a limited list of what the analyst takes to be the crucial features or attributes which distinguish particular characters. Assuming that no two characters are identical, a rather limited set of attributes needs to be drawn up, attributes that (in a simple system) a character can either have or not have, such that no two characters are assigned an identical set of attributes. In this way, the hope is, we shall get a simple and useable schematic picture of all the *crucial* ways in which particular characters are the same as others and different from others. (The approach is based on distinctive feature phonology and componential semantic analysis: influential methods of analyzing the fundamental dimensions of sounds and meanings, respectively, in a language. For introductory discussion of these methods see, e.g., Fromkin and Rodman, 1978; or Bolinger, 1981.)

An interesting demonstration of distinctive feature (or **semic**) analysis of characters is to be found in Fowler (1977: 36–8). This focusses on *The Great Gatsby*, and in particular Daisy's rough macho husband, Tom Buchanan. Fowler applies over twenty attributes to him which seem either explicit or implicit in the two-page introduction of him early in the novel:

> restlessness, physical strength, virility, athleticism . . . dandyism, wealth, materialism, extravagance, vulgarity, possessiveness, jealousy, untrustworthiness, selfishness, care-lessness, cruelty, physical violence, aggression, arrogance, cyni-cism, contemptuousness, insolence, fractiousness, prejudice, shallowness. (Fowler, 1977: 36)

This is a long list, with several overlapping terms; whether the list is overlong is a question taken up in the notes and exercises. But in general, in attribute selection, the following observations from Bal will hold:

> The *selection* of the relevant semantic axes involves focussing, out of all the characteristics mentioned – usually an unmanage-ably large number – only on those axes that determine the image of the largest possible number of characters, positively or negatively. Of the axes which involve only a few or even one character, only those are analysed which are 'strong' (striking or exceptional) or which are related to an important event. (Bal, 1985: 86)

All this really only becomes interesting when what is predicated of Tom is compared and contrasted with what is predicated of other characters:

> Tom 'overlaps' with Jordan Baker in respect to some semes (athleticism, competitiveness, hardness), with Daisy in other respects (handsomeness, selfishness, restlessness). The three of them share some semes with Gatsby (wealth, ostentation, selfishness) but are polarized from him by others (Gatsby's romantic idealism). . . . The semes 'idealism, romanticism, purposefulness' excuse his materialism and criminality; the Buchanan set and the Wilsons, dissimilar in most other attri-butes, are all distinguished from Gatsby by a pointed lack of any seme of spirituality like the idealism which Nick attributes to Gatsby; they are all classified as purposeless, hopeless, spiri-tually dead. (Fowler: 37–8)

Although Bal suggests we might extend the modelling to note variations in degree (how weak or strong?) and modality (how probably?) of attribute manifestation, this would be departing some way from the analytical simplicity of the basic technique. That technique, within its own limits, is interesting in its high-lighting of essential distinctions between characters *as the analyst sees them*. There need be no requirement in distinctive-feature characterology (as there would be in standard componential feature semantic analysis for different speakers of the same dialect), that all reader-analysts see the same set of features appropriately present or absent in a text's characters. I am perfectly free, at some variance with Fowler, to posit 'entrepren-eurial quality' as a crucial feature of Gatsby, who 'undertakes', takes ambitious risks, and so on, a feature starkly absent from all the other characters, who merely live, act, work, until the unex-pected and catastrophic entrepreneurial turn that Wilson's character takes when he sets out to avenge his wife's death by killing Gatsby. Such variant emphases in analyses are in them-selves, and in their reflection of analysts' assumptions, an indi-cation of ideological divergences.

There are other things to say about character analysis. One interesting and delimitable aspect that often attracts attention is the way a character is *designated* in a text: the deployment of a proper name or names, of definite descriptions, and of pronouns in making reference to an individual. The effects of irony or sympathy, approval or distaste, can be quite complex, given that there is usually an ongoing designating of several characters in any stretch of text by these varied means. In the well-known opening paragraph of Henry James's story 'The Pupil' (discussed in Leech and Short, 1981), for example, the young man applying for the position of resident tutor is named, in sequence, in the following ways:

> The poor young man . . . him . . . he . . . (his) . . . he . . . he
> . . . he . . . (his) . . . he . . . the candidate for the honour of
> taking [the boy's] education in hand . . . this personage . . .
> he . . . (his)

None of these means, we may surmise, would be adopted by the man to describe himself or his position (we learn his surname, Pemberton, only in the second paragraph). Embedded in the given text, the definite descriptions in particular are a simple means of characterization which is also subtly evaluative, covertly creating a tone of distanced sympathy for Pemberton, distanced

enough to permit ironical treatment of his situation. The picture
is further complicated in that, for example, in

> [the little boy] looked straight and hard at the candidate for
> the honour of taking his education in hand

the description of Pemberton is *as if* it were the boy's view of the
situation. And that example is a small indication of the complications that arise and cannot be neglected once we consider the
varied *sources* from which our information about characters can
come (the character him- or herself, another character, an
external narrator, and so on).

Another heavily exploited means of characterization, often with
the assumption that outer surfaces reflect inner essence, is
description of characters' outward appearance – especially clothes
and facial features. Given the rarity of surgical adjustments, we
tend to think of the latter as attributes a character is simply blessed
with or stuck with, and certainly reject any claimed causal link
between appearance and personality (such theories of physiog-
nomy and phrenology, popular in the nineteenth century, influenced writers such as Balzac and Dickens). On the other hand
Cyrano's protruding nose *is* one of his more significant attributes,
as is Falstaff's vast belly or womb; and the smallpox that (merci-
fully, temporarily) disfigures Esther Summerson does threaten her
likelihood of marrying and so threatens to alter the course of the
story. Then again, some features of physical appearance such as
body shape, hairstyle, facial expression (propensity to frown, with
head lowered, *v.* a smiling disposition with an enquiring tilt of
the head) are judged to be partly under a character's control,
something for which they can be held accountable. Falstaff's
great waist reflects his culpable great waste, as the textual pun
insists, and is much more an effect of self-indulgence than, as the
man himself indulgently pretends, a cause of fecundity.

The source of character apperception that I have neglected
most severely is the business of *implicit* characterization, based
on how a character *acts*. As Rimmon-Kenan notes (1983: 60–1),
twentieth-century fiction has tended to opt for the indirectness of
presentation, a 'showing' of character that respects the ability of
the reader to infer, evaluate, and draw conclusions on the basis
of presented behaviour, rather than direct (and directive) presentation, an authoritative 'telling' of how a character is.

Setting   4.5

I have space only to touch on a few key aspects of the role of setting in narrative text. Perhaps the first thing to say is that, though less fundamentally essential to narrative than event and character (we require a narrative to contain a sequence of events involving change, and prefer those changes to involve or affect individuals with whom we can sympathize or identify), the establishment of an identifiable setting is a strong psychological preference in most readers. We like, in our reading of narratives, to know where we are, and look for clear spatiotemporal indications of just where and when a thing happened.

However, this specificity requirement seems relative to genre, story type, and so on. Thus a story about a hen that outsmarts a fox, a fable-like text whether for adults or children, does not need precise anchorage to some particular farm of specified layout, with its fields, machinery, and livestock described. Such particularity would even strike us as bizarre, where the story's power rests in its generic truth, its 'pan-situational' universality. We can even cope quite happily with stories about hens and foxes where the word 'farm' never appears: unless we learn to the contrary, we simply assume a stereotypical rural background. Relatedly, in Fielding and Austen novels that revolve around big houses and their estates, parsonages, inns, and so on, the particularities of those backcloths are rarely important. Settings in broad terms are of course important here, for example, the fact that Fanny Price's parents live in a poky little house in Portsmouth while her uncle and aunt live in a grand house at Mansfield Park. And, in the same novel, it is important that the library in which the younger people present their entertainment is not quite a suitable setting, just as the whole enterprise of the play is not quite suitable. But the details of these settings are rarely so, since they are rarely instrumental in plot development or a refraction of character.

In many modern novels, however, where the humane cohesion between members of society of a similar rank is displaced by a widespread atmosphere of alienation, anomie, and interpersonal relations made more complex by industrial and technological developments that have depopulated the country while turning cities into monstrous battlefields, the situation is different. Setting here may be much more than backcloth; it may be instrumental – like another character – in leading a character to act in a certain way. This fuller role for setting – quasi-animate, menacing or soothing, chorus-like or emblematic – goes back in the English novel at least as far as Dickens, and continued to develop and modulate in the work of George Eliot, Hardy, Lawrence, and many others. In American fiction it seems to have been prominent from the earliest literary writings: in Cooper's Leatherstocking novels, in Poe copiously (most memorably, perhaps, in 'The Fall of the House of Usher'), in the Gothic tradition that descended through Hawthorne to Faulkner, in Twain (what would *Huckleberry Finn* be without the raft and the river?), and so on.

In simple terms, the relations between setting on the one hand, and character and events on the other, may be causal or analogical: features of the setting may be (in part at least) either cause or effect of how characters are and behave; or, more by way of reinforcement and symbolic congruence, a setting may be *like* a character or characters in some respects. Under causal relations we might include Miss Emily's decaying house in Faulkner's 'A Rose for Miss Emily' – as Rimmon-Kenan rather mildly puts it:

> Its decay . . . is a result of her poverty and her morbid temperament. (1983: 66)

Obvious examples of setting as either cause or effect in Dickens would be the Chancery environment in *Bleak House* and Miss Havisham's dining room in *Great Expectations*, respectively. Vivid examples of setting as analogous to characters, noted by Rimmon-Kenan (1983: 69), come in Charlotte Brontë's *Wuthering Heights*:

> Catherine and Heathcliff . . . are similar to the wilderness in which they live, just as the nature of the Linton family parallels the peacefulness of their dwelling place.

Perhaps more common than clear instances of causality or analogy are those texts indeterminate between these two types of relation. Hardy's 'characterizations' of Egdon Heath in *The Return of the Native*, for example, are so distracting and compelling partly because we sense, but cannot fathom, the influences the heath has on specific characters.

But if many of the examples above tend towards the broadly Gothic or personifactory, it seems clear that much more conventional, 'undramatized', settings play an important part in promoting versimilitude and indirect characterization. Senior civil servants have to live in a 'civil servant' style of housing (unless there is good reason for the unexpected in domiciliary setting): that is the unmarked option. Here the broad details of the house (detached; with several bedrooms, a large kitchen and a detached brick garage; in Surrey or Berkshire), and the garden (half-acre; well-kept; lawn, roses, and fruit trees), in their emphases on the comfortable, rational and unostentatious, will be assumed to be characterizing. So too will the specifics of the internal furnishing (the living room has an original Victorian landscape over the genuine and occasionally-used fireplace, the comfortable armchairs are from Heal's, no television can be seen, but the hi-fi – with compact disc player – is well-stocked with Deutsche Grammophon recordings, etc.). All such details of setting articulate their owner's intelligence, conservative good taste, moderate wealth, cultured values – and utter remoteness from the Northern jobless or the women of Greenham Common.

The above stereotyping need not be very accurate to the facts of real senior civil servants' homes and interests – some of them may be so vulgar as to vote Labour and drink beer from the can while playing Slade records. The point is that, in simplifying and standardizing the world around us, we construct stereotyped portraits of civil servants – and doctors, and spies, and politicians, and farmers, and teachers, and milkmen, and welders – and of how they live. In particular texts – again, unless there is good reason for things to be to the contrary – we expect particular spies and farmers broadly to match our stereotypes.

In much of the foregoing concentration on stereotyping, extratextual, knowledge-based inferencing, and expected familiarity and predictability of characters and their behaviour, there has been the danger of giving the impression that characters are mere assemblages of devices, artificial constructs whose seemingly natural properties are themselves convention-bound, being the kinds of attributes particularly valued or 'privileged' by the societies from which those narratives happen to emerge. This view of character as convention-based and convention-bound is evident in Fowler (1977) and pervades structuralist treatments. But such a conclusion may be questioned as involving a preoccupation with the structural similarities in characterizations within and between texts to the neglect of those differences not amenable to structuralist explanation. We are back here to an asserted richness of texture – not 'natural' of course, but still too distinctive and, yes, unique to be merely conventional – involved in what Forster called a 'rounded' character. What *would* Dorothea Brooke have done if she had met Ladislaw before Casaubon? How would Lambert Strether have lived if he had stayed on in Paris? Did Cash spend the rest of his life with Anse Bundren and his new wife? We may speculate, but we can hardly project mechanically, for these characters are neither so static nor so predictable.

If these points are plausible, a revaluation of Bradley's analyses of Shakespeare's characters seems in order. His approach – obviously, I would have thought – cannot claim to furnish adequate accounts of the tragedies as aesthetic wholes, but, as Chatman shows in a spirited and persuasive defence, Bradley's work is a coherent and legitimate procedure of trait-analysis, leading to original and plausible interpretative conclusions. Chatman's entire discussion of character is invaluable (1978: 107–38) and his conclusions are worth quoting:

> Characters do not have 'lives'; we endow them with 'personality' only to the extent that personality is a structure familiar to us in life and art. To deny that seems to deny an absolutely fundamental aesthetic experience. Even fantastic narratives require inferences, guesses, and expectations according to one's sense of what *normal* persons are like. . . . When fictional characters are psychoanalyzed as if they were real people, hard-nosed critics may be right to challenge the effort. But characters as narrative constructs do require terms for description, and there is no point in rejecting those out of the general vocabulary of psychology, morality, and any other relevant area of human experience. (1978: 138)

4.6 Character and setting in 'The Dead'

A focussing in on the textual means by which these narrative facets called character and setting are articulated now feels overdue. For this purpose, I will concentrate on the final story in Joyce's *Dubliners*, 'The Dead'. The story's opening is as follows:

> Lily, the caretaker's daughter, was literally run off her feet. Hardly had she brought one gentleman into the little pantry behind the office on the ground floor and helped him off with his overcoat than the wheezy hall-door bell clanged again and she had to scamper along the bare hallway to let in another

guest. It was well for her she had not to attend to the ladies also. But Miss Kate and Miss Julia had thought of that and had converted the bathroom upstairs into a ladies' dressing-room. Miss Kate and Miss Julia were there, gossiping and laughing and fussing, walking after each other to the head of the stairs, peering down over the banisters and calling down to Lily to ask her who had come.

It was always a great affair, the Misses Morkan's annual dance. Everybody who knew them came to it . . . (175)

This opening is focalized from Lily's orientation, and bears many traces of her speech which we may remark on later in this chapter. But here the chief things to note are that three named individuals are introduced, the first an employee of the other two. We do not yet know whether any of these will play a major role in the story, but in the given situation at least, it being 'the Misses Morkan's annual dance', the two sisters will be prominent since they are the hosts. And the setting is evidently a modest private house, one which is both a residence and a place of work, if the reference to the ground-floor office is rightly interpreted. For this special occasion – an *annual* dance – pro tem conversions of a ground-floor pantry and an upstairs bathroom, into dressing-rooms, have been contrived.

Already the indices of genteel standards upheld despite straitened financial circumstances are numerous. We note again, in the setting description, the 'wheezy hall-door bell', the 'bare hallway', and the evidently short distance separating Kate and Julia at the head of the stairs from Lily down below. This is no grand house, nor one that is opulently furnished. Modest means, and a sense of things worn but still functioning (the bell is wheezy, but works) seem to be the tenor. Perhaps, analogously, the Misses Morkan are 'worn but still functioning', but we cannot yet be certain of their age. They're old enough to throw – annually – a party for ladies and gentlemen, and we may associate their 'fussing', in particular, with stereotypical spinsterly behaviour. But equally important are the indications that they go together, behave alike, and have a shared life: they are named together in a coordinate phrase, we are told (analeptically) that they had resolved the dressing-room problem together, and they respond identically to their sense of excitement, 'walking after each other to the head of the stairs', and so on.

On the basis of the above evidence, we are already entertaining quite elaborate ideas about the women introduced and their manner of living. All this is under way even before the second paragraph, a mixture of analepsis and descriptive pause, which reports that the residence is a

> dark gaunt house on Usher's Island, the upper part of which they had rented from Mr Fulham, the corn-factor on the ground floor (176)

and that the Misses Morkan's only niece, Mary Jane, lives with them and is now 'the main prop of the household'. Typical of the revisions we may often have to make in our constructions of character and setting, we now – in the light of the reference to the corn-factor on the ground floor – have to cancel any supposition that the ground-floor office is the Morkans' place of work. Other inferences are confirmed, however: the sisters are old – Julia is quite grey, Kate is too feeble to move from the house. Yet these women are resilient, independent, committed to certain standards: from Lily's focalizing perspective, they consume 'the best of everything: diamond-bone sirloins, three-shilling tea and the best bottled stout', and 'would not stand . . . back answers'.

To begin on a distinctive feature or trait analysis we need simply to draw up a list of characters, set out across the page, and a list of attributes set out down the page, and note the occurrence or otherwise of each attribute in each character. Notice here that an ambiguity lurks when we note the absence of a trait: absence may mean 'no indicators of the presence of' or 'evident lack of'. For example, if a character is marked '+strongminded', does the negative counterpart denote average strength of mind or downright pusillanimity? Here lies a problematic difference from distinctive feature phonology; there, anything not +labial is inescapably −labial, but we cannot similarly say that anyone not strongminded is automatically weakminded. I proceed below on the assumption that, in the case of gradable attributes such as youthfulness (by contrast with absolute attributes, such as male/female, single/married), I am marking only presence or absence of the specified trait, with no further assumption that absence of a trait implies the presence of its opposite. Thus, in terms of the example above, we will need to note positively weakminded characters on a separate trait dimension from that of ±strongminded.

This table, let me emphasize, is just a first approximation. On

Character-trait inventory

	Kate/Julia	Miss Ivors	Gretta	M. Furey	Gabriel	D'Arcy
female	+	+	+	−	−	−
young	−	+	+	+	+	+
old	+	−	−	−	−	−
married	−	−	+	−	+	−
vulnerable	+	?	+	+	−	−
vigorous	−	+	−	−	+	?
passionate	−	?	?	+	−	−
emotional	+	−	+	+	?	−
'generous'	+	?	+	+	?	−
'mortal'	+	+	−	+	−/+	−
frank	+	+	+	+	−	+
covert	−	−	−	−	+	−
fussy	+	−	−	−	?	+
narcissistic	−	−	−	−	+	+
superior	−	−	−	−	+	+
humble	+	−	−	+	−/+	−
self-conscious	−	−	−	−	+	+
erotic	−	+	+	+	?	−
prosperous	−	?	+	−	+	+

rereading the story several of these may be dropped from the reckoning as not being particularly salient, while others may merit inclusion. And some of these attributes are greatly in need of annotation. Thus the important adjective 'generous' I attribute to Kate and Julia (the party puts them to real expense they can ill afford, their concern for their guests seems utterly genuine), to Gretta in the generosity of her memory of Michael Furey, but not to Gabriel, despite the numerous *textual* attributions to him of generosity. For all those attributions are suspect or qualified in some respect, whether it is his self-restoring tipping of Lily; or his wife asserting 'You are a very generous person, Gabriel' (217) even as Gabriel, fired by covert physical desire for her, strives 'to restrain himself from breaking out into brutal language about the sottish Malins and his pound'; or the 'generous tears' that fill his eyes later (223), which are not so much tears for Michael Furey but a self-pitying sorrow that he, Gabriel, has never felt so selfless a passion for a woman. Similar qualificatory annotation should accompany the trait 'mortal' − by which I mean whether or not a character seems to have a sense of his or her own mortality. In this respect, and perhaps in others (from −[sense of] vulnerability to +vulnerability?), it seems clear that Gabriel develops and changes in the course of the story. In the table I have separated earlier and later attributions with a slash mark. Some such marking of characterological development – where that occurs significantly – does require representation.

I shall leave the reader to explore what the table implies about individual characters and 'overlapping' characters. I will simply note that it does draw our attention to the extent to which Gabriel is more like D'Arcy than he is like Michael Furey, and the extent to which Gretta is more like Michael Furey than she is like Gabriel. If we set aside the first four attributes (none of which are conditions on the basis of which we could reasonably pass a moral judgment on a character), it is quite striking that, at least at the outset of the story, Gabriel and Michael Furey contrast on practically every trait.

If we turn to setting in the story, we find subtle exploitations of the ambience of setting, of change of ambience with change of setting, and of noticeable inappropriateness of behaviour to setting. There is first the public setting of the drawing room, where the music and dancing goes on, and the more private back room, where the drinks are dispensed. In very broad terms, there seem to be styles of interaction appropriate to those domains, but it may be that the major determinant of these styles is the fact that one room has the music and (predominantly) the women while the other has the alcohol and (predominantly) the men. The public discourse of the drawing-room setting can degenerate into the inconsequentiality of Mrs Malins's ramblings (rendered in free indirect discourse),

> Her son-in-law was a splendid fisher. One day he caught a fish, a beautiful big big fish, and the man in the hotel boiled it for their dinner. (191)

while in the drinks room a discordant note may be struck when the prevailing tenor, of masculine familiarity, is over-extended, as when Mr Browne speaks 'a little too confidentially' to the young ladies. This refreshments room undergoes a change of status, however, when it becomes the supper-room dominated by a table laden with Christmas delights, the stage for Gabriel's speech of thanks extolling 'genuine warm-hearted courteous Irish hospitality' (203), 'good fellowship' and 'the Three Graces of the Dublin musical world' (204). But particularly telling are the arhythmic awkwardnesses of atmosphere in the transitional scene that takes place in the hall as various guests prepare to leave. This is the occasion both of D'Arcy's needless but revealing rudeness and of his rendition (distantly) of 'The Lass of Aughrim', a song that stirs such strong memories in Gretta (whose outward reactions stir such strong but unrelated feelings in Gabriel).

Because the main dialogue takes place in the hall itself, but the characters and their words also relate both to the pantomime with the cabman out on the street and to D'Arcy singing upstairs, complex spatial relations between the near and the far develop. If the antics with the cabman are a farce which the audience impatiently waits to depart, the song, expressing tragedy, is a performance the audience yearn to draw near. The song retells (brings near again) an old grief, but only works properly when heard at a distance – D'Arcy's voice is 'made plantive by distance' (210). (Here, in fact, is a spatial articulation of grief that we can set beside the temporal one I sketched in 3.2.1.) And it is just the special configuration of perspectives and focalizations that Gabriel experiences – 'a woman standing on the stairs in the shadow, listening to distant music' – that makes him think of this as a picture, as symbolic. The reader, relatedly, is prompted to interpret this 'audio-spatial' scene symbolically – but with the enrichment that Gabriel, too, is within the symbolic scene.

But nowhere in 'The Dead' is setting more powerfully used than in the closing paragraphs, as Gabriel lies down beside his sleeping wife, and reflects on the evening's events, which have concluded in such an unforeseen way with his wife's revelations. Critics continue to dispute whether Gabriel here 'transcends' his earlier limitations and inversions of vision and sympathy. But what seems beyond dispute is that setting here takes on the role of companion and herald, then catalyst, and finally, in the ubiquitously falling snow, of essence. There is a challenge here to the stylistic analyst to chart the linguistic means by which, quite rapidly, the categories of character and setting begin to dissolve, the text announcing at one point 'His own identity was fading out into a grey impalpable world' (223).

The grammaticization of character and situation 4.7

In the final section of Chapter 2 I suggested a number of ways in which the special status of certain clauses in a narrative, as main carriers of the plot, may be typically reflected in the grammar of those clauses. A similar claim can be made, perhaps with more confidence, about the grammar used in portraying characters and settings. The claim is that the grammar is often an index to, and matches with, the nature or conditions of characters. In making such a claim it is necessary to stress that I am using the term 'grammar' in a relatively enlarged sense, to denote not merely a formal description but a meaning-oriented functional description of the language in question. By grammar, then, I mean the systematic account of all the principles governing choices of words and sequences of words within a language, with the additional requirement that the account is attentive to the meanings that speakers associate with those choices. One of the most useful and usable contemporary meaning-oriented grammars of English is that of Halliday (1985). Below I sketch that part of his grammar, namely choices in the **transitivity** (see glossary) of clauses, which seems most relevant to the analysis of character and setting.

For Halliday, transitivity concerns rather more than purely syntactic questions such as whether or not a particular verb takes a direct object (cf. *smile* v. *embrace*). Halliday assumes that the semantic processes and participants expressed by particular noun phrases and verb phrases in a clause are a representation of *what we take to be going on* in the world. By means of choices from among limited sets of processes and participant roles, expressed in the grammar of the clause and, in particular, its verb, we characterize our view of reality.

A process consists, potentially, of three components:

1 the process itself (typically realized by a verb phrase)
2 the participants in the process (typically realized by noun phrases and, in the case of attributes, adjectival phrases)
3 circumstances associated with the process (realized by prepositional phrases, adverbial phrases, and adverbial subordinate clauses).

Transitivity (or process) analysis is a simple semantic parsing. That is to say, the analyst is identifying the process or action that a clause expresses, whether there is an animate individual intentionally doing the action to another entity (these participants are labelled the 'agent' and the 'affected' respectively), or whether the action is rather one of saying something or thinking something or unconsciously doing something (verbal, mental and behavioural processes respectively). The entire business of representing the processes and participants of reality is what Halliday has termed the **ideational** function of language. In relation to this ideational function, the clause is the basic vehicle for representing patterns of experience. Below I offer a few more explanatory notes on the major types of process and participant in the English clause (these notes are heavily indebted to the lucid lecture hand-outs of my former colleague, Anneliese Kramer-Dahl).

Material processes: processes of doing

Material processes entail verbs of doing, and doing to. These involve agents, affecteds, effecteds and, sometimes, forces, instruments, and agent/affecteds. Compare:

John lit the bonfire with paraffin

(where John is agent, the paraffin is instrument, and the bonfire is the affected),

The lightning hit the tree

(the lightning is not an agent, nor a controlled instrument, but simply a force),

It is raining

(where there is really only a process, and no participant),

Emma painted a large watercolour

(where the watercolour *comes into being* through the process, but is not there to be 'affected' at the outset: hence an effected participant),

Oliver collapsed

(where Oliver's experience is hardly intentional: he is chiefly an affected participant, like the orchids below)

The orchids grew quickly

John wrecked his car

(where, though acting unintentionally – usually – John is both perpetrator and victim, hence best labelled agent/affected).

Mental processes: processes of sensing

Mental processes entail verbs of feeling or mental reaction (like, fear), perception (see, hear), and cognition (think, believe). These involve a human or human-like participant, the experiencer, and a thing or fact that is perceived, felt or thought, the phenomenon or mental focus (either label will do). Note that some mental process verbs take an active, engaged agent rather than a mere experiencer: the processor who listens, watches, learns, etc., is more agentive than the one who merely hears, sees, or understands. The former processes are more developmental, and can take a progressive aspect.

Relational processes: processes of being

Relational processes entail intensive verbs, and verbs expressing circumstantial or possessive relations:

1 intensive: 'x is y'
2 circumstantial: 'x is at/about/like y'
3 possessive: 'x has y'

Each of these may be attributive or identifying (the latter are syntactically reversible).

The participants involved are a carrier and an attribute (current or resultative) or an identified (always in subject position) and an identifier.

types	attributive	identifying
intensive	Emma is clever	Oscar is the leader The leader is Oscar
circumstantial	The concert is on Tuesday	Today is the tenth The tenth is today
possessive	Ted has a piano	The piano is Ted's Ted owns the piano

Note that in complex transitives, the object carries a double role, e.g. as both affected and identified:

They made John the chancellor

Behavioural processes

Behavioural processes are processes of physiological and psychological behaviour, like breathing, coughing, smiling, dreaming. They are grammatically halfway between material and mental processes, with, typically, just one participant, the behaver.

Verbal processes

Verbal processes are processes of saying or telling in a broad sense, with a sayer, a said, and a receiver (the addressee):

He told me he was sorry.

Other participant roles

Sometimes, with ditransitive verbs (verbs that take two objects), we have a recipient role:

Smith gave Mary a box of chocolates.

Sometimes, such is English usage, we find verb + object structures which don't really involve an affected as object, but an element specifying the scope of the process, to be labelled 'range':

He sang me a song
He played tennis very well.

The tennis and the song are not so much an independent participant, but a delimitation of the process itself.

The reward for carefully analyzing character portrayals in relation to this semantic grammar should be clear. We rapidly obtain a preliminary picture of who is agentive, who is affected (for whatever reason: they may be passive, or powerless, or just lazy), whether characters are doers or thinkers, whether instruments and forces dominate in the world represented, and so on. Invaluable applications of the transitivity analysis apparatus in the description of characters – their dispositions, ability to control things and infer causal connections, or their powerlessness – include Halliday (1971), Kennedy (1982) and Burton (1982). Hallidayan transitivity will be applied extensively in the course of analyses in Chapter 7.

4.8   Achieving immediacy in the narration of thoughts

Although Bertha Young was thirty she still had moments like this when she wanted to run instead of walk, to take dancing steps on and off the pavement, to bowl a hoop, to throw something up in the air and catch it again, or to stand still and laugh at – nothing – at nothing, simply.

What can you do if you are thirty and, turning the corner of your own street, you are overcome, suddenly, by a feeling of bliss – absolute bliss! – as though you'd suddenly swallowed a bright piece of that late afternoon sun and it burned in your bosom, sending out a little shower of sparks into every particle, into every finger and toe? . . .

Oh, is there no way you can express it without being 'drunk and disorderly'? How idiotic civilisation is! Why be given a body if you have to keep it shut up in a case like a rare, rare fiddle?

'No, that about the fiddle is not quite what I mean,' she thought, running up the steps and feeling in her bag for the key – she'd forgotten it, as usual – and rattling the letter box. 'It's not what I mean, because – Thank you, Mary' – she went into the hall. 'Is nurse back?' (Katharine Mansfield, 'Bliss')

As we proceed through these memorable opening paragraphs of 'Bliss', we are (at least to some degree) aware of a masterfully controlled kind of storytelling. It is a telling in which external facts about a character on the one hand, and a version of her intimate thoughts on the other, share the same sentential envelope without strain. Thus the routine information that there is a woman called Bertha Young who is aged thirty gives way to disclosures of her sudden impulses to run, dance, laugh at nothing, and so on. Such disclosures appear without either noisy signalling or dis-coursal strain, and this is partly due to the avoidance of either cumbersome clauses of self-perception (She realized that, she felt that . . . etc.), or any sudden appearance of confessional first-person pronouns ('I want to . . .', 'I feel . . .'). That much of this – from around line 3 onwards – is a subtle rendering of Bertha's thoughts and emotions is to some extent confirmed by the belated appearance of a 'she thought' in paragraph 4.

But our first intimation of a veiled immediacy of telling comes with the unexpected phrase 'like this' in the opening line. The expression rather swiftly aligns us with the character Bertha's own immediate orientation to her world, 'like this' being not so much cohesive, tied to some co-textually specified moment, but rather expressive and deictic, alluding to the current moment, one we would have no difficulty identifying were we Bertha herself. From that phrase onwards, for the entirety of the story, we can argue that Bertha is the internal character-focalizer (and often, of course, the focalized too).

Notice too, in that first paragraph, how cleverly we are led to assume that Bertha *is*, at this point in the narrative, walking along a street, on a pavement, in the open air – though none of this is directly *reported*. All that is directly reported are her blissful impulses – and these are strictly consonant with the character sitting up in bed, eating lunch, or whatever. Yet no such situation comes to mind as we read the paragraph: we assume that reported impulses to frolic in the street indicate that the woman is actually in the street, although perhaps only the exophoric definite article used in the reference to 'the pavement' is an explicit formal cue. In what follows, we shall attempt to explore more systematically these subtle techniques, and their equally subtle communicative consequences. But we have already informally recognized that, with an art that conceals art, the narrative has modulated from the distanced description of the character – 'Bertha Young was thirty'; to the immediacy of the relaying of Bertha's thoughts in, especially, paragraph 3; and back to the externality of the direct speech in paragraph 4. Those modulations have also involved switches in tense, from past to present to past – but we are too distracted on a first reading by the larger textual effect, its representation of bliss, to notice such mechanics.

Isabel noted afresh that life was certainly hard for some people, and she felt a delicate glow of shame as she thought how easy it now promised to become for herself. (1) She was prepared to learn that Ralph was not pleased with her engagement; but she was not prepared, in spite of her affection for him, to let this fact spoil the situation. (2) She was not even prepared, or so she thought, to resent his want of sympathy; for it would be his privilege – it would be indeed his natural line – to find fault with any step she might take towards marriage. (3) One's cousin always pretended to hate one's husband; that was traditional, classical; it was a part of one's cousin's always pretending to adore one. (4) . . . You could criticize any marriage; it was the essence of a marriage to be open to criticism. (5) How well she herself, should she only give her mind to it, might criticize this union of her own! (6) She had other employment, however, and Ralph was welcome to relieve her of the care. (7) Isabel was prepared to be most patient and most indulgent. (8) He must have seen that, and this made it the more odd he should say nothing. (9) After three days had elapsed without his speaking our young woman wearied of waiting; dislike it as he would, he might at least go through the form. (10) We, who know more about poor Ralph than his cousin, may easily believe that during the hours that followed his arrival at Palazzo Crescentini he had privately gone through many forms. (11) (Henry James, *Portrait of a Lady*: 338)

In this passage, as in that from 'Bliss', we see the subtle narrative presentation of a character's thoughts, with the same attenuated sense that any narratorial figure is *relaying* those thoughts. On the contrary, no matter how audacious Isabel's views become, no narratorial voice of 'true judgment' intrudes to censure the character, dissociate itself from Isabel, and alert the reader to the errors being broadcast. That is not James's way.

And yet that this passage is still narrated seems clear. In particular, Isabel continues to be designated by the third-person pronoun, *she*, as someone different from the teller (who is always an *I*), and the tense continues to be the past tense of narration, rather than the present tense of direct experience. Furthermore, the passage begins by telling us what 'Isabel noted' and by reporting as the text of an intrusive omniscient narrator (Fowler's type B narrator, described in 3.8) what she thought and what she felt as she thought. But by sentence 4 that narrator has withdrawn, his omniscience giving place to Isabel's own limited wisdom – a wisdom that confidently and blindly assumes that Ralph, 'classically, traditionally' always pretended to adore her. Pretended, the reader asks? The mismatch between Isabel's gapped and distorted picture of things and the reader's own fuller one is too striking to ignore. The narrative mode adopted so as to narrate Isabel's thoughts in an uncensored form engages the reader in the computing or construing of many such ironies. The irony just noted may be chiefly poignant. But when, in sentences 5 and 6, this newly-engaged young woman announces to herself that the essence of a marriage is its openness to criticism; that she could – if she thought about it – criticize her own impending union, but that she had other things to do, then a more comprehensive defectiveness of judgment is laid bare.

The narrative mode at work here, in sentences 3 to 7, 9 and the latter half of 10, is free indirect discourse. The mismatches it can be used to quietly expose – mismatches between a character's judgments of the world-of-the-text and our own judgments of that world – are of many kinds. Note, for example, how despite Isabel's insistence on her own patience towards Ralph, her indulgence, her refusal 'to resent his want of sympathy', she *does* resent his unspoken reservations and wearies of waiting. Or, somewhat differently, consider the narrator's clever collusion with the reader – 'We, who know more about poor Ralph than his cousin' – when he picks up Isabel's complaint 'he might at least go through the form' (i.e., wishing her joy and happiness, etc.), and uses the same phrase in the next sentence in a tellingly different sense.

Direct and indirect discourse   4.9

Just one of the attractive features of **free indirect discourse** (known as FID) is that most readers are not consciously *aware* of it being at work. We may think of it as a sort of foregrounded narrative, neither pure narrative nor pure character-expression. And, as we shall see, it has two sub-types, not always easily distinguished, **free indirect speech** and **free indirect thought** (henceforth, FIS and FIT respectively). The former of these is often easier to perceive so I will turn to it first, though we should subsequently spend more time on FIT, which is far more common and important in modern fiction.

As is well recognized, two long-established conventional means of reporting characters' speech are available to narrators; each is exemplified below:

1 He said to her, 'I cannot see you now, but if you return tomorrow, we could spend the day together.'
2 He explained to her that he could not see her then, but that if she returned the next day they could spend the day together.

Both the above modes of presentation are extremely widespread in traditional novels, as well as in other discourses in which the speech of individuals is reported. Consider the language of newspapers, for example, which are very heavily dependent on direct and indirect speech reporting of the actual words of politicians, judges, and people in the news.

Direct speech purports to be a *faithful verbatim report* of a person's actual words (although we accept, in literature, that all sorts of likely pauses, reformulations, repairs, and dialectal features are partially if not completely removed). In *indirect* speech, the narrator or reporter purports to provide an accurate *version* of what the speaker said, but not by simply reproducing that speaker's own words: instead, the narrator's words and deictic orientation are retained. As you might be able to see, it is possible for indirect speech versions to be fairly remote versions of their hypothesized direct speech source. Thus Leech and Short (1981: 323–4) note the use of quite summarized and remote versions of indirect speech. A summarized report of the direct speech above might be:

> He explained that although he couldn't see her immediately, they could get together the next day.

We can begin to specify our grasp of the distinctions between various ways of reporting speech by comparing and contrasting two sentences that feel roughly synonymous:

(a) She said, 'I want you to come here today'.
(b) She said that she wanted him to return there that same day.

We can list some of the formal ways in which the second (indirect speech) version differs from the first (direct speech) one:

1 absence of inverted commas (speech marks), and hence a different interconnection of the two clauses, as now syntactically related **hypotactically** rather than **paratactically** (see glossary);
2 presence of subordination relation made explicit by the presence of the *that* subordinator (optional);
3 first and second person pronouns in the direct speech replaced by appropriate third person pronouns. Notice that this makes the indirect speech more explicit than the direct with respect to the sex of the addressee (*him* v. *you*);
4 where the direct speech version uses the present tense, the indirect version uses the past tense (*want/wanted*);
5 present-time-and-place deictic elements in the direct speech

(*here, today*) contrast with ones denoting a past and distant deictic orientation (*there, that same day*);

6 the verb of specific directional movement, implying movement *towards*, contrasts with the use in the indirect speech of a verb with non-specific directional movement. Note the awkwardness and counter-intuitive feel of collocating *go* with *here*, and *come* with *there* –'I like to come there every Sunday'; while *return* is more neutral as to direction (it's a going *back* in a direction that must be previously specified).

In the list above I have repeatedly talked in terms of 'absence of' and 'presence of'. If I had talked in terms of 'removal of' (*e.g.*, speech marks) or 'insertion of' (*e.g.*, the subordinator *that*), I would have been implying that (b) was a transformed version of (a), and that (a) 'must have come first', before (b) was derived from it. Although there is a conventional logical dependency of real-world indirect speech upon real-world direct speech, bear in mind that this is in itself by no means unproblematic (people often 'report' things that their reportees never said), and certainly – as noted earlier – this dependency carries no guarantees about the *form* of the indirect speech report.

If the above are the formal differences between direct speech and indirect speech report, what may be the differences in effect on readers? These are much less easy to specify, but we might suggest that we feel a greater *distance* and detachment from characters and their words when these are mediated via indirect speech. Informally, we may think of direct speech as an environment where characters are in control and speak for themselves, while in indirect speech the narrator is more overtly still in control, and reports *on behalf of* the characters. (These appearances of character control become deceptive if we put too much stress on them: behind all the fictional individuals, of course, is the controlling teller, as is made newly vivid when, for example, stretches of direct speech are set in sharply evaluative framing contexts – see Sternberg, 1982.)

An additional sign of narratorial control in indirect speech is the frequent possibility of narratorial tinkering with the phraseology (as noted above). Thus the *here* of the direct speech version could be replaced not merely by *there*, but by any prepositional phrase (such as *to the house*) which did not alter the facts implicit in (a) and (b). The indirect rendering is thus often felt by readers to be both a less vivid and a less authentic expression of the character.

The two versions of speech rendering I have discussed so far are best seen as prototypes or standard styles of speech reporting: there are many variants which depart from the prototypical formats. At the 'direct' end of the spectrum, we can talk of free direct speech, discarding the reporting clause (*He said*, etc.) and/or the speech marks:

I want you to come here today.

At the 'indirect' end, more indirect than indirect speech, is narrative reporting which condenses, summarizes or recasts characters' speech, so that only the gist is reported:

She urged him to visit her at once.

Such narratorial speech-summarizing is useful in reporting unimportant conversation, where a verbatim account seems aesthetically undesirable – or for referring a second time to a conversation that has been previously presented to the reader more fully. It is accordingly quite widespread in novels.

4.10 Free indirect discourse

The most fascinating styles, however, are those that lie between orthodox direct and indirect speech, revealing some formal features of each of those two formats:

(c) She wanted him to return there today.
(d) She wanted him to come there today.
(e) She wanted him to come here today.

These styles of thought and speech representation, neither direct nor indirect according to orthodox prescriptions, but mixings or mergings of narratorial indirectness with characterological directness, all fall under the designation of free indirect discourse (henceforth FID). But the phenomenon is often referred to by other names. Perhaps commonest, from a very long list, are: free indirect style, *style indirect libre*, represented speech and thought, quasi-direct discourse, *erlebte Rede*, and combined discourse. If it is right to talk at all of a prototypical FID style (we may come to see that some of the best FID is that which resists easy categorization), then (e) may be thought of as more fully FID than (c) or (d).

All three of these show in a simple way why they are thought of as free indirect style, a freed version of indirect reporting: the character's words are freed from syntactic domination by any reporting clause (*She said* is absent), and from a more important sense of 'mental' domination – of the character by the narrator, who is the source of that *She said*. But this format is also a freer, less refracted, reporting in its tendency to adopt the orientation, in deictic words, of the reported character rather than any reporting individual. It does so despite retaining third-person pronouns and (typically) past narrative tense.

The distinct formal characteristics of FID may be briefly enumerated:

1 no reporting clause, and thus no *that* subordinator either (in this, akin to free direct discourse);

2 third-person pronouns used to refer to the implied speaker or thinker of whatever is reported as said or thought, together with the text's established narrative tense (typically, past) (in these respects, akin to both pure narrative and indirect discourse);

3 proximal deictics (*here, now, this, today*, etc.) – just as in direct discourse;

4 syntactic inversion, in questions, of the clause subject and the finite element in the verb – 'Was she quite mad? How did he have the time to keep coming over to see her?' (in this, akin to direct discourse question format);

5 more prominent use of modality markers, which we judge to emanate from a character rather than from the narrator. In particular, FID reveals frequent use of modal verbs (*must, had to, could, might, would*) expressing judgments (from the *character-*'speaker') about the probability or obligatoriness of the denoted action or state actually happening:

What he *ought to do* was go down to Norfolk and settle down and get married. (Dos Passos, *1919*: 56; cited in McHale, 1978: 265)

Modal 'sentence adverbials', all of degrees of probability (*certainly, perhaps, possibly*, etc.), operate in the same way:

and Old Ben too, Old Ben too; they would give him his paw back even, certainly they would give him his paw back . . . (Faulkner, *Go Down, Moses*: 329)

As indicated above, all such modals are to do with disputable judgment. They prompt an FID reading in just those cases where we find it implausible to imagine that it is the teller who, perhaps rather abruptly, intrudes into the story to tell us what some character ought to do, or what possibly had happened or would happen. (Again, note that with a limited-knowledge, first-person witnessing narrator, like Nick Carraway in *The Great Gatsby*, such modals would make narratorial sense.) A simple framing or commutation test that is sometimes useful here is to compare and choose between versions which explicitly cast the utterance as a narrator-to-reader communicative act:

> I, the narrator, tell you, the reader, what he ought to do was go down to Norfolk . . .

or as a character-to-self-or-other-character communicative act:

> I, the character, say/think to myself, what I ought to do is go down to Norfolk . . .

(Note the need to shift tense and pronouns in the second version.)

6   use of the vocatives, evaluative words (*poor, dear*), fillers (*well, of course*), expletives, interjections, and dialectal or idiolectal distinctivenesses, and emotive language in general, that we associate with the character rather than the narrator. Informally, we may think of all this as a reinstatement of the 'fruity' flavour of a character's direct speech. Fruity because, conforming to a long but flexible tradition, *most* of the narratives we read have or imply a sober, restrained, standard-English-speaking narrator with, by contrast, characters' own speech appearing somewhat franker, less inhibited, and so on. A particularly visible marker of distinctive 'fruitiness' is a switch – still within text which purports to be sober narrative – to eccentricities of spelling and writing in general, intended to reflect the eccentricities, or at least non-standardness, of a character's words.

But these are patterns rather than rules. By contrast we can easily encounter a non-standard-English-speaking narrator dialectically at odds with the very 'proper' speech – and FID – of various reported characters; or, similarly, a vivid and earthy narration of the life of a dull bureaucrat (himself stilted in word and thought), which style gives way, where the character's discourse is conveyed by either the direct or free indirect discourse methods, to a noticeably plodding banality, decidedly arid and unfruity! As elsewhere in narrative study, it is the perception of *difference* between character speech and narrator speech, which is the true criterion. Obviously, then, this fifth diagnostic is simply inoperative where there seems to be no difference between the narrator's dialect and a character's, where there is only a single shared lect, as in many of Henry James's novels and stories.

Who speaks, who thinks?   4.11

If the crucial question in focalization was 'From whose spatiotemporal/psychological/ideological orientation is this conveyed?', here in FID it is 'To whom do we attribute these spoken words or articulated thoughts?' In direct speech it is definitely the character who speaks, in indirect speech it is definitely the narrator who speaks, while in FID it seems to be really the character who speaks, but that speech appears embedded in the narrator's framing speech.

Deciding whom to attribute any particular discourse to is, in a sense, very simple – it is either the narrator or some particular character. The choice seems easily made. There is very often *nothing*, in the way of blatant ill-formedness or textual ludicrousness, to prevent the reader ascribing FID sentences to a narrator and that narrator alone. There is no unresolvable, impossible dilemma of 'undecidability'. Rather the dilemma rests in the fact that whatever choice you make, attributing sentences to whomever you will, there's no way of confirming or verifying the correctness of your choice. The problem is chiefly, then, one of 'unconfirmability'. But more of this later.

The 'Who is saying/thinking this?' question is useful to keep in mind, since FID is a very open category, with – as Leech and Short show (1981: 328–33) – *no* necessary formal markers of its presence. Narratives in the present tense (with the result that there is no tense-difference between direct and indirect discourses), or with first-person narrators, can thus just as easily contain FID as other types. As Leech and Short show in the following two examples, a single character-attributed expletive, or – even slighter – a single character-expressive punctuation mark, can signal the presence of FID, and not mere indirect discourse:

He said that the bloody train had been late.
He told her to leave him alone!

If we have marks of the presence of FID here, note that what we don't have are clear indications of its extent. Here is another unverifiable dimension. Do we say that the entire clause 'leave him alone!' is FID, or only 'alone!', or merely '!'? Or should we reject such a question as a misleading irrelevance, emphasizing that what is more important is the perceived presence of FID, and its larger narrative effect?

FID is a long-established technique that can be usefully related to such classical literary distinctions of narrative method as those between showing and telling, or **mimesis** and **diegesis**. While the former places the emphasis on a direct characterological representation or impersonation, the latter places it on a more indirect, detached teller-oriented conspectual presentation. In the narration of events, as we saw earlier, mimesis is associated with a scenic presentation, while diegesis is linked to a condensed or 'edited' summarized account – with, relatedly, a greater overt role played by the teller who condenses or edits. Mimesis presents 'everything that happened' in one sense, but really only everything as it would be revealed to a witness within the scene; in these latter respects it is rather partial and non-comprehensive. And as Stanzel (1981) notes, it typically comes with internal character-focalization. Diegesis presents 'everything that happened' in another sense, but only everything that a detached external reporter decides is worth telling – a reporter who is able to reflect, reorganize, decide upon the point or teleology of the story prior to narrating it. We can accordingly predict that diegetic narration will have more manipulations of temporal order, duration and frequency, more evident ranking or hierarchical ordering of event-presentation; that diegesis is hypotactic while mimesis is paratactic.

In FID, then, we encounter a fascinating narrative mode where formal grammar and the unpredictabilities of creative language use meet. We *can* identify a cluster of typical grammatical indices of FID; but we cannot determine in advance what is or is not FID, since the lexicogrammatical features have to be seen in the larger literary and pragmatic context. As McHale (1978: 269) has written:

The decisive indices of FID ought to be not the marks of its syntactical distinctiveness, or even its traces in the surrounding context, but the signs of its mimetic character, whether formal signs (the 'words' of a character, his characteristic registers and idiom) or semantic signs (the 'content' of utterances, the 'thoughts' or 'intended meanings' of a character as distinguished from those of a narrator). This account thus overturns the priorities of orthodox stylistics: FID is not so much the syntactical frame which 'permits' the appearance of otherwise inadmissible mimetic material, as it is formal or, more problematically, semantic materials which evoke a 'voice' or presence other than the narrator's, and conduce to the recognition of free indirect syntax.

Because the FID indices are in a sense optional, or may simply not occur relevantly in particular contexts, the separation of FID from pure narrative is often problematic. It is not that FID is incontrovertibly 'there', and that some students have difficulty seeing it: it is rather that it is an open question as to whether we decide there is an FID departure from a pure narrative (PN) norm at all. In good structuralist fashion, we examine the system of the narrative text, and have to make judgments as to the perceptibility of significant differences, analogous to the perception of significant difference between utterances phonemically rendered as /pet/ and /bet/. But what, we need to know, is the criterion for determining significant difference? The /pet/ *v.* /bet/ contrast will be judged significant or not depending on whether those strings fill different places or have distinctly different values in the larger system of the language they are judged to come from. Similarly, judgments about perceived significant differences that we relate to a switch from PN or ID to FID will be largely based on our view of how that fluctuation or dialectic fits in with our larger encompassing reading of the text as a coherent structured whole.

FID: functions and effects   4.12

In the neo-Platonist terms mentioned earlier (mimesis and diegesis), we can think of FID as a mimetic diegesis (a telling that shows or presents aspects of the character's 'own' words or thoughts). There are no end of ways of characterizing FID, in fact: as substitutionary narration; as combined discourse; as a contamination, tainting or colouring of the narrative; as a dual voicing. My own preference is for viewing it as a strategy of (usually temporary or discontinuous) *alignment*, in words, values and perspective, of the narrator with a character. I like the word 'alignment' because it doesn't prescribe whether that closeness of narrator to character is going to be used for purposes of irony, empathy, as a vehicle for stream-of-consciousness or the clashing of two voices, or whatever: the alignment is perceived, then the function (or 'naturalization') is worked out by the reader. The term 'alignment' perhaps also helps us keep in mind that, in terms of lexicogrammatical markers and aesthetic/narrative effect, there is a continuum from pure narrative words to pure character words, with any number of points on that continuum.

A few remarks on the relations between FID and stream-of-consciousness (SOC) may be in order. As McHale (1978: 276ff.) implies, SOC is a cover label for any verbal rendering of a character's thoughts in a way which is not overtly governed by framing narratorial verbs of internal communication (*he thought to himself, he realized*). FID is one of the two major ways of effecting this SOC rendering: the other, much more widespread, I think, is free, and compacted, direct thought (also known as **direct interior monologue**). FID seems less widely used as a mode of SOC because it does retain many marks of the narratorial voice and presence. Thus to describe FID as the formal realization of the conceptual category labelled **indirect interior monologue** is not entirely happy, because the persistent pres- ence of narratorial marks means that FID is never pure mono- logue, is always – and definitionally – dialogical.

Jefferson (1981), taking a historical look at the emergence and enthusiasm for FID in literary circles, shows that it was endorsed as a powerful mode of presenting characters in an (allegedly) authentic-cum-realist way. FID entails

1 escape from an omniscient narration, total (and implausible, even boring) disclosure of the contents of characters' minds, and
2 escape from the boringly one-voiced telling of an external, constantly and dully distant narration.

A happy compromise, it is an honest recognition that authors or narrators do always hold the strings and control what is told, but that they don't always feel happy with the authoritarian control they have of characters' minds and thoughts. So FID is a sporadic, intermittent movement towards perceptive/intrusive/aligned understanding and disclosure of characters, not the straitjacket of total perception/intrusion. The 'fastidiousness' about entering and disclosing a character's thoughts may well relate to the teller's aesthetics or ideology.

Jefferson, like McHale and others (Pascal, 1977; Ginsberg, 1982), recognizes that a key source of the impact of the FID sentence is its ambiguous mixture of proper narrative and proper speech or thought (we shall find that a theorist of rather different orientation, Banfield (1982) takes the contrary view that no ambiguity is possible):

> The dual voice of FID which is responsible for the superficially realist effect of immediacy is also an ambiguity which is highly unrealistic. From a realist point of view, FID is a doubly disconcerting use of language: its ambiguities cut it adrift from the two points at which we commonly imagine language to be anchored to reality, the speaker and the referent. It is neither fully expressive nor fully referential, and this *invraisemblance* [lack of the faithful 'realistic' representation, in literature, of the real world: a convention of 'realism' that many novels foster and many readers demand] differentiates it most profoundly from other forms of reported discourse. (Jefferson, 1981: 42)

Actually, a realist explanation of FID is futile – an approach based on dualizedness or 'impossible' infiltration, dialogism, the clashing of two voices, is needed. FID is a flawed or problematical mimesis, since it is discourse that cannot fit any one speaker or speech situation. And its problematic nature means that it itself is foregrounded or made the object of attention, rather than being a mere channel or vehicle for directing attention to something else (e.g., a picture of a particular world). This is an enlightened kind of formalism;

> In a theory of dialogism which sees self-criticism rather than mimesis as the main function of criticism, the dual voice is freed from the embarrassment of its *invraisemblances* and becomes an exemplary rather than an anomalous stylistic mode . . . (Jefferson, 1981: 43)

Banfield's theory of unspeakable sentences   4.13

Before leaving the topic of FID, I want to discuss a recent radical and linguistically explicit critique of more orthodox treatments of it (such as that outlined above). That critique is contained in Ann Banfield's ambitious interpretation of narration and discourse, and their syntactic bases (Banfield, 1982). And though this section is partly a negative report, focussing at some length on various objections to her approach, I must stress at the outset that Banfield's book merits this extended attention because it is a model of sustained argumentation using linguistic description and methodology in the study of narrative.

Basic to Banfield's discussion are distinctions she makes (elaborating Benveniste, 1966), between language-as-discourse and language-as-narration. Most language use is discourse, which she defines as text (spoken or written) that is both communicative (in that it involves an addressee, at least implicitly marked in the text by, for example, second-person pronouns) and expressive (in that there is a speaker, whose subjective orientation is encoded in the text by means such as, among others, tense and pronouns). While discourse is both communicative and expressive, narration is neither: it is text without a genuine addressee (or any textual traces of one), and text without a genuine expressivity-disclosing speaker. One dizzying conclusion of all this is that in narration nobody speaks, narration is 'unspeakable' and narratorless.

In Banfield's scheme, sentences that are communicative *and* expressive are speakable discourse. Both DS (direct speech) and IS (indirect speech) would be included amongst such speakable discourses, together with most of our everyday uses of language, where an identifiable speaker addresses an identifiable addressee, conveying in the message their own subjectivities of orientation where these are relevant. At the opposite extreme, the sentence of narration is said to be devoid of either communicative or expressive functions: it's just there, and even if there is first-person narration – an 'I' in the text – there is still no real 'you'. Between these two lies FID (which Banfield terms 'represented speech and thought'), where there is plenty of expressivity (which we attribute to the character whose words are being represented) but again no genuine communication, no genuine I–you interaction. Hence, like other types of narration, FID is unspeakable. As should be clear, Banfield's thesis is wide-ranging and original: I urge the interested reader to turn to it, together with related material listed in the 'further reading' section of this chapter. In what follows I can only raise some of the problems in her approach, as these bear more directly on the treatment of FID.

Consider the following sentences of direct and indirect speech:

(a) John said to her 'I am tired'.
(b) John said to her that he was tired.

In direct speech, a speaker expresses his self (his subjective, self-oriented perspective on events) to a hearer/addressee. The selfhood (subjective orientation) expressed is that of the speaker, explicitly present, and the self-speaker identity is reflected in the present tense, proximal deictics, and first-person pronoun. (We should bear in mind – an obvious point perhaps – that by the direct speech, in (a), we mean only that text inside the speech marks.) The preceding *John said to her* portion we attribute to some narrator or reporter. Thus in (a) there are two distinct speaker-selves: first the reporter/narrator, and then, marked by overt textual and grammatical signals, a switch to the character John as speaker-self.

In indirect speech such as (b), according to Banfield, John has the bare sense of his utterance reported, but John's selfhood, his own expressive and subjective orientation, is wholly absent. The speaker-self expressed in indirect speech is rather, and invariably, that of the reporter responsible for the entire utterance, including the verb of communication. Put another way, this means that one speaker cannot express the subjectivity (deictically-oriented selfhood) of another in indirect speech.

This absolutely crucial step in Banfield's argument is, however, at best controversial. More importantly, it's a step which, if taken, will guarantee the correctness of her subsequent rejection of any 'dual-voiced' dimension to FID. But is her claim here, that in indirect discourse only the reporter's subjectivity can be expressed, persuasive? Like any generative hypothesis, it cannot be evaluated without our paying proper attention to the language (sentences) that it generates and the sentences it rejects. On the basis of Banfield's claims we will find all the following sentences rejected, disallowed, by her 'strong' theory of unitary, paratactic-clause-bounded, selfhood:

Lily asked where were her paints.
Clarissa insisted that, concerning Peter Walsh, she was never wrong.
She replied that they might be parted for years, she and Peter.
Laura exclaimed what nice eyes he had.
Laura blurted out how very nice workmen were!
Gerty revealed that she had paid three and eleven for those stockings on the Tuesday, no the Monday before Easter. (In a footnote Banfield says this is acceptable if the 'correction' comes from the quoting speaker.)

Now it won't do just to say 'Yes these may be OK somewhere,

but not in IS', for that is to beg the question of just what IS is. We must treat these sentences as IS rather than FID, despite the traces of the latter, because they retain the 'un-free' dominating initial verb of communication. If we exclude all the above sentences from IS, where shall we put them? Nor will it ever do for Banfield to say 'Well, that's OK in your dialect (some dialect!) but not in mine.' Plenty of native speakers accept the above sentences, and such sentences are precisely the problem that an adequate theory of speech- and thought-representation must aim to account for and explain, not simply reject. These sentences fall foul of Banfield's prescription that expressivity can only transfer from one speaker to another across non-embedded sentences; the fact that readers accept such sentences, in suitable narrative contexts, suggests that no such prescription (a prescription that looks overly oriented to language-as-discourse) applies to narrative text. If we accept the double-expressivity and dual-voicedness of such sentences we are drawn to conclude that dual-voicedness can emerge even outside FID sentences, viz., in coloured or contaminated IS. Nor, incidentally, should we imagine that double-expressivity IS is a freak production found only in the rarefied world of modernist fiction. The following instance is one of many I have found in the thrillers of Dick Francis. It begins with the first-person narrator's account of how he gets Mrs Palissey's simple-minded son to help him in his wine shop, but concludes with Mrs Palissey's 'voice' very evidently overlaying the narratorial frame:

> He might not be able to read, but I had found he could recognise the general appearance of a bottle and label if I told him three or four times what it was and he now knew all the regular items by sight. Mrs Palissey said at least once a week that she was ever so proud of him, considering. (Dick Francis, *Proof*, Pan, 1985, p. 34)

Banfield's insistence on the impossibility of two selves getting mixed up in a single sentence is particularly highlighted in her discussion of the following sentence (1982: 94):

> Yes, she could hear his poor child crying now.

If we treat this as FIT (her 'represented thought'), then all the self-expressive elements (*Yes, poor, now*) must, in her view, be attributed to the same individual (the *she*), with no possibility that the evaluation 'poor child' could be merely the woman's ironic echoing of, for example, a father's tiresome indulgence of that child. (See McHale, 1983: 35, for convincing contextualization where this latter, subtler possibility is confirmed.)

In FID sentences, Banfield claims, a subjectivity or selfhood is expressed, but lacks any genuine traces of a speaker, an I-figure addressing listeners/readers. The FID sentence is a strictly unspeakable sentence; no one could utter of themselves the sentence:

What a fool he had been!

where the subjectively-oriented selfhood is *not* tied to any speaker. Absence of speaker is reflected in absence of speaker-oriented deixis: present tense, proximal deictics indicating a genuine here-and-now-ness. The now of FID is a *past* now, not a genuine and authentic present one. Thus FID is expressive of a selfhood, but not communicative of a speaker's position in relation to a hearer/listener. Similarly, while in discourse we have a speaker, an actually-present addressee, and a 'genuine' present (one representing the actual real time of utterance), in narration there is typically no present, no here and now (instead, past tense and non-proximal deictics), and never an addressee. There is no 'you' addressed in narration as there is in discourse. Even 'worse' than FID, not only is narration not communicative, it is not genu-inely expressive either – its deictics and lexis do not express a self. The sentence of narration narrates events but is anchored to no now.

On the issue of narration as 'narrator-less' it would be nice to effect a reconciliation of views by suggesting that Banfield's thesis is simply a bolder confrontation of the puzzle which third-person narrative creates. All theorists agree that talk of a 'third-person *narrator*' is woefully misleading, although traditionalists hypost-asize an attenuated narratorial presence, a shadowy figure, invis-ible, removed, but still 'there'. Is Banfield simply like the boy confronting the Emperor in his superfine new clothes, and pointing out there are no clothes there at all? It is tempting to conclude so, especially given my own criticisms of the prolifer-ation of narratorial and quasi-authorial roles that some theories have promoted (see Chapter 3). It would be nice to conclude that Banfield simply denies the existence of any extradiegetic narrator, instead reinstating the author as teller. I suspect quite a number of tradionalists would not object to that revision. But such a reconciliation rather assumes that in all cases in which we have conventionally thought of there being a text-internal narrator, i.e., all first-person narratives, Banfield would allow that that narrator does exist. But she does not.

To be sure, she accepts that in certain types of first-person stories (which we might think of as yarns), akin to what the Russian formalists called *skaz*, a narrator is present (so that these stories are discourse, not narration). But there remain many other first-person narratives, in her scheme, which are technically narratorless. Just why, for example, the 'yarn' version of Faulk-ner's 'Spotted Horses' tale, which has appeared as a separate short story, should be narrated discourse, while the novel-embedded version that appears in *The Hamlet* should be narratorless first-person narrative, seems to depend on the following factors:

1 In the *skaz* version, there is an audience implicit within the text, sometimes addressed as 'you'.
2 In the *skaz* version, there are plentiful indications of characterol-ogical dialect and pronunciation – 'He come outen that barn like a chip on the crest of a busted dam of water, and clumb onto the wagon.'
3 The telling is given a precise time in the *skaz* version only, not in the novel.

It seems ill-judged to propose a fundamental contrast of narrated communicativeness and narratorless non-communic-ativeness on such tenuous and disputable grounds. The differ-ences 1–3 are important and merit a place in the discussion of narrative poetics and technique, but we might well argue – as McHale implicitly does in his review of Banfield's book (McHale, 1983) – that explanation should relate to questions of narrative function, motivation, and 'naturalization'. 'Spotted Horses' as a story, and the 'same' incident in *The Hamlet* (almost three times as long in the telling, Banfield notes) are simply different narra-tives with different logics, but not so different that one is non-communicative in any fundamental sense.

Point 2 above, for example, relates to Banfield's claim that narrative lacks all marks of dialect, pronunciation, these allegedly only appearing in discourse. But this, to a linguist, is simply incoherent. All forms of written English – as is true of most written languages – convey plentiful indications of pronunciation or 'signs of actual pronunciation', and learning to read English would be a far more tortuous process if this were not the case. Written

English, including the standard written English that Banfield privi-
leges as the 'proper' English for narration, carries numerous
markers of pronunciation and is itself, of course, a dialect. As a
transcript or mimesis of pronunciation written English is always
problematic, however – always, whether we're looking at direct
speech or indirect speech, a standard dialect or a non-standard
one.

Thus, contra Banfield, we should recognize that marks of the
spoken form are always there as a background in the written
form – reflecting the latter's historical derivation, and continued
interrelations, with the former. In some texts, however, marks of
pronunciation are particularly foregrounded, typically to render a
more vivid sense of a character's distinctiveness, whether that
character is Lawrence's Mellors or Dickens's Stephen Blackpool.
(Distinctiveness can be good or bad – in very general terms, it
seems that, increasingly, fictional characters' distinctive dialects
and accents are intended as an index of virtuous qualities rather
than, as was once usually the case, vicious ones.)

It is clear why Banfield does not want to allow marked pronunciation as proper anywhere but in direct speech and the extended
direct speech of *skaz*. Real narration is supposed to be unspeakable, 'never spoken', so what right would such marks of speech
have to contaminate the unspeakable and noncommunicative? If
there is something dogmatic about introducing the term 'right'
that I have used here, then that reflects Banfield's dogmatism,
which in turn leads her to strained defence of her overly rigid
demarcations. Thus when faced with some clear cases of foregrounded characterological pronunciation in Lawrence –

Mrs Morel usually . . . sympathized with her fruit man – who
was a gabey, but his wife was a bad un . . .

she denies that these really render the speaking voice, but claims
rather that they 'capture an attitude by specific dialect words
which are primarily expressive' (116).

One basic problem with Banfield's argumentation seems to lie
in the fact that her methodology and grammar are resolutely
sentence-based. Full stops and quotation marks are held in
particularly high esteem by her, as unquestionable markers of
sense boundaries. Accordingly, subtle expressivity shifts within
the clause are simply neglected, or positively disallowed, in the
model. She simply denies the legitimacy of slippage or modu-

lation from ID to FID intrasententially – and so, inevitably, sees nothing to warrant or sustain a 'dual-voice' hypothesis.

There has been much unresolved debate between Banfield and the dual voice theorists as to which of their two distinct accounts of FID is preferable, more coherent, informative, and explanatory. However, it might be worth recognizing the considerable degree of agreement between the two camps on how to interpret the facts. Thus both sides acknowledge and emphasize a kind of 'impossibility' that attends FID, although Banfield casts this as 'unspeakability' while the Pascalians insist on dialogism – in the sense of two positions, two voices, not set apart and alternating as in conventional dialogue, but both inhabiting the *same* utterance (sometimes at the level of single words). But what unites these two theories is an emphatic recognition that no ordinary speaker, speaking to us face to face (rather than, for example, narrating) would produce the kind of discourse that FID inhabits. That is because in such FID-coloured narrative two radically distinct situations of utterance are simultaneously implied: situations with quite different participants (character-to-character *v.* narrator-to-reader) and quite different spatiotemporal settings (the 'then' of the story *v.* the 'now' of the telling/reading), and with convergence only in the area of subject matter (a character's represented thoughts or speech are experiential subject matter for that character, but also the subject matter of the narrative for its reader). The oddity of encountering two amalgamated situations of utterance should be evident if we reflect upon Lyons's invaluable characterization of 'the canonical situation of utterance':

> This involves one-one, or one-many, signalling in the phonic medium along the vocal-auditory channel, with all the participants present in the same actual situation able to see one another and to perceive the associated non-vocal paralinguistic features of their utterances, and each assuming the roles of sender and receiver in turn . . . There is much in the structure of languages that can only be explained on the assumption that they have developed for communication in face-to-face interaction. This is clearly so as far as deixis is concerned. (Lyons, 1977: 637–8)

Another ground of similarity between Banfield and the dual-voicers is the emphasis on the heightened reflexivity and literariness of FID-coloured narrative. Thus Banfield opens her first chapter with an observation that could as easily have come in the essays by Jefferson, Ginsberg, or McHale:

> [In the special reflexive forms developed for reporting speech] the speaking subject and his utterance become, not merely the transparent vehicle of expression and communication, but the object of a self-conscious attention on the part of language turned back upon itself. (Banfield, 1982: 23)

Of Banfield's broader conclusions, then, I am sceptical. Even FID's unspeakability is, for me, an unspeakability based on grounds other than hers. For her, FID is unspeakable in its lack of an addressee; for me it is unspeakable since it involves *two* addressees (a character and the reader). And her more sweeping assertion that narration is speakerless seems more a riddle than an explanation. For me all language, and not merely language-as-discourse, by definition entails a speaker who, in the absence of others, becomes the addressee also. And if narratives are dynamically constructed by processing readers bringing their knowledge to bear as they make sense of or with texts, then our theory of narrative cannot be grounded solely on context-free grammar. McHale's criticisms seem particularly germane here:

> Operating with a pragmatics-free grammar of English, [Banfield] aims to establish the *essence* of various types of narrative sentences, what they *are* in isolation from any real or constructed context of utterance and use. From this essence, in turn, she derives her definition of what a narrative text is; of what fiction is; of what literature is. Nowhere does the theory make contact with the facts of context, whether textual or historical. (McHale, 1983: 43)

That passage is a salutary reminder of the larger shaping contexts of narratives. It is relative to those shaping contexts that we must finally assess any proposed set of procedures for the study of narrative.

Further reading

Yet again, the best places to begin further reading on character and setting are Rimmon-Kenan (1983: 29–42, and 59–70), and Bal (1985: 25–36, and 79–99). Fowler (1977: 33–41), cited in 4.4, demonstrates the application of a distinctive feature approach to character and setting in *The Great Gatsby* with his typical lucidity. I particularly recommend Chatman (1978: 96–145) for its discussion of the concept of 'trait', for its narratological revaluation of A. C. Bradley (and the 'personificatory' impulse in readers' construing of characters), and for its sensitive reading of the role of setting in 'Eveline' (see discussion below). Culler (1975a: 230–8) makes many valuable points about character. Interesting literary critical discussions of character include Price (1968), Harvey (1965), and Bayley (1963), while Frow (1986) is an influential theoretical critique. Lodge (1977: 73–124) contains an extended thesis to the effect that there are two most fundamental and contrasting means of discourse-development: the metaphoric (where inherently disparate things are somehow linked and some illuminating context-specific similarity is posited), and the metonymic (where inherent associations between things are drawn upon, and consequently a richer, more textured picture of a single area of reality is achieved). Risking gross distortion we might say that the metaphoric involves a move from (a conjoining of) the one to another, while the metonymic involves a move from one to the next. Lodge's theoretical account, based on work by Jakobson, leads to original and insightful analyses of just how the depiction of setting proceeds in many literary texts, including the openings of *Bleak House* and *A Passage to India*.

The literature on both the theory and literary exploitations of free indirect discourse is simply voluminous. A good starting place is Chapter 10 of Leech and Short (1981). Pascal (1977) is a clear and detailed account of FID's role in, especially, nineteenth-century European fiction; McHale (1978) is an authoritative survey and demonstrates well the ramificatory consequences that different views of FID may have for quite fundamental issues in the theory of poetics or language. Also to be recommended in this vein are Hernadi (1972) and Ginsberg (1982), while longer innovative studies include Cohn (1978) and Stanzel (1984). More linguistic discussions of FID begin with Bally (1912), and include Voloshinov (1973), Bickerton (1967), Jones (1968), Bronzwaer (1970), Fillmore (1974), Dillon and Kirchhoff (1976), McKay (1978) and of course Banfield (1982). McHale's (1983) review article of Banfield's challenging study is also invaluable. Advanced studies of FID and related topics continue to appear. Sternberg (1982), for instance, is an important reassessment of the indirections of direct speech, while many original papers appear in the Winter 1981 issue of the journal *Poetics Today*, devoted to 'Narrators and Voices in Fiction'.

Notes and exercises

1 The issue of what kind of realism we may reasonably look for in narratives is one that will run and run. Lodge (1977: 53) quotes Bedient's assertion (1969: 84) that

> When we read the problems of Lydgate's marriage, or about Casaubon's 'inward trouble' or about Bulstrode's public fall, it doesn't occur to us that these are *imagined* realities.

and suggests we may be inclined to respond 'speak for yourself'. Consider these two different reactions to the characters of *Middlemarch*, the involved and credulous versus the detached and sceptical. Is there a way in which both responses are right, is it possible that both responses may be coherent, even in the same reader, depending on just what perspective she is taking up on the text and the act of reading?

2 Despite my sympathies with much of Chatman's (1978) discussion of character, there are – perhaps unguarded – moments where he seems to assume a rather too direct, too simple linkage between text and world. On what grounds might we challenge the following claims he makes (1978:120) concerning 'Eveline'?

> A trip to Dublin cannot but help us understand the special quality of paralysis attributed to its denizens by Joyce, and meeting a Dublin working-class girl, even in 1978, will give us deeper insight into Eveline's predicament and personality. . . . I have never been to Ireland, but I know that the peculiar sort of 'strutting' that Eveline's father does would be clearer if I had.

3 Fowler (1977: 35) prefaces his discussion of core character traits with the following observations:

> The novelist and his readers make reference to a stock of physical, behavioural, psychological and verbal attributes out of which fictional characters may be put together in somewhat the same way as the police assemble an 'identikit' picture out of a set of pictures of segments of different kinds of faces. In modern 'realistic' fiction, the semes tend to reflect the clichés and stereotypes in terms of which the society which supports the literature sees itself: aggression, materialism, possessiveness, piety, innocence, naiveté, ambition, sensitivity, physical

power, femininity, introversion, elegance, verbal wit, rationalism, status, alienation, etc.

As Fowler adds, these are only guesses for illustrative purposes, and as we might add, in the light of my emphasis on extratextual knowledge and ideology in section 4.3, they are guesses that reflect Fowler's own partial facts-and-views reading of texts. In 'distinctive feature characterology' we shall always face such complications: in claiming to present the features that are really salient in a text or texts, the analyst is partly presenting only what she *sees* as really salient. In theory, no such dilemma confronts distinctive feature phonology, where the analyst builds a description on two resources. These are:

1 widely-accepted native-speaker intuitions (e.g. that /p/ and /b/ are significantly different sounds, in English, so that /pet/ and /bet/ mean significantly different things); and

2 sophisticated technical measuring devices that will confirm that there is indeed a really salient phonetic difference between /p/ and /b/, namely the attribute of voicing, of whether or not the vocal cords vibrate.

Fortunately no such elaborate back-up machinery can apply to text analysis. But a rudimentary procedure analogous to appealing to native-speaker intuitions *is* commonly invoked, however. That is to say, readers do seek out agreement from other readers that Tom Buchanan's most salient attributes are his materialist potency combined with his sheer poverty of ideals, morals or vision. Literature tutorials may sometimes implicitly concentrate very closely on determining just what the most salient attributes are in, for example, the world of *Troilus and Criseyde*, and on who has them, who hasn't, and what consequences those distributions have for story events.

Taking Fowler's list of semes as a starting point, try to determine how well they fit less mainstream types of modern literature, such as third world literature from the Caribbean or India, feminist novels, or the ideologically 'right on' kind of fiction now being produced for teenagers. Presumably the semes that are the positive attributes of a hero in a feminist novel will not be the same as those we would attach to Natty Bumppo, James Bond, Ike McCaslin, or Hemingway's Robert Jordan in *For Whom the Bell Tolls*, or Lawrence's Gerald Crich in *Women in Love*. Or if the same seme figures in feminist and 'patriarchal' novels, we might expect it to be positively weighted in one, negatively weighted in the other.

4 A common entry point for discussion of characters is the paying of particular attention to their names. Dickens is commonly cited, with his long roll-call of evocatively, characterizingly-named individuals: Podsnap, Pecksniff, Scrooge, Fagin, Gradgrind, Bounderby, Jupe, Wackford Squeers, and so on. But one can take the names of characters in very many modern fictions and analyze them for their expressivity, for their semiotic quality. There seems almost a compulsion, in both authors and readers, to make character names be message-bearing. I am not sure – could I be? – that Bellow intended that his main character's name in *The Dean's December* should be expressive, but for me Dean Albert Corde's surname is a recurring reminder of his problems of the heart (physical, social and moral). The man who has long been his friend and rival, now a media star, is a charming and extrovert all-American, marvellously named Dewey Spangler. That the name Pnin, in Nabokov's novel, is message-bearing for the reader seems incontrovertible (just *what* it connotes, for each reader, may vary a great deal). Take any recent novel and consider just what kinds of semiotic 'freight' the character names carry. Conversely, try to find novels where the names are 'transparent', semiotically null: are such novels from particular authors only, or in one genre only?

5 Perhaps the commonest and most important element in fictional settings is the house. Everywhere in English fiction, from *Mansfield Park* to *Bleak House* to *The House of the Seven Gables* to *Howards End* to *Brideshead Revisited* to *The Mansion* on to *The Hotel New Hampshire* – the list is endless – we find novels whose titles themselves are names of houses that are an essential, mood-determining, story-shaping, *arena* for characters and events. Take a novel by any author of your choice (even at random), and examine the extent to which allusions to the house(s) therein go beyond the basic required notation of place. Speculate as to the possible reasons for such 'excesses' of attention.

6 Jefferson (1981) argues, among other points, that FID is effective in 'Eveline' since it expresses and articulates Eveline's personality from within, even though on the surface Eveline is clearly a fairly inarticulate person. FID in 'Eveline' is also discussed in

Chatman (1969) and Leech and Short (1981). Jefferson also questions the appropriateness of carving up a passage, reallocating phrases 'to their supposedly original speakers':

> Who is the source of the sentence 'One time there used to be a field there in which they used to play every evening with other people's children' (p. 36)? It could be the narrator, but it could also be Eveline. And since it could be either it could also be both: *each word* has what Voloshinov calls a 'double intonation' . . . and this duality makes it impossible to read the passage as the record of an actual voice, narrator's or character's. (1981: 41)

Actually the sentence Jefferson cites may not be so hard to attribute to Eveline – notice the Irish English 'one time', the repeated 'used to'. But even so, the narratorial *frame*, of third-person pronouns and past tense, remains in place, giving rise to an effect of duality.

On the other hand much of the narrative of 'Eveline' is *not* plausibly FID, and close attention to the text reveals a highly fluid, even volatile, style of narration that moves from intrusive narration, summarizing her thoughts, in sentence 1 below, to the almost entirely impersonal report – except for the word 'mournful' – in sentence 2, to the probable FID of sentence 3:

> She felt her cheek pale and cold and, out of a maze of distress, she prayed to God to direct her, to show her what was her duty. (1) The boat blew a long mournful whistle into the mist. (2) If she went, tomorrow she would be on the sea with Frank, steaming towards Buenos Ayres. (3) (40)

Similarly, there is no question of such sentences as the following, the work of an intrusive omniscient narrator, representing Eveline from within:

> As she mused the pitiful vision of her mother's life laid its spell on the very quick of her being – that life of commonplace sacrifice closing in final craziness. (40)

A careful charting of the strategic changes in narrative orientation in 'Eveline' will uncover many complexities – and authorial risks.

7 I have argued in 4.13 that Banfield is too prescriptive, no longer aligned with native speaker intuitions, in categorically disallowing sentences such as

Laura blurted out how very nice workmen were!

In appropriate (and more extended) textual situations, readers do tolerate such sentences, despite their conjunction of the reporter's subjectivity (*I* say she blurted) and the reported character's (Laura said 'How very nice workmen are!').

However, Banfield's identifications of the syntactic ways in which – in her view – a reported speaker's expressivity is barred from occurring in indirect speech are still invaluable. We can use them as we sort out just which cases she is right about – cases where some syntactically-describable feature seems unquestionably unacceptable in indirect speech – and which cases she is wrong about. Readers are urged to read Chapters 1 and 2 of Banfield closely for themselves. But sentences including those cited in 4.9 that I find acceptable as a kind of creative IS seem to involve only either movement transformations that are unexpected in the embedded clause of IS (subject–auxiliary inversion; topicalization), or the similarly unexpected presence of language-mixing or attitudinal disjuncts (*frankly*, etc.). Expressivities which I, with Banfield, would bar from IS include her 'non-embeddable expressive elements', namely, incomplete sentences, subjectless imperatives and direct address. Can we suggest that there are different orders of self-expressivity in these two broad clusters?

8 Chatman identifies three interacting settings in 'Eveline': (a) her home, where everything is 'grimy and poverty-ridden'; (b) her mind, where home-and-family are more positively framed (before the fire, the Howth picnic, her father larking with her mother's bonnet); and (c) outside the home, where 'everything is exotic, frightening, and finally unacceptable' (Chatman, 1978: 142). If Chatman is correct in positing just these three settings, we ought to be able to find linguistic support for his claims by means of close analysis of the language. In particular, three simple 'searches' may be useful:

(i) We might conduct a distinctive feature analysis of each of these settings, just as we did for characters in 'The Dead'. In this way we should be able to identify and differentiate more clearly the 'character' of each setting – if indeed, as Chatman claims, they do have different characters. Again, as in 'The Dead', we may need to consider developmental *change* in these settings. Is setting (c), for instance, outside the home, menacing from the beginning of the story, or does it only become so?

(ii) We might draw up a list of all the evaluative adjectives used to describe all non-human (i.e., non-character) elements in each of the settings. On that basis, the third paragraph of the story, which begins with the exclamation 'Home!', contains the following setting-evaluations: *familiar* (objects), *familiar* (objects), *yellowing* (photograph), *broken* (harmonium), *coloured* (photograph). This procedure is both simple and fairly unproblematic once we remember to exclude from the list the *many* of 'for so many years', which is a temporal qualification, not a description of (any part of) the setting, and the *casual* of 'her father used to pass it with a casual word', which is part of a description of her father's manner of speaking (the word is not a 'thing' in the setting). Again, these lists of evaluations should highlight differences, emphases, modulations. By emphases I mean the sort of reinforcement apparent in paragraph 3 where the teller uses the evaluation *familiar* twice in close succession, even in the course of Eveline's reflections about her family and her family home.

(iii) We might probe the degree to which each of the three settings is represented as agent-like, as the *cause* of processes or actions that affect some other entity (perhaps the character Eveline). Broadly, this is a matter of examining all text in which setting is mentioned to see when – if ever – any element of setting is in subject position (in active sentences) with a transitive verb and an affected object. My initial impressions are that the domestic setting – tame, unthreatening – comprises objects that are also syntactic objects, things affected by a human agent (Eveline 'had dusted' the familiar objects once a week for so many years); while the quayside setting includes elements that are quite agent-like, at least to the extent of taking up subject position in either transitive or intransitive sentences, with no mention of a human causer: 'A bell clanged upon her heart', 'All the seas of the world tumbled about her heart'. Does a more detailed analysis support those initial impressions of contrast?

9 Along the lines suggested in exercise 8, you might compare and contrast the two basic settings in 'That Evening Sun' – Nancy's cabin and the Compsons' house (actually there are clearly sub-domains within the latter: the kitchen is a somewhat different setting from the library). Setting plays a prominent role in this story. It might be argued that 'change of setting' *appears* to amount to a solution to Nancy's problems: if she can stay with the Compsons and sleep on their kitchen floor she will be all

right, she says. But this is a solution that the Compson parents are evidently quite reluctant to accept.

10 Guided by the account of free indirect discourse offered in the latter half of this chapter, reconsider the opening sentences of 'The Dead' quoted in 4.6 and try to identify those features of the passage that would lead you to attribute much of it to Lily rather than to a more neutral and detached narrator. That much of this discourse is Lily's, rather than a neutral narrator's, is suggested in the very first line: would we expect a literate Joycean narrator to misuse *literally* in the way that it is when Lily is said to be 'literally run off her feet'?

11 Chatman also notes, in 'Eveline', the very effective use of 'climactic metaphors precisely at the moment of the heroine's greatest anguish' (1978: 142): the bell clanging upon her heart, all the seas of the world tumbling about her heart, Frank 'drowning' her in those seas, and so on. The particular metaphors used in this suddenly melodramatic scene are especially well motivated since, at the quayside, there are, in the actual setting, a clanging bell, tumbling seas, and so on:

> What makes the metaphors powerful is the way they fuse character and setting, subject character to the onslaught of setting, make setting almost a character – Frank and the seas collude, the strange and sinister outer world threatens to over- whelm her. The narrator permits himself the luxury of clustered metaphors only once in this story, and it is at the most telling point. (142–3)

What is also striking is just how parallel the narrative manipu- lations are at the close of 'Eveline' and, as discussed in 4.6, at the close of 'The Dead'. Using Chatman's words, could we not say that Gabriel's drifting, dissolving consciousness is subjected to the onslaught of setting. And what is that setting? The rented room, a temporary home and symbol of human transience on earth; the snow, general over Ireland, drifting and dissolving as Gabriel feels himself to be. (You might compare this setting with that of Quentin and Shreve's reconstruction work in *Absalom, Absalom!*). We might look further in *Dubliners* to see whether this gradual promotion of setting into a character, a shaping influence, applies to other stories in the collection. Note that the title *Dubliners* itself is an act of defining characters *by* their setting.

5 Narrative as socially situated: the sociolinguistic approach

5.1 Labov and narrative structure

A great deal of exciting study of naturally occurring narrative – particularly the narratives of ordinary people in their extraordinary everyday lives – stems from just two seminal essays by the American sociolinguist William Labov. The first of these, written jointly with Joshua Waletzky, appeared in Helms (1967), under the title 'Narrative analysis: oral versions of personal experience'. The second, to which I will refer more, appeared as Chapter 9 of Labov's *Language in the Inner City* (1972), and is titled 'The transformation of experience in narrative syntax'. In most respects it is better to focus on the later paper, since it is largely a revision and extension of the earlier one. But I will begin with the former essay.

Labov and Waletzky's hypothesis is that fundamental narrative structures are to be found in oral versions of personal experience – the ordinary narratives of ordinary speakers. They wish, by looking at many narratives, to identify and relate formal linguistic properties of narrative to their *functions*. Like all structuralists, their analysis is based on the perception of a delimited set of recurrent patterns – some things (here, linguistic forms) have to 'be the same' or 'do the same job' in a range of data, otherwise the analysis of structured patterning cannot get started. And again in broadly structuralist fashion, they resolve to set aside what they take to be surface differences in their pursuit of the deeper structural similarities:

> We will be relying upon the basic techniques of linguistic analysis, isolating the invariant structural units which are represented by a variety of superficial forms. (Labov and Waletzky, 1967: 12)

Labov and Waletzky want to relate those identified linguistic-structural properties to functions, and they nominate two broad functions in particular as more or less essential as soon as narrative is viewed *within the human context*. The first of these they term, not entirely happily, the referential function; by which they mean the function of narrative as a means of recapitulating experience in an ordered set of clauses that matches the temporal sequence of the original experience. We have encountered versions of the 'sequential recapitulation' function before, in our definitions of story or bare narrative. The second function has been less universally emphasized, partly because – as my italics earlier in the paragraph intended to suggest – narrative has not always been properly related to its contexts of occurrence, its role as an instrument or resource for its human 'users'. The second function then, which Labov and Waletzky term 'evaluative', attends to the users of narratives, and notes the strong requirement that a narrative has a *point*, is worth telling, as far as the teller (and preferably the addressee also) is concerned.

Unlike Propp, whom they claim focused on 'large semantic units' (13), Labov and Waletzky focus on

the smallest unit of linguistic expression which defines the functions of narrative [i.e., the smallest unit which can ordinarily realize those functions] – primarily the clause . . . (13)

And their first task becomes that of attempting to relate

the sequence of clauses in the narrative to the sequence of events inferred from the narrative. (20)

This task is made rather more manageable by their own (quite open) simplifications. In particular they opt to look solely for narrative clauses that tell the events of a story *in the same order* as those events originally occurred. Even having travelled this short distance into Labovian analysis we may see both a continuity and contrast with the complexities of narrative discourse studies previously discussed. Just as Banfield concentrates on the sentence (i.e., clause) with a resulting distortion, dismissal or neglect of subtle intra-sentential effects, so here there is a potentially impoverishing privileging of the clause (and, as becomes evident later, the independent clause) as the focus of inquiry. On the other hand, in contrast to all the analyses of narration we have considered, there is a sharp exclusion, from the Labovian study, of the techniques of temporal reordering. It is clear that the notion of *order* in the following sentence lacks the resonances of Proustian complexity that it has for (and from) Genette:

The basic narrative units that we wish to isolate are defined by the fact that they recapitulate experience in the same order as the original events. (20–1)

In just these terms, the following sample constitutes a narrative:

Well, this person had a little too much to drink and he attacked me and the friend came in and she stopped it.

while the following version, where there is presentational reordering through subordination, is simply not a narrative in Labov and Waletzky's terms, though it is an acceptable recapitulation of experience:

A friend of mine came in just in time to stop this person who had had a little too much to drink from attacking me.

This is not by way of disparagement of Labov and Waletzky's work, however, but simply a warning that their assumptions and procedures differ in some respects from those we have previously looked at. The attraction of their principles lies in their clarity, replicability, and their search for a basic pattern from which more complex narratives might be derived. And their differences from the narration analysts should not be overstated: after all, Genette no less than they develops his taxonomy of diegetic variations on a foundational 'natural' order of event recapitulation.

5.2   Fixed narrative clauses, free evaluative clauses

The Labovian thesis, then, is that true narrative clauses, the backbone of narrative as they narrowly define it, are temporally ordered independent clauses that must occur in a fixed presentational sequence. There is a 'shiftability' of subordinate clauses, around the main clause on which they depend, that excludes them from consideration as fully narrative clauses. The fixity of sequence of properly narrative clauses is quite crucial for Labov and Waletzky. But note that this is not an assertion of the impossibility of reordering narrative clauses as such, but simply the impossibility of doing so *while still telling the same story*. Compare

1 John fell in the river, got very cold, and had two large whiskies.

with

2 John had two large whiskies, fell in the river, and got very
   cold.

Clearly, despite many similarities of form, the differently-ordered
clauses here represent two radically different stories, with different
cause-and-effect relations between events, and different probable
evaluations by teller and hearer (the listener might comment
'serves him right' about the second John but could hardly do so
about the first).

   Labov and Waletzky present a rather more formal account of
the non-shiftability of narrative clauses (relative to each other) by
specifying the **displacement potential** of clauses in narratives.
Setting a narrative out on the page with just one main or independent clause per line of text, and labelling the clauses alpha-
betically, they annotate the letter-label of each clause by noting,
either side of it, the number of previous and subsequent clauses
that any particular clause could displace. Accordingly we could
set out narrative 2 above as follows:

OaO   John had two large whiskies,
ObO   fell in the river,
OcO   and got very cold.

thus indicating that in our judgment none of the three clauses
could be displaced 'leftward' or 'rightward' without 'changing the
inferred sequence of events' (Labov and Waletzkty, 1967: 21) in
the original experience. But note that if we add, at the story's
close, the observation

This happened when he was still at school

it seems that this is freely shiftable to any position earlier in the
story without interference with the inferred sequence of events:

John had two large whiskies – this happened when he was still
at school – fell in the river, and got very cold.

So now, if in fact this additional comment came at the end of
the sequence, we should analyze the full text, in Labov style,
thus:

OaO   John had two large whiskies,
ObO   fell in the river,
OcO   and got very cold.
3dO   This happened when he was still at school.

The annotation 3dO states that clause 'd' may occur as many as three clauses earlier, but no later, in this particular narrative, without alteration to the inferred sequence of actual events, the essence of the narrative. The previous three clauses, on the other hand, continue to be locked into their given interrelated positions. A clause like 'd', describing the circumstances *surrounding* the fixed sequence of events of a narrative and with the potential of being moved anywhere in the text, is known in Labovian terminology as a **free clause**.

Narrative and free clauses are the most sharply contrasted pair of clause types that Labov identifies. Each is the basic means for enacting the two functions of narrative cited earlier: the 'referentially' ordered recall of temporally ordered experience, and the 'evaluative' staging of the story so as to convey its point and tellability. But there are one or two in-between cases, of clauses with partial shiftability and functions which are a variable blend of narrative ones (reporting the ordered experience of the interrelated events) and free ones (reporting the context of the events, the participants' perspectives, etc.). There are some narrative clauses, for instance, usually only pairs or triads, that can be reordered 'freely'. These Labov calls **coordinate clauses** – the coordination here being not so much in terms of grammar as in terms of narrative sense. Many grammatically coordinated clauses are not coordinated in this special sense of permissible narrative reorderability ('She took arsenic and died', for example, is grammatically but not narrationally coordinate). And it is quite possible for clauses lacking any overt grammatical coordinator (linked by a simple comma, in writing, or a pause, in speech) to be narrationally coordinate If we revise our 'drunken drenching' story, we can demonstrate Labovian coordination:

OaO	John had two large whiskies,
ObO	fell in the river,
Oc1	got very cold
1dO	and ruined his suit.
4eO	This happened when he was still at school.

Note the amended clause classifications: the order in which we report John's getting cold and ruining his suit is freely reversible without alteration to the basic narrative.

Conversely, there are some free clauses that are not entirely freely shiftable to just any other place in the sequence. They have a limited domain of occurrence and are termed **restricted clauses**. In the following version:

Oa2	John got this urge to be the star of the party.
ObO	He had two large whiskies,
OcO	performed a standing somersault on the embankment wall,
OdO	fell in the river,
Oe1	got very cold
1fO	and ruined his suit.
6gO	This happened when he was still at school.

Clause 'a' here is a kind of comment in parallel to the main action, and – arguably, at least – could come a little later: after clause 'c', but no later than this, if we interpret the contents of 'd' as an unintentional lapse from starlike behaviour (he fell, he did not simply jump). The event that 'd' reports, we imagine, must have considerably dampened the urge that 'a' discloses. But a greater degree of arguability of the analysis enters with the notion of restricted clauses: some readers may contest the analysis offered above, and might even want to reclassify 'a' as a wholly free clause. We may expect, then, that in more complex narratives these restricted clauses will be a source of much satisfying analytical-interpretive trouble as they generate uncertainties and larger debates about the 'what happened when, and why' of particular texts.

What then, for Labov, is a narrative? Minimally, and similar to my own definition in Chapter 1,

> a minimal narrative [is] a sequence of two clauses which are *temporally ordered* . . . a minimal narrative is defined as one containing a single temporal juncture. (Labov, 1972: 361)

And by **temporal juncture**, as we have seen, is meant the non-reversibility of two narrative clauses without change of the original semantic interpretation of the story. Having characterized narrative clauses, Labov and Waletzky go on to specify the heads of those clauses: these are, as we might expect, the main clause finite verbs, and usually occur in the simple past or present. Progressive aspect (*he was performing somersaults*) and perfective aspect (*he had performed two somersaults*) are rare though not impossible in narrative clauses: such aspectual elaborations are much commoner in restricted and, especially, free clauses. Procedures are also outlined for isolating the **primary sequence** of any narrative, a postulated simplest unmarked order of clauses, but such refinements need not occupy us here.

We should instead consider now Labov's essay of 1972, which, as noted above, revises and expands the earlier one, and more specifically applies the established model to actually-occurring narratives from New York Black English vernacular culture. In this later paper a six-part structure of a **fully-formed oral narrative** is posited:

1 **Abstract:** What, in a nutshell, is this story about?

2 **Orientation:** Who, when, where, what?

3 **Complicating action:** Then what happened?

4 **Evaluation:** So what, how is this interesting?

5 **Result or resolution:** What finally happened?

6 **Coda:** That's it, I've finished and am 'bridging' back to our present situation.

These are related in Labov's famous 'diamond' picture of the progression of an oral narrative, which I reproduce below. Notice how evaluation, while associable with a 'most expected' place in the progression of a narrative, is shown – by the spreading waves

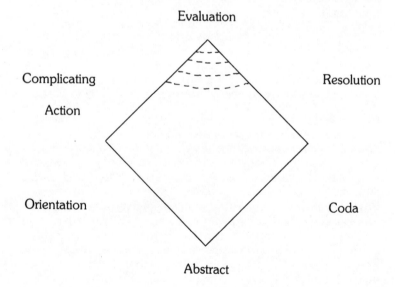

– to be something that can permeate throughout the telling, occurring anywhere.

What follows are more detailed commentaries on the six structural parts or phases of this model. Besides reproducing some of Labov's own examples, I will quote copiously from the account of Mr Casey's story of the 'famous spit', which he tells at the Christmas dinner table, early in Joyce's *Portrait of the Artist as a Young Man*. Besides being a magnificently crafted story, set with a richness of highlighted contextualization that seems particularly available in literary narratives, the story seems to exemplify the similarities between ordinary narratives and literary ones. (Actually, since it is presented as spoken by Mr Casey and yet known by us to have been written by Joyce, we could argue that as a type the story lies somewhere between the purely oral narrative and the purely written one.)

Abstracts and orientations   5.3

Together with the coda, the abstract can be thought of as one of the optional margins of a narrative. Complicating action, on the other hand, the phase in which most of a story's positionally fixed narrative clauses occur, is the **obligatory nucleus**. I am here borrowing terms standardly used to describe the structure of the English syllable: the syllable is orthodoxly said to contain a vowel sound as obligatory nucleus, this being optionally flanked by an **onset** and **coda**, each of which comprises one or more consonants. Interestingly, the alternative British terms for the margins of a syllable, **arrest** and **release** seem applicable to narratives too: an oral narrative arrests the flow of multi-party talk, buttonholing the addressees; with the story's completion there is a freeing-up of the suspended turn-taking possibilities and a release, too, from the state of being absorbed and 'caught up', as teller or listener, in an experience of the narrative.

A typical abstract outlines the story that a teller intends will follow. (I choose that form of words, rather than 'intends to tell', because – as we shall see – one person can produce an abstract intending that someone else goes on to tell the fuller story.) An abstract may then sketch a narrative in a severely abridged form, but it is never a proper telling of it, as the following examples should indicate:

1 An' then, three weeks ago I had a fight with this other dude

outside.
He got mad 'cause I wouldn't give him a cigarette. Aint that a bitch? (Labov, 1972: 356)

2 – Tell me, did I tell you that story about a very famous spit?
– You did not, John, said Mr Dedalus.
– Why then, said Mr Casey, it is a most instructive story. (Joyce, *Portrait of the Artist*, 34.)

But abstracts also do something else (at least in the view of many sociolinguists), as example 2 indicates. They often contain requests for the extended turn at talk necessary to tell a story. The teller's addressees are thus politely given the opportunity to indicate their preference not to hear the story, for whatever reason (they may be pushed for time, they may have something very important they want to say first, or they may have heard the story before). Even here, however, we should be alert to the fact that as bids for the floor between casual friends, abstracts may have few marks of a polite request and rather more marks of a friendly battle for attention. This is reflected in a third common dimension of abstracts, besides those of story summary and request for telling rights: abstracts are often advertisements or trailers for stories, making exaggerated claims for what will follow, promising more than gets delivered.

This latter dimension of abstracts is noticeably absent both from Labov's data and from his characterization of the element. But that abstracts performing requesting, advertising or floor-wresting functions are absent from Labov's corpus is hardly surprising: typically his informants are supplying stories after they have been invited so to do, so that for any of them to then request-to-narrate would be rather odd, indicative of some misunderstanding, or an extreme of timidity or politeness. In sum, then, abstracts in one respect mark an exiting of direct interaction in their summary heralding of the monologue text that is intended to follow, but in another respect they remain interactive in their functions of checking or announcing – or insisting upon! – the *tellability in principle* of a narrative.

A variant of the normal pattern in which a single teller provides both abstract and following story is that where a co-conversationalist supplies an abstract of a story considered worth the telling by way of prompting or inviting another participant to tell it. This technique may appear in any setting where at least two of the participants know each other well, but I have noticed it particularly in the behaviour of married couples at social gatherings. One interesting consequence of the technique is that worries about tellability are no longer, as usually, directed at one's addressees: the prompter has effectively gone on record as asserting the tellability of a story, and the prompted teller has the luxury of proceeding or not, depending on whether *he* thinks the story is tellable.

The collaborative story introduction is, however, fraught with uncertainties when compared with the solo story introduction. We might compare it to the difference, in soccer, between shooting at goal yourself or passing to a teammate for *him* to shoot at goal. Some prompted tellers dislike being 'forced' into telling a story, but are also aware – as is everyone else – of the awkward 'misfire' feel if he declines to proceed. Such an action puts either the prompter or the prompted in a bad light, and may be adjudged uncooperative if it is viewed as a refusal to make a contribution that has been explicitly requested (see Grice, 1975, on the cooperative principles said to underwrite our construction and reception of utterances in conversations). Even with cooperative good will, however, a prompted teller may fail to tell a story, or fail to tell it adequately, due to poor recall of the detail of the story events. In such cases the initiating prompter has made a mistaken judgment as to just how well his partner remembers the story – a clear case of poor teamwork.

As indicated above, orientation specifies the participants and circumstances, especially of place and time, of the narrative, and is equivalent to what we have sometimes called setting in earlier discussions. Labov notes that while orientation material can be embedded within opening narrative clauses, it more commonly comes in a block of free clauses prior to the development of the narrative action. Or at least we might think of the position between abstract and complicating action as the unmarked and logical position for orientation. In the orientation we can expect verb forms other than extensive verbs (i.e., transitive or intransitive verbs involving action) in the simple past tense. Thus here we may find past perfectives and past progressive verb phrases, and intensive verbs (*be, become, seem,* etc.) in relational process clauses specifying attributes and identities (as described in 4.7).

But, as Labov notes, the most interesting use of orientation is where components of it are strategically delayed, and we are told salient facts about the setting late in a narrative. This, like analepsis, may create effects of considerable surprise, even of shock. It may be particularly used where the teller himself, as a participant in a sequence of events, only belatedly learned some salient facts of a situation and wants to put his audience in a similar experiential position.

5.4 Evaluation

Evaluation consists of all the means used to establish and sustain the *point*, the contextual significance and tellability, or report-ability, of a story. It may take very many forms and appear at almost any point in the telling, although it is often particularly clustered around the 'hinge' or climactic point of the action, just before – and in effect delaying – the resolving action or event. It is the pre-eminent constituent by means of which the narrator's personal involvement in a story is conveyed. In Labov's words, it is

> the means used by the narrator to indicate the point of the narrative, its raison d'être: why it was told, and what the narrator is getting at. (Labov, 1972: 366)

The Labovian sub-types of evaluation are first distinguished according to whether they appear inside or outside the fixed-position clauses of narrative. Evaluations appearing outside the narrative clause are of five sub-types.

1 Wholly external evaluations – as external as you can get; here the narrator breaks the frame of the story-telling itself to address the listener directly, interrupting the narrative to express a speaker's current or still valid general evaluation of the distant events:

> It is a most instructive story . . . the story is very short and sweet . . . (Joyce: 35, 36)
> It was the strangest feeling.
> It was quite an experience . . .

2 Evaluation embedded as a comment reported as made by the teller-as-participant at the time of the events themselves:

> And I said to myself: 'This is it!'

3 Or embedded as a comment made by the teller-as-participant to another participant:

> And I said to Mary: 'This is it!'

4 Or embedded as an evaluation coming from another participant:

And Mary said: 'This is it!'

5 Evaluative action: how some participant responded in physical rather than merely verbal terms to the ongoing events:

I never prayed to God so fast.
I was shakin' like a leaf.

(Notice, in the first of these two examples, reflecting one set of cultural assumptions, prayer is implicitly classified as a kind of evaluating rather than a kind of doing. Prayer here is not conceived of as narrative action, occurring at a fixed point in a sequence of causally-linked events. Devout believers of many creeds might see things differently, interpreting any happy outcome that followed the prayers as *caused by* (the deity supplicated in) those prayers.)

As Labov notes, all the above modes of evaluation involve a temporary suspension of the action, a brief 'time out' from the telling of the story proper. When well placed, such manoeuvres do indeed create suspense, set apart whatever narrative follows (often the concluding resolution), and heighten the listener's interest. But all such external suspensions can be contrasted with the narrative-clause-internal modes of evaluation to which I will turn in section 5.6. Before doing so, a few observations on a central assumption of Labovian method may be useful.

Doing and saying   5.5

Perhaps the most basic point to emphasize is that Labov works on the broad assumption that *what is said* (by yourself or others) will not be the core of a story; that, rather, *what is done* (by you or others) will be. The 'what is done' then becomes (or may become) the core narrative text of clauses – actions – while the 'what is said' becomes evaluative commentary *on* those actions. Now this pattern is common enough to be a reasonable assumption in many cases, and one can immediately see why 'danger of death' stories of the sort Labov elicited would promote identification of a sharp division between salient actions such as physical assaults and accidents on the one hand, and verbal reactions on the other. But more complicated imbrications of words and actions are also possible, where the sayings are the most important doings – are the 'action' of the narrative – revealing a fixity of sequence of those sayings, temporal juncture, and so on. From the work of the philosopher J. L. Austin has developed a renewed recognition that our use of words in interaction is typically a performing of actions and not merely an asserting of true or false (hence evaluative) statements. Labov's own informants demonstrate this vividly in other interactions that he analyzes (1972): as their enhanced skills of duelling, rapping and sounding make very clear, there can be verbal fights as well as physical ones.

But no narrative of sayings, you might complain, can break your bones, put you in danger of death. Again, however, we might question this assumption. There are too many recorded cases of individuals suddenly driven murderously mad by what someone else has said; or getting to the verge of this state, and then being very carefully 'talked down' by individuals who are themselves at risk. There, sayings may indeed put you in danger of death. In a very different situation, that of trial for murder, the conflicting narratives of events that prosecution and defence attempt to persuade the jury of, by recourse, as substantiation, to the sayings of witnesses, have the consequences of weakening or strengthening the possibility that the accused will face execution. What things are said (alleged), and the order in which these things are said, is the basic narrative, fixed in experiential order and narratorial recapitulation, of a legal trial.

And in our increasingly verbal worlds, where growing numbers of us make our living through our verbal work rather than our non-verbal actions, we may predict that 'what is said (written/promised/denied/argued/etc.)' will more commonly constitute the essential complicating material in narratives. Not least in literature: in the 'famous spit' story of Mr Casey, for example, the 'doing' that makes up the complicating action to be evaluated is a verbal 'doing': the old woman's series of increasingly offensive insults. And the terminate or resolutory action of spitting itself is reported less as a doing (Casey does not announce 'I spat at her') than as a saying:

I bent down to her and *Phth!* says I to her like that.

Casey's *Phth!* has some of the marks of external-evaluation of type 3, but we know it is also a crucial sequentially-fixed action: an inextricable merging of evaluation and narrative action, of saying and doing. Similarly we can ponder the old woman's reaction to this verbal-cum-nonverbal action:

> O Jesus, Mary and Joseph! says she. I'm blinded and drowned.

We infer, from Mr Casey's accompanying gesture of clapping his hand to his eye, that the old woman reacted in other ways than simply saying these things. But again, the woman's verbal response is itself very important to the story: the unpleasant physical consequences of the spit are far less to the point, but in any event do not include literal blinding or drowning. The tellable reaction is the verbal one, directly mimicked, with its lower-class non-standardism, its ludicrous Chaucerian hyperbole, its possibly profane invocation on the lips of this self-declared defender of the faith and guardian of morality.

The above unravelling of the narrative/evaluative dichotomy is broaching a very important topic, for in Labov as in other *fabula/sjuzhet* theorists the separability of the plot from surrounding or interpolated discoursal elaborations and recastings is an operational necessity. And in working with that dichotomy, notice that all our language reflects an assumption that plot is core, that the clauses of narrative action are the heart of the matter, the inner narrative, and that evaluation is to a degree external, and always intrusive. Now that assumption is one I am prepared to accept, with the caveat voiced above (that core narrative clauses may be ones of speech rather than action, and look very like evaluations) and a further caveat I will now introduce.

This is that adopting the categories of fixed narrative clause and freer evaluative clause is not in itself a claim about the 'status in reality' of the actions and sayings these report. In particular, it is not an assumption that material presented as main-clause narration 'really did' happen the way the narrator claims. Put thus the warning seems obvious, that narrators 'aestheticize' their experiences, assert cause-and-effect chains where no chains are there, and so on; but the point is dwelt upon in Culler (1981: 184–5) in his critical treatment of Labov. Actually Labov emphasizes a duality of motivation and function rather more than Culler acknowledges, but the latter's point is still worth remembering. If we imagine that first we have the sequence of actions (narrative) then we work on the reporting of them to enhance their point or tellability (evaluation), we are ignoring the possibility of a reverse order of impulses, namely that, guided by the prior awareness of the tellability-requirement, our evaluations shape our plots.

5.6 Internal evaluation

Narrative-clause-internal evaluation is categorized by Labov into four sub-types:

1 **Intensifiers:** here are included gestures (often accompanied by deictic *that*),

> He turned aside and made the act of spitting. . . . He clapped his hand to his *eye*.

expressive phonology,

> *Phth!*; 'I'm drownded!'

exaggerating quantifiers such as *all*,

> such booing and baaing; paid all her attention to me; right into her eye

repetitions,

> I let her bawl away (2); *Phth!* says I to her like that (2);

and ritual utterances. Unlike the following three types, this type does not significantly complicate the syntax of the narrative clause.

2 **Comparators**: these evaluate indirectly, by drawing attention away from what actually happened by alluding to what might have been, what could be, but what doesn't happen. The main types of comparators are expressions of negation,

> You never heard such booing and baaing; I couldn't say a word;

modality and modulation,

> We had to make our way to the railway station;

and futurity:

> I won't sully this Christmas board.

All of these are encoded in the auxiliary verbal elements; also included are questions, imperatives, and, most overtly, comparative or superlative phrases. All of the above involve an indirect evaluative departure, in the lexicogrammar, from the simple direct telling of the narrative actions. A more complex departure is the use of simile or metaphor, when these occur in narrative clauses (we may surmise that they would be more common in free clauses).

3 **Correlatives:** these bring together events in a single independent clause, and require complex syntax (and are hence often beyond the control of young narrators): progressives (*be* + V-ing), and appended participles (adjacent verbs in non-finite V-ing form), both of these emphasizing simultaneity of occurrence of actions,

> She kept dancing along beside me in the mud bawling and screaming.

double appositives,

> there was one old lady, and a drunken old harridan she was surely

double attributes,

> a drunken old harridan

and 'left-hand' participles or 'deverbal' adjectives (e.g., 'an *unsavoury-looking* character').

4 **Explicatives:** These are appended subordinate clauses which qualify, or give reasons for, the main events reported: for example, clauses introduced by *while*, *although*, *since*, *because*, and so on:

> sure I couldn't say a word in any case because my mouth was full of tobacco juice.

Such clauses contribute to the establishment of a story's tellability, its point, by more fully specifying the extent or motivation for a particular action.

Coda   5.7

We can think of codas and abstracts as related. A coda signals the 'sealing off' of a narrative, just as an abstract announces the 'opening up' of one. There seem to be two most common devices within codas. One is the explicit declaring that the narrative proper is over, so that for an addressee now to ask 'And then what happened?' would be absurd. The element is often realized by a near-redundant narrative-external comment, using pro-forms that are both textually anaphoric (pointing backwards to earlier co-text for interpretation) and distancing in their deixis:

1 And that is the end of the story.

2 And that was that.

3 And that – that was it, you know.

In sentences 1 and 3 we have the item *that* cohesively tied backwards to some previous text in which a state or conclusion has been rendered, but also deictically pointing to that state or conclusion itself, and now locating that conclusion at a distance from the speaker and her current position (*that*, not *this* or *here*), no matter how vivid and immediate parts of the telling of the narrative might have been.

This brings us to the second device common in codas. As the above indicates, codas are commonly the site of a deictic shift, especially in the more involving narratives of personal experience. In telling such narratives, the teller who is also a principal partici-pant often switches the deictic anchorage to the spatiotemporal orientation of himself-as-participant, selecting items such as *this*, *here* and *now* relative to that individual, rather than relative to the currently present one telling the story to an addressee. But it would make no sense, once the story was finished and the interac-tion was in the process of returning to conversational mode, in 'real' present time, to persist in using present-time deictics of the past story. Putting this another way, we can suggest that the teller seems best advised to *signal*, before the close of his long narrative turn, that he has exited from the marked past narrative to present deictics mode, and that all can resume normal use of present deictics to designate relatedness to the present context of situ-ation. Accordingly, tellers often do signal such a switch in their codas

4 And ever since then I haven't seen the guy 'cause I quit, I quit, you know.
No more problems.

5 And you know that man . . . is a detective in Union City and I see him every now and again.

using distal deixis (*the* or *that*) now to denote elements of the story, and present tense (with or without perfective, 'current relevance', aspect) to denote the shared current time of the speaker-as-conversation-participant, no longer speaker-as-narrative-participant. Labov talks of codas as having

> the property of bridging the gap between the moment of time at the end of the narrative proper and the present. They bring the narrator and the listener back to the point at which they entered the narrative. (Labov, 1972: 365)

Again, we should note that codas bridge a *contrived* gap, mutually agreed upon in the abstract, which creates a distinctive space for the narrative to occupy.

Relatedly, we may look for a reverse counterpart of the coda's deictic switch and orientational bridging early in many stories. This does seem to occur, although less commonly, and more centred in the orientation than the abstract. Thus abstract 1 in section 5.3 above alerts the addressee to orientational switch by alluding to 'this other dude' (cf. 'another dude' or 'some other dude'), and by marking the temporal gap from the present ('three weeks ago'). While abstract 2 does not perform an orientational switch, Mr Casey's very next turn, which is both orientational and externally evaluative, does:

> – Why then, said Mr Casey, it is a most instructive story. It happened not long ago in the county Wicklow where we are now. (Joyce, *Portrait of the Artist*: 34)

The seeming redundancies of the second sentence here should give us pause. Why, we might ask ourselves, doesn't Casey simply say

> It happened here not long ago.

or, at the most,

> It happened not long ago here in the county Wicklow.

Is the loosely-appended adverbial tellable material at all? Ordinarily not, but here we might conjecture that the sentence as a whole is a nicely-judged establishment of both the story's detachment from the present *and* its heightened current relevance (the time was 'not long ago', the place was hereabouts). Casey is a very cunning storyteller, and this story's underlying purpose is to suggest that the foul-mouthed old woman within the story, and Dante, who is one of its addressees, are analogues, meriting analogous treatment (to be spat upon). The seeming redundancies of Casey's introductory turn highlight the situational contiguities just as, later, the old woman's heaping of abuse will be reported as if parallel to Dante's censure.

But having dwelt at length on the form and function of codas, it must be stressed that these codas are often absent from personal narratives, especially those told in the course of casual conversation where, by contrast, sequences of stories may get told 'back to back' by a single teller or a range of tellers. In such sequences it may happen that some aspect of the resolution of one story serves, in some direct or remote way, as the trigger of the next – but the associative links that particular tellers construct, so as to enhance a story's sense of being 'locally occasioned' and 'sequentially implicative' (Jefferson, 1978) are of many types.

5.8   Stories in societies

Another approach to the evaluations in stories, to the point of telling them, less directly attentive to linguistic form than Labov, more interested in community-wide motivations, comes in the work of Polanyi (1978; 1981), who has argued the very plausible position that the kinds of stories (and story contents) we choose to tell each other, and in particular the kinds of things that we seem to agree are the kind of issues that make stories 'nonpointless' and tellable, reflect and disclose our cultural presuppositions and values. Similarly, Tannen (1979) demonstrates in some detail how our 'structures of expectation' based on past experience influence the particular ways we construct our stories, and interpret those of others. This in turn would predict that the kinds of stories that get told, and are valued, in one cultural milieu may differ quite considerably from those that get told in another.

Such seems to be the case, not simply when we compare stories and story points in two quite different societies, but even when contrasting stories and their evaluation between two communities within the same larger society. This was the finding of Heath (1983), in her comparative study of language use in two small-town working-class communities in the rural southeast of the United States, one black (Trackton), the other white (Roadville). These two communities reveal quite different views of stories and storytelling, as Romaine (1985) summarizes:

In Roadville stories stick to the truth and are factual. They maintain strict chronicity, end with a summary statement or moral, and serve the function of maintaining values and reaffirming group membership. Any fictionalized account is a lie. Trackton stories, on the other hand, are hardly ever serious. The best stories are 'junk', and the best storytellers are those who can 'talk the best junk', i.e. make the most wildly exaggerated comparisons and tell outlandish fictional narratives. (Romaine, 1985: 102–3)

And as Heath (1983: 189) concludes, of these radically diverging norms of behaviour:

For Roadville, Trackton's stories would be lies; for Trackton, Roadville's stories would not even count as stories.

In the face of Heath's findings, which are supported by extensive data, it should be evident that reading off cultural values or ideology from the kinds of points that a community's stories have will not be so easy as Polanyi sometimes implies. This is because, as the Trackton–Roadville comparison shows, it is not the case that everything else besides a story's main evaluated point is kept constant across communities. It may well be that communities have different kinds of story points because they have different perspectives on the proper functions and nature of storytelling. If that is so, we are driven back from the easier task of correlating delimited story points with possible cultural values, to the harder task of holistically assessing all of a community's tendencies in narrative use in relation to inferred cultural values.

Narrative performance   5.9

Over the past few years a number of sociolinguistic studies have appeared using the folkloristic term **performance** to describe a certain type of particularly involved and dramatized oral narrative. The term has been adopted and espoused despite resistance from some traditional folklorists, for whom the term standardly denotes the retelling of stories that are part of a tradition, are collectively known, and are non-innovative.

The idea that narratives are often performances seems to have first emerged in the work of Hymes and Goffman, and has received its fullest sociolinguistic exposition in Wolfson (1982). Wolfson's work is most directly relatable to Labov's; but she makes reference to a larger corpus of stories, told in a greater variety of contexts (of situation, of formality, of familiarity, age, sex and status of tellers and addressees, and so on). Working with this large and distinct set of possible variables, Wolfson probes in detail the varying formal reflexes of individuals' experiential involvement in their storytellings as **dramatized reenactments**:

> When a speaker acts out a story, as if to give his audience the opportunity to experience the event and his evaluation of it, he may be said to be giving a performance. (Wolfson, 1982: 24)

To perform a story is to furnish one's addressees with a more vivid and involving experience of that story, while exploiting special performance features as resources for highlighting the story's main point. Wolfson's performance features are the following:

1 direct speech
2 asides
3 repetition
4 expressive sounds
5 sound effects
6 motions and gestures
7 conversational historic present (CHP), alternating with narrative past tense.

Clearly, many of these are already incorporated in some part of Labov's typology of evaluation devices. Thus direct speech, whoever the participant, is embedded evaluation outside the narrative clause, while items 3 to 6 are types of intensifiers. In fact only items 2 and 7 are noticeably new to us. I will comment briefly on asides, before dealing more fully with CHP. Asides are a rather sophisticated device understandably absent from most adolescent narratives. In an aside a teller exits briefly from the time reference of the story dialogue he is recounting in order to add some comment about the content which has continued relevance in the present time of the teller and listeners. Such comments highlight, for the listeners, the teller's own viewpoint and sympathies with regard to the interrupted dialogue. Thus asides are an interruption of direct speech, and are therefore somewhat related to that mode of evaluation; they are also somewhat like external evaluation, with time reference to the present time of the teller-as-conversationalist; while in their explanatory function they are rather like Labov's explicatives.

The most interesting and controversial contribution that Wolfson (1982) makes is in her account of the use of historic present tense in story-telling. In particular she contests the traditional grammarian's view that historic present, in conversation-embedded narratives, is there to make a story more vivid and immediate. Historic present, as used in conversation-embedded narration, has a distinct function for Wolfson (hence the emphasis on *conversational* historic present), and that function relates not directly to the occurrence of CHP itself, but to the patterns of *switching* between historic past and present tense. The switches or alternations, she says, create three main effects: (a) an intervention by the teller; (b) a focussing of attention on certain portions of the narrative; and (c) a dividing-up of the flow of action into distinct events.

Now these three claims, in so far as they are clearly testable, have met with considerable resistance from other theorists. If we posit consistency of tense as the unmarked option in story-telling, we may accept that tense-switching is marked, noticeable, an extra technical complication added by the teller. But it remains only one of very many mechanisms of teller intervention – if we can accept the idea of a teller intervening in his own story. On the particular type or effect of this intervention, and on the evidence that there is a special focussing achieved by tense alternation, Wolfson is less than explicit. We are drawn to her third claim, the most intuitively plausible, that tense-switching has a segmenting effect on the material, 'chunking' it into stretches in present tense and stretches in past tense. But again we must beware of overstating the case in our efforts to escape the criticism of stating the trivially true. Do the tense-switches really create the chunks, or do they merely accompany a prior separation of the flow of action into distinct events, a separation made on other grounds? Or is the argument merely circular, i.e., are we identifying chunks of discourse as events only because they are bounded by tense-switches?

Schiffrin (1981) reviews these issues, and finds historic present tense almost wholly confined to the complicating action of the narratives she analyzes. This is significant because complicating action is precisely the section of stories where tense does not have to do any special task of temporal orientation (since temporal and presentational order can be assumed to be congruent):

The most typical pattern is one in which the complicating action begins with past-tense verbs, switches after a few clauses to the HP, possibly switches between the HP and the P[ast] a few more times, and then concludes with past-tense verbs . . . . There is a tendency for verbs in the same tense to cluster together . . . Sequences with rapid alternation between the HP and P are not typical. (1981: 51)

In elaborating support of Wolfson's claim about tense-switching co-occurring with the boundaries of events, Schiffrin focusses on the Labovian criterion of interclausal temporal juncture. She finds a relatively high correlation of clauses with both temporal conjunctions and tense-switching and, in view of independent grounds for assuming that temporal conjunctions occur when there is some break in events, registers qualified support for the claim that tense-switching is *one* event-separating device. But for Schiffrin tense-switching is only a possible device, and not a necessary one, in event-isolation. Other devices – including temporal conjunctions – may separate out events, while tense is maintained rather than switched due to other constraints.

Besides qualified support for the event-separation view of HP, Schiffrin also offers qualified support for the more traditional view that HP (frequently in the progressive) is a special kind of present tense when the latter is used to refer to present events, and that it thereby

makes the past more vivid by bringing past events into the moment of speaking . . . (Schiffrin, 1981: 58)

Accordingly,

HP is an INTERNAL EVALUATION DEVICE: it allows the narrator to present events as if they were occurring at that moment, so that the audience can hear for itself what happened, and can interpret for itself the significance of those events for the experience. (58)

And when HP combines with progressivization (a correlative event-aligning device) the evaluation is particularly saucy.

But a fuller examination of the varying relative weightings of different evaluative devices in narrative still remains to be done. Wolfson's work on CHP specifies a number of variable factors which seem to influence a teller's decision to perform or not perform a narrative:

1 similarity (or not) of sex, age, ethnicity, occupation, status, between teller and addressee
2 whether the teller and audience are friends
3 the teller's assessment of the audience's similarity of attitudes and background
4 whether the speech situation itself is conducive (e.g., the interview situation is not conducive)

and, more directly to do with the story itself:

5 whether the story topic is appropriate to the audience
6 whether the events are recent or not
7 and whether the story includes physical or verbal interaction or not.

What Wolfson has done for the cluster of performance features taken as a group could clearly be done, in principle, for any other evaluative device or group of devices. Nor can we expect the simple trends that Wolfson found, where, predictably, performance of stories is more likely where conversationalists are the same sex, of similar age and status, similar in attitudes, background, and so on. For – and perhaps this now needs to be restated – evaluation undertakes a larger, more crucial task, than that of performance: the task of articulating the point of a story and persuading the audience of its tellability. Thus while performed stories give the impression that they contain a number of extra evaluative features added to stories told between intimates but not between people remote from each other in various ways, a reverse trend may apply when we compare the amount of evaluation in the stories of mature tellers. In other words, it may be the case that the fewer the dimensions of similarity between conversationalists the greater the role that evaluation devices may have to play, in spelling out the significance of a tale for a teller to a listener who does not share unspoken understanding.

Diffuse, embedded, and group oral narratives   5.10

There are other types of personal narrative, more subtly interleaved with the ongoing conversation, than those Labov extracted. Polanyi, for example, draws attention to the 'diffuse story' (1978: 109ff.), in which a chunk of story is followed by a chunk of multi-party conversation glossing, clarifying and amplifying aspects of the story chunk just told. In such a format, story evaluation can become a collaborative exercise. Diffuse story format shades into practices of embedding where, for example, several short stories are spread out and interrupted by conversational interludes, but can also be treated as the several sections of a single, overarching story.

Uppal (1984) has just such an example, a story comprising four conversationally embedded stories (I am most grateful to Ms Uppal for permission to reproduce data from her study). The stories emerge in the casual conversation of a mixed-sex group of Singaporean university students, good friends, reminiscing about their schooldays. I have glossed (in square brackets) only very few of the many features of colloquial Singaporean English in the teller's speech, and trust to the wit of the reader to make sense of these utterances.

(1) S: My one ah- my one ah- I was saved by my intelligence y'know. Because ah- I was in 6A, y'know. Eight of us were caught gambling, y'know. Seven 6-repeat-2. That time they got 6-repeat-once, -repeat-2 y'know. Repeating the second time repeating the first time. Seven 6-repeat-2. Then 6A. All public caning. Because the teacher caught us gambling y'know. So all public caning. Some more [= what is more] I prefect y'know. Kena [=caused to happen] lost badge, all. Everything gone nah, koyak. So kena, er, public caning. *Some more I gabrah, boy.* Some more public is like, principal office no sweat, y'know, but public is like they call your parents round.
   V: Huh?
   S: Ya, so parents will stand by the side, know.
   G: Ayooo!

   [some dialogue ellipted]

   S: Because, because it seems that you know is so- the son something goes wrong, parents have to be notified y'see. So they give public caning. Then- some more standard (2) y'know. Okay next, come ah. Fellow'll squeeze your bums all, know. Because beginning stages I think someone put book all. /katabah/ Got sound, y'know.
   G: [uninterpretable]
   S: So the fellow he squeeze squeeze your bum all. He make sure soft, know # Cushion # You see funny funny things ah. The fellow is, ah, the senior assistant is the one who

canes nah, not the principal. Principal was a woman nah,
so senior assistant. He feel feel. Then he smile at the
school, y'know. Then he take out wallet. Beautiful wallet
Three handkerchiefs. Take out all. One by – ((S makes
lashing sound)) Wahh Lan. I tell you cry, dah. *6-repeat*
boys crying, dah. 6-repeat that time you respect. Wah,
that time the terrors of the school.

B: This one your grandfather stories, ah?

S: Public caning terok, y'know. I tell you.

V: Is it really that painful or because of the ( ).

H: *Pain* boy

S: Damn pain na, I tell you. Damn pain. I never kena but I
know damn pain. See boys cry, I know damn pain. The
canes also got different ones, know. You know Kim Seng.

(3)   I escaped because I was in 6A. The principal came. He
saw- he saw all 6-repeat. Then he called down my
teacher. 'Explain why your 6A boy is doing with the 6-
repeat student.' The teacher got no explanation. So he
said, 'I want you to account for his behaviour.'

N: Like real, ah?

S: Then I excused y'know, I excuse. Go back. My teacher
to account for my behaviour for the rest of the year lah.
So I kena sit sit in front. Smile smile everyday.

N: So unfair, know. How come you never kena?

S: Exactly. I kena- after the six boys moody already.

N: Ya boy.

H: No members [= friends] na, alamak.

N: Some more, never mind. They are the terrors of the
school, y'know you go home nah-

(4) S: But they- they're okay nah. The reason I got to know
them was badminton. You see, I played badminton for
school, y'know. Then the whole school team formed by
6-repeat students, except I. Only 6A feller playing
badminton for school. So slowly lah. Slowly got into the
ideas of life lah. Then ah you know school, afternoon
school. Twelve o'clock come. What do you do?=

G: =True=

S: =All first started with the Saturday, know, play Saturday.
Carry on. Then slowly switched to five cents nah.

G: ((/))

S: Then slowly slowly switched to ten cents, twenty cents.
Then after that ting-tong already.

G: Mm
S: Move lah, advance. Ting-tong, kena sway sway. *Cards only kena caught. Moody. Advance through what.*
G: ((/))
S: Actually we tell them, know. We say, 'Sir, this one second time only.' Tell them, 'Gambling playing for fun.'
G: Mm
S: Actually six months ago we started already.

Story 1 supplies an abstract, orientation, and some complicating action, story 2 adds further orientation and evaluative description, story 3 contains the resolution, while story 4 is a flashback explaining how the situation at the beginning of the complicating action was arrived at. But each of these stories is itself adequately formed, with temporally-ordered action and resolution, and all four come from a single speaker.

To strengthen the claim that they are not merely a ribbon of loosely-related stories but rather also constitute a single 'macro-story', we should at least require some degree of temporal juncture between these stories, and further evidence that these four parts all cohere around a specific topic and resolution. Here the main story we might call a 'danger of caning' one: the teller recalls how, when he, a model student, was caught at school gambling for money with boys from another 'repeat' class, he alone escaped the pain and humiliation of a public caning. The main story resolution is as follows:

> Then I excused y'know, I excuse. Go back. My teacher to account for my behaviour for the rest of the year lah. So I kena sit sit in front. Smile smile everyday.

This appears towards the close of subordinate story 3. Prior to it, story 1 perfunctorily reports the fact that the boys were caught gambling, and the minor actual resolution (the teller is stripped of his prefect's badge) plus the *possibility* of a more major resolution (public caning). But most prominent in story 1 is emphasis on the crucial orientational facts that the other boys are in a repeat stream, distrusted hard cases, while the teller was in the prestige fast stream. Story 2 tells the embedded story of public canings in general, and the caning of his co-gamblers in particular, all the more vivid and hilarious in colloquial Singaporean English:

> So the fellow he squeeze squeeze your bum all. He make sure soft, know .... He feel feel. Then he smile at the school,

y'know. Then he take out wallet. Beautiful wallet. *Three* handkerchiefs. Take out all. One by – ((speaker makes lashing sound)) Wahh Lan. I tell you cry, dah. *Six repeat* boys crying, dah.

Now it will be clear that the public caning reported in 2 must have been preceded by the conditional letting-off of the teller-as-participant reported in 3, and that orderliness of event recapitulation has not been maintained (the order of actual occurrence of events reported in the stories being 4–1–3–2). On the other hand we may still maintain that here is a well-formed macro-story if we classify story 2 as evaluative within the larger context, an extended comparator exploring the path of punishment that, to the teller's relief, was not taken in his case. As noted earlier, the main point of this macro-story is not what happened to the other boys, but how *this* boy got away lightly. Story 2 effectively heightens our interest in just what treatment the teller will receive, artfully suspending the action before that resolution.

If the above is accepted as a type of diffuse story (the term 'diffuse', with its negative associations, seems to me less than ideal as a description of such virtuoso multi-phase monologues – a story elaborately structured of other stories), the more common phenomenon is for stories to relate more directly to surrounding conversational discourse and prior stories in noticeably relevant ways. Usually the onus is on conversationalists as individuals to insert their stories appropriately, showing attentiveness to what others have said, and so on. But sometimes group stories are told, by all or several conversationalist-participants working together: a narrating that does not involve suspension of the turn-taking mechanisms.

At first glance the group story appears to be an admirably democratic storytelling mode, built on a heightened degree of interdependence. The division between tellers and listeners falls away, as does anxiety over tellability, and a spirit of benevolent mutual indulgence may prevail: all are contributing to a story that each already knows. But, in some ways, and with more scope than usual, a competitive rivalry may shape the several contributions to the telling, there may not be full agreement on the point, on whom among the teller-participants comes out of the story well, and so on. In some ways, given the general familiarity with the broad story outlines, the exercise may become more oral-literary, with great attention paid to the most effective and entertaining methods of verbal expression.

As Polanyi notes (1978:143) the group story is an area where greater fictionality may be tolerated; credibility or *vraisemblance* is not a prime concern, since focus is less on any particular teller than on the tale for the tale's own sake. Or, as Bennett (1983) notes of her related story type, the group saga, the retelling is for purposes of reminiscence and social binding, with the emphasis less on the incidents themselves than on painting a rich picture of the situation. But again we should avoid being overly stipulative. In practice, as Uppal (1984) notes, a group story may become more a series of hypotheses or conjectures about what might have been the case (the true resolution, the proper evaluation) concerning some set of events, particularly where all the group-tellers were detached witnesses of those events, with limited inside knowledge. And the more that a group's talk becomes an unordered set of overlapping conjectures, the more the talk returns from narrative mode to that of ordinary conversation or gossip. Putting things the other way around, it may be that a collective style of telling is more frequently adopted where there is individual and collective uncertainty about just what happened and just how things ended up: each in the group helps to piece the story together.

Along these lines, we may see crime and detective fiction as a literary genre partly built upon the group story principle. When P. D. James's Superintendent Dalglish pieces together the testimony of a range of individuals connected in some way to a crime, he and the reader must process a radically diffused and potentially defective group story. The diffusion lies in the fact that there is – typically – no Aristotelian unity of time or place as far as the characters' contributions (within the story) are concerned. And – an extreme form of intra-group dissent – defectiveness and contradiction are probabilities since one or more of the group may construct their contributions so as to conceal their own guilt: fictionality with a vengeance, for self-protective and not merely aesthetic purposes.

5.11   From Labov to literature

A particular attraction of the Labovian six-part analysis of the oral narrative of personal experience is that it seems to underlie the structuring of many literary narratives too. Chapter 2 of Pratt

(1977) presents numerous examples of novels and short stories revealing various forms of abstracts, orientations, and so on. Of course the sheer scale of a novel makes for huge differences of magnitude of these narrative components by comparison with a brief oral narrative. Thus Pratt notes that Hardy's *The Return of the Native* opens with an entire chapter of orientation, and really only a small part of orientation at that: a description of the Egdon Heath landscape on a particular November afternoon. Pratt adds:

> The human characters and complicating action do not arrive until the second chapter, aptly titled 'Humanity Appears Upon the Scene, Hand in Hand with Trouble.' (Pratt, 1977: 53)

Furthermore, as Pratt notes, all sorts of departures from the 'underlying' unmarked or canonical narrative format, with adequate abstract, orientation, and so on, are to be found in literary narratives. Nor, in the face of such creative departures from the standard format, are we inclined immediately to reject the text as a defective narrative: we are used to paying more attention, working harder, being more challenged by literary texts than non-literary ones. Thus many novel- and story-openings project us *in medias res*, into the middle of ongoing events, with insufficient orientational briefing, as if we were already familiar with the world and actors depicted. Cast into this position, we sometimes feel we indeed become familiar with the world presented very rapidly; on other occasions, however, we remain somewhat disoriented throughout our reading of the text, and effects of mystery, disorder, obscurity, lostness, are achieved (intentionally or otherwise). In several plays by Beckett and Pinter, for example, the persistent 'undersupply' of orientation is something some playgoers cannot bear.

The broad point Pratt makes, by further copious exemplification of forms of resolution, abstract and coda in literary narratives, is that no radical gulf separates literary from 'everyday' narrative: the same devices, used for the same purposes, emerge in both.

> What is important about the fact that literary narratives can be analyzed in the same way as the short anecdotes scattered throughout our conversation? To begin with, it casts grave doubt on the Formalist and structuralist claims that the language of literature is formally and functionally distinctive. . . . Unless we are foolish enough to claim that

people organize their oral anecdotes around patterns they learn from reading literature, we are obliged to draw the more obvious conclusion that the formal similarities between natural narrative and literary narrative derive from the fact that at some level of analysis they are utterances of the same type. (Pratt, 1977: 67, 69)

Further reading

Labov and Waletzky (1967) and Labov (1972) are obviously the place to begin further reading. Labov (1981) gives some indications of his more recent thoughts on personal narrative. This essay is also interesting since, in its particular focus on speech actions and violent physical reactions, it bears out the points I wanted to make about saying as a kind of doing in section 5.5. Thereafter, Chapter 2 of Pratt (1977) is full of interesting applications of the Labovian model to literary examples; see also Carter (1985), Watts (1984) and Toolan (1988), while Culler (1981: 169–187) contains useful critique.

Among the sociolinguistically-oriented studies that have applied Labov's model are: Carter and Simpson (1982), Bennett (1983) and Polanyi (1982). The last of these explores the literary complexities in ordinary stories. Discussions of Conversational Historic Present and narrative as performance include Wolfson (1978; 1979; 1981; 1982), Schiffrin (1981), and Silva-Corvalan (1983). On cultural presuppositions and expectations and their shaping of the stories we tell, see Polanyi (1978), and Tannen (1979).

A great deal of attention is now being directed to the question of the ways in which spoken and written discourse differ. For a revision of the prevailing assumptions about the greater syntactic complexity of written narratives see Beaman (1984). and for an approach to the structure of written narrative that sees it as combining the syntactic complexity of writing with the spoken discourse features used to enhance interpersonal involvement – hence merging oral and literate strategies – see Tannen (1982). Ultimately we may need to pay more conscious attention not simply to the sociolinguistic environment but also to the wider cultural setting from which a story emerges. For recent anthropologically-minded study of narratives see Bruner (1984) and Bauman (1986).

Notes and exercises

1 There is no better place to start, in seeing how effective the Labovian scheme of narrative analysis is, than with data that you yourself have elicited. Record a story from someone you know well. The story could be prompted by, for example, asking them if they have been in a car crash, if they've ever had an operation, or whatever, or the choice of story topic could be left up to the informant. The recording could be open or surreptitious. Just whom you record, obviously, will make a very great difference to the type and structure of story told: five-year-olds produce stories somewhat unlike those of teenagers, who produce ones somewhat unlike those of octogenarians. And the teller's closeness to you, the recorder, will also cause considerable differences. (The question of how similar or dissimilar the stories of children and adults are will be returned to in Chapter 7.) But at this stage the chief thing is to 'get' a story.

Once that is done, you will need to transcribe it. Again, at this stage, it might be best to trust to your own judgement, simply setting out as full a written record of the taped material as you can. Very soon you will come up against tricky questions of specific practice and general theory in the most direct way. Should one measure pauses, are they sometimes an evaluative device? Are there different kinds of pauses? Should one annotate stress and intonation, changes of pace of delivery? What about eye contact – or lack of it – between teller and listeners; and both the teller's and listeners' body movements? Can we legitimately ignore these dimensions of the speech event? If the answer is no, doesn't this suggest that an audio-tape may mislead us more than it assists? All empirical study must resolve such questions: for useful discussions of sociolinguistic methodology see Wolfson (1976), Stubbs (1983:218–46) and Ochs (1979).

Now at last you can test out the Labovian model outlined in this chapter on your sample narrative. Identify the orientation, complicating action, resolution, and abstract and coda (if any) of the narrative. Is there any significantly delayed orientation, and if so, are such delays motivated or accidental? We must be alert to the fact that many tellers are imperfectly competent, forget to include important background, and may even neglect to relate important narrative events. Focussing now on evaluation, is there a distinct section of this, as Labov's diamond diagram suggests, prior to the resolution, and/or is evaluation dispersed throughout the text? Are certain types of evaluation device more prominent than others (e.g. many intensifiers, few explicatives or comparators); is this a performed narrative, in Wolfson's sense? (Many of these questions only become really interesting once a comparative analysis of a number of narratives is attempted.) Finally, in what ways do you feel – or suspect – that the Labovian model is inadequate relative to your target narrative? Is there temporal reordering of the kind disallowed by Labov in the narrative? Are there dimensions of evaluation that his categories seem not to cover?

2 Labov (1972) draws attention to the absence of adequate evaluation material in children's narratives of vicarious experience that he studied – specifically, in their retelling of the plots of a television spy series, *The Man from UNCLE.* Now this rather absolute absence in Labov's data has not been replicated by other researchers, who have found some evaluation present in certain vicarious-experience narratives. If we were to speculate as to why evaluation is sometimes absent or inadequate, however, one factor we might consider is that a child narrating such a story cannot be reliving or reperforming the events – as both Labov and Wolfson suggest is often the case in personal narrative – but merely retelling. She doesn't evaluate fully because the story didn't happen to her, and as far as the teller is concerned the story may not have much point, may not be terribly tellable – but something has to be told because the story has been elicited.

Elicit and record – or just listen to – narratives produced by children recounting stories from television series they are addicted to. Do you really find no evaluation? In a larger study, you might be able to begin to see whether evaluation varies with the age, sex, or class of the child. (The first of these is unquestionably a shaping factor: with age will come, if not always greater absolute quantities of evaluation – we surely don't want more and more of this, *ad infinitum*, as the years go by! – then a greater repertoire of different means of conveying evaluation.) Another important variable besides the three mentioned above must surely be whether the child thinks or knows that you are familiar with the basic situation of, for example, an *A-Team* story – the characters, the kind of assignments they tackle, their resort to ingenious 'alternative technology' that can convert an old washing machine to a flame-thrower which – equally miraculously – never causes

serious injury to any baddy, etc., etc. In what the child tells, and
in how she evaluates what she tells, she may be guided very
much by her judgments of your extratextual knowledge – factual
and ideological – of the kind outlined in Chapter 4.

3 Attempt a six-part (abstract, etc.) analysis of Joyce's 'The
Dead'. How satisfactory does this seem to be? Does it help if we
treat the text as *two* narratives – the story of the Christmas party
and the story of Gabriel and Gretta's night at the hotel – each
with its own trajectory from orientation to resolution? Argue the
case for or against this proposal, taking into consideration the
kinds of sequential cause-and-effect relatedness that each
approach might highlight. Think also of the possible evaluative
function of the text's recurring references to warmth, generosity,
mortality, darkness, coverings, and so on. These may operate at
a level of narrative texture, mentioned at the opening of Chapter
4, which I have entirely neglected. Thus, in the copious references
to darkness and covering and gauntness, from the 'three mortal
hours' it allegedly takes Gretta to dress, to the lugubrious conversation about the monks who sleep in their coffins – a macabre
topic which is 'buried in the silence of the table' (201) – there
are numerous allusions to the fact of dying. These, too, the reader
incorporates into his sense of why the story is being told.

To say so much is not, however, to claim that the 'point' of
'The Dead', or any moral or message, can be easily extracted
and summarized in a sentence or two. That this is so first begins
to be apparent when we try to decide where (if at all) resolution
leaves off and coda (if any) begins. Is Gabriel's dreamlike sense
of dissolving, at the close of the story, a coda appended to the
already-past events of the party and of Michael Furey's life and
death? Or, more integrated into the narrative, are these
concluding thoughts a kind of resolution to all the preceding
events, selfconscious as codas often are, but inescapably a result
as a resolution is? Is our choice between seeing this as coda or
resolution affected by whether we feel the revery is genuinely
revelatory insight, or maudlin self-indulgence?

4 But at least as interesting as applying Labov to such large
narrative units as whole novels or stories is applying the model
to the stories within stories. Here in 'The Dead', analyze Gretta's
direct speech account of her involvement with Michael Furey,
and comment on any oddities in the structuring of her story
that emerge. Why might one conclude that Gretta's story about

Michael Furey still ends up telling the reader rather more about its addressee, Gabriel?

5 Where are the evaluation elements in Faulkner's 'That Evening Sun'?

6 In this chapter I have emphasized that in order to justify the telling of a story, what gets told must be to some degree special, and that non-trivialness must be adequately communicated.

On the other hand, from the famous ethnomethodologist Harvey Sacks has come an emphasis on another aspect of peoples' stories, an aspect potentially at variance with the non-trivialness condition mentioned above. This is that, to protect our stories from dismissal as outrageous fabrication, immediately suspect, we render our stories as ordinary as possible. Sacks suggests that the stories we typically encounter in everday interaction are 'overwhelmingly banal', and that people strive to establish the 'nothing happened' sense of truly catastrophic events. Thus ordinary people have to work their way between the Scylla of the 'so what?' question (by making their stories not uninteresting) and the Charybdis of the 'I don't believe you!' reaction (by making their stories not incredible).

It would be interesting to explore the repertoire of linguistic means that we might identify as, in part at least, performing this task of 'ordinariness construction'. Again, we need recordings or transcripts of narratives of incidents that we know (from personal involvement or further questioning of the teller) to be extraordinarily ghastly, fortuitous or whatever. Some of the means we might predict will contribute to 'ordinariness construction' might include downtoning modifiers (*rather, a bit, somewhat,* etc.); hedges (*sort of,* etc.); less emotive predicates (*hit* instead of *smash*); plentiful description of all the routine events, settings and background; a flattening off of pitch and volume variations; and restricted changes in pace of delivery. Sacks's ordinariness hypothesis would be to some extent confirmed if we could find a teller telling the same story twice over, once to close friends, once to more distant acquaintances, and found more downtoning in the latter case than in the former. It may also be the case that the expression of ordinariness varies with different tellers: more prominent in the stories of introverts, relatively neglected in the stories of extroverts.

7 Compare and contrast a spoken and written telling of the same

story. If you are lucky, the informant you used for exercise 1 might be persuaded to write down the story she has told you. It's probably best not to mention you'd like a written version of the story until you have extracted the oral version, even if that informant declines to continue. And perhaps the most crucial thing to do is to keep the data manageably short: many informants just won't do a good job of writing up a story that, in the oral telling, took ten minutes or more. The best way to grasp what, as a data-gatherer, you are up against is to do the exercise yourself: produce oral and written versions of some brief narrative from your own life before inflicting this chore on others!

Now compare the two versions of the 'same' story in any ways you think appropriate, but focussing especially on the formal differences. Are abstracts, codas, evaluations, etc., 'done' the same way in the different media? Despite differences of form, are there pairings or counterparts: for example, are there elements of the written form that do the job done by stress and intonation and pace of delivery in the spoken version?

8 The single most delimiting aspect of Labovian description seems to be the requirement that only independent clauses can carry the fundamental, fixed-order clauses of narrative. As we saw in 5.2, a consequence of this insistence that subordinate clauses cannot carry superordinate events is that many narratives that listeners readily accept are excluded. And what is true of listeners is even more evident when we consider readers of written narratives. There are many narratives, then, spoken and written, that are not 'Labovian oral narratives of personal experience'. The issue principally concerns two cases:

1 subordinate clauses in general, some of which *may*, contra Labov, carry crucial, action-complicating events

2 subordinate temporal clauses in particular, introduced by *before*, *after*, *when*, and so on, which often seem to carry important events and are freely shiftable either side of their dominating main clause:

The king died of grief when the queen died.

Labov's motivations for his restrictive definition of narrative have less to do with what listeners might accept than with what his informants actually did. And, in practice, he found sufficient apparent observance of a main-clause/main-event pairing to suggest that this was a requirement – a requirement, at least, in the kind of narratives, from the kind of speakers, in the kind of settings (etc.), that he studied. The requirement also makes sense in that it fits in with other Labovian expectations, particularly the expectation that, in personal narratives, people will recapitulate their tellable past experience in its original order of occurrence. There is an iconic simplicity in this pattern, where events a, b and c, are recalled (even performed) in main clauses in the sequence 1, 2 and 3. This is a direct matching, which we may reasonably think of as the basic format, from which more complex reorderings and subordinations are more artful derivations.

Look, in both spoken and written narratives of personal experience, for instances of main-event reordering: do these appear in particular types of subordinate clauses (e.g., of time and reason), do they relate to particular types of happening (e.g., hidden motivations), are they more common in the written narratives than the spoken, does the temporal distance of the narrated events from the teller's present time seem to affect any tendency to reorder and – widening the net now – are they more frequent in narratives of vicarious experience than of personal experience?

⑥ Children's narratives

Stories *for, by,* and *with* children   6.1

The topic 'children's narratives' covers many sub-branches: this section's title only begins to discriminate them. Within stories *for* children (as within those *by* and *with*) we can observe very many sub-types: oral *v.* written; oral face-to-face *v.* oral 'removed' (e.g., radio or cassette); oral face-to-face and one-to-one (typically, from a caregiver) *v.* oral face-to-face and one-to-many (typically, from a teacher in a classroom); oral, face-to-face, one-to-one, and spontaneously constructed *v.* situationally similar stories that are to a degree text-dependent (regardless of the status of that 'text': a printed book, a family saga, a garbled memory of some folktale). The above are just a sample of the subdivisions within one branch of types of stories for children, supplied chiefly as a reminder of the multiple dimensions along which such stories may well vary. Differences of situation may cause the same teller (whether adult or child) to tell utterly different kinds of narratives; and even if the same basic story is told, we can expect that the influences of situation will reshape that basic material in many ways.

As I have implied above, the potential dimensions of situational variation are numberless. However, a very useful preliminary categorization of situations can be achieved by considering Halliday's three macro-dimensions of discourse, which he calls the **field**, **mode**, and **tenor**. Field designates, broadly, the nature of the social activity that is going on (e.g., children sharing a personal-experience story with their teacher and peers). Often an important question to ask *within* the dimension of field is 'What is the *topic* of talk, what is the talk *about*?; but it is crucial to grasp that field addresses the larger behavioural question, that of understanding what type of social activity is in progress, and so involves the discourse under scrutiny. Like other Hallidayan categorizations, then, field is insistent upon the motivated 'fit' between language practice and cultural practice, where a society's language patterns articulate or signify its view of the world. Mode encompasses variations in the medium of the text and the 'channel' between addresser and addressee (e.g., whether the text is written or spoken, planned or unplanned, integral to some ongoing activity or a detached reconstruction, and whether the addresser–addressee relation is one of immediacy or distance). Tenor concerns participant relations as shaped by the statuses and roles that are being observed (e.g. friend to friend, father to son, doctor to patient, sales assistant to customer). For much fuller discussion of field, mode and tenor see Halliday (1978) and Halliday and Hasan (1985). A final very important dimension of mode, sometimes termed **functional tenor**, concerns the rhetorical purpose of a text: what goals or effects it is intended to achieve (e.g., entertainment, instruction, persuasion, etc.).

The above reminders of situation-dependent variations are also relevant to two interrelated qualifications, which might be summarized as caveats about teller assessment and tale assessment. The first concerns the use of data from children's performance with stories (skills at constructing, comprehending, summarizing, and so on) as evidence of their cognitive skills or linguistic competence more broadly defined. If situation-dependency makes major differences to the stories tellers produce, we must be extremely circumspect about moving from an assessment of a particular performance in a particular (perhaps highly problematic) situation, to any general assessment of narrative (to say nothing of cognitive) ability. The second concerns the need for circumspection in our critical analysis of a child's tales: again, if our judgments are dominated by unexamined preconceptions as to what a 'good' story should be like, and neglect the likelihood that what is good in one set of circumstances may be quite inappropriate in a different set, then any conclusions we make may be valueless, if not positively harmful. We should never end up with the young wag dogged by his tale.

On the other hand, even as we are mindful of the very different kinds of objects that different 'children's narratives' may be, we should also look for patterns of similarity and relationship across a range of cases: without such findings we fail to identify connections within what we can intuitively accept as a coherent area of study. Ultimately linguistic analysts of children's narratives will want to consider some fairly sharp issues of relatedness. These would include the question of whether specific linguistic evidence can be identified to support the frequent claim that children's oral storytelling is a preparation for written narrative composition. Similarly, if written narrative is a distinct **register** (or kind of writing) and a competence-base from which older primary-school children build their developing .control of other varieties of language such as argumentation and description, which particular linguistic features of the known variety are a help, and which are a hindrance, in progress towards these 'target' varieties? Are children's narratives evaluatively and structurally simplified versions of adult ones, modelled on the narratives they hear from adults, or are they constructed according to quite other principles; what linguistic evidence is there on either side? Can we nurture production of more complex stories (written or spoken) in children – and if so, how? What role do recall exercises, probe questions, and shared retellings play in the development of narrative skills? How does reading narrative relate to writing narrative, should the former be graded for optimal effectiveness, and if so how do we determine grades of narrative complexity or difficulty?

Storytelling and emergent literacy   6.2

An increasingly well-explored area of children's language development is that of the child's nurtured receptiveness to writing and reading, and familiarity with some of the disciplines and constraints of writing and reading, somewhat before she is formally taught to read or write. The fundamental recognition here is that, as the introduction to one recent collection of studies of children's emergent literacy puts it,

> Practically all children in a highly literate society such as ours do bring knowledge about literacy to school with them. (Farr, 1985: vii)

A number of related theses, which I have space only to list in summary fashion here, accompany this basic insight. Literacy begins at home, these studies show, where that home is characterized by valued relationships with parents, siblings, and friends. Recurringly, close ethnographic studies such as those reported in Farr (1985) and Bissex (1981) show that where the interactant is highly attuned to the child's current stage of writing competence, is supportive and enthusiastic and not overly corrective of 'errors', then that interactant can be instrumental in developing the child's literacy skills in a greater variety of ways and more rapidly than if the child were left to his own resources. It also seems that the value (in terms of results or impact) of the support an interactant offers cannot be separated from the value the child puts on that interactant not so much as a role-model, or rival, but as an individual. Here is another bald reminder of the non-autonomous nature of narrative productions and receptions: what you give and what you get (or think you've been given) may vary sharply depending on the interpersonal ties – of respect, affection, antipathy, etc. – between addresser and addressee. Halliday's notion of tenor, introduced earlier, attempts to address at least the lexicalized and grammaticized aspects of these complex and changing ties.

The idea of the interactant as an essential ally in the assault on 'forward positions' of language development, otherwise beyond the individual child's current powers, is based solidly on the psychologist Vygotsky's notion of the **zone of proximal development**. Indeed Vygotsky's theories of cognitive development in the individual are the dominant theoretical underpinning of much current research in the field. While Piaget's theories have the attraction of indicating quite explicit stages in cognitive development which, at differing pace, all children must go through in the specified order, following a 'biological timetable', those theories have been felt to concentrate on development driven by interaction between the learner and the object-of-knowledge (e.g., a language) to the neglect of development driven by growing and changing cultural and personal interaction. In a sense Vygotsky is more comprehensive than Piaget, allowing biology a role but arguing that cultural development, fostered by interaction with significant others in one's immediate environment, dominates. And from that interaction, as Vygotsky famously asserted, internalization proceeds: 'An interpersonal process is transformed into an intrapersonal one' (Vygotsky, 1978: 57). That which was learned through social interaction becomes knowledge in the individual. And Vygotsky's emphasis on the social environment makes it all the easier for researchers to expect and allow for variation in different children's orders and manner of narrative development, given different social environments and different interests and purposes in the child. The above is an impertinently brief sketch of Vygotsky's principles, supplied simply to give some indication of the theoretical background of current orientations in child development research.

The specific strategies adopted by kindergarten teachers in the nurturing of children's skills of writing and storytelling are of many kinds. But most commonly discussed are the activities of 'sharing time' (reviewed in the next section), dictation, and dramatization. In dictation, a child dictates a new story, or retells a familiar one to a teacher-scribe. The teacher-scribe is thus in a position to monitor the telling as it is in progress: suggesting improvements, pointing to information gaps, etc., while the child retains responsibility for the production. Dictation is in effect 'doing writing without doing the writing', and gives the child a particularly immediate sense of how marvellous a knack it is to be able to record one's own story productions with fixed graphic symbols (reproducible, increasingly unmysterious). Dictation entails a degree of detachment from the events of a story that we noted earlier was essential for consistency of orientation in any telling, and it also nurtures reflexive self-awareness. The dictated story is usually read back to the child, with the teacher checking with the child that she is happy with the story as it stands: the larger world of 'second thoughts', self-correction and assisted improvement, of verbal production as 'out there' and separate from you but your responsibility, begins to take shape. All this is taken a step further when such dictated stories are then dramatized, with the teacher declaiming the story, in chunks, as its original teller and other children act out its events: the teller learns the need for a story to be coherent and tellable to its addressees in the most direct way possible. In acting out a story the children reconstruct the world of events which the teller's words represent, and in the process awkwardnesses of match, between words and world, can become newly apparent.

Differing styles, differing orientations   6.3

In 5.8 I mentioned Shirley Brice Heath's findings that what *counted* as narratives in two small-town North Carolina working-class communites (one black, one white) were drastically different. How easy is it, one might wonder, for anyone from Trackton to tell a good, appreciated story in Roadville – or vice versa?

And not just in Trackton and Roadville. A great deal of research now underway from psycholinguistic, sociolinguistic and social psychological perspectives is uncovering just how much cultural specificity and relativism attends narrative practice. Let a hundred ways of telling what we wish to tell flourish, the *laissez-faire* liberal might suggest, but the situation is less simple where our 'ways' converge. All styles are equal, but some are more equal (i.e., preferred, by someone) than others. And sometimes the exponents of the preferred style get more rewarded, even without the rewarders being aware that it is chiefly to differences of style that they are responding so differentially. One sample of this kind of problem is that probed in the work of Martin, discussed in 6.5. Heath (1982) shows vividly what moral and educational dilemmas emerge as the number of ways of being oriented to literacy, and of being inducted into one's own community's way, multiply. Here she contrasts Trackton and Roadville, mentioned above, with the mainstream, middle-class, school-oriented culture of Maintown. Some of the tacit 'rules in literacy events' (such as bedtime stories) that she suggests Maintown children learn to observe will strike most of us with a shock of recognition:

> (3) From the time they start to talk, children *respond to conversational allusions to the content of books; they act as question-answerers who have a knowledge of books. . . .*
> (7) When children are about three years old, adults discourage the highly interactive role in bookreading children have hitherto played and children *listen and wait as an audience.* No longer does either adult or child repeatedly break into the story with questions and comments. Instead, children must listen, store what they hear, and on cue from the adult, answer a question. Thus, children begin to formulate 'practice' questions as they wait for the break and the expected formulaic-type questions from the adult. It is at this stage that children often choose to 'read' to adults rather than to be read to. (1982: 53, original emphases)

Nevertheless, what is recognizable to us may be quite foreign to others; Heath demonstrates that orientation to literacy in general, and to narrative more particularly, and adjustment to school and schooling, is as different in Roadville and Trackton as either is from what prevails in Maintown. And this is so despite the fact that all three communities hold the view that school is important and that children who do well there will do well in life. The danger that 'non-recognition' of style difference will lead to misrepresentation and even disregard on the part of teachers, employers, and out-group fellow citizens, is abundantly clear. And yet such dismissive misconstruction is made easier by the narrowly normative research of social scientists themselves. As Heath points out in a telling footnote:

Numerous studies of behavioural phenomena (for example, mother-child interactions in language learning) either do not specify that the subjects being described are drawn from mainstream groups or do not recognize the importance of this limitation. (Heath, 1982: 74)

Another persuasive elucidation of the problems broached here is charted in the work of Michaels (1981, 1984, 1985), who shows that

> [first-grade] children from different backgrounds come to school with different narrative strategies and prosodic conventions for giving narrative accounts. (1981: 423)

This matters because 'sharing time' activities in which, prompted and supported by the teacher, individual children describe things or narrate past experiences to the whole class, are an important and widely-used educational resource; they are a potentially rich practice ground for using (and learning) *literate* discourse strategies. Michaels found, in an empirical study, that children whose already-established discourse style matched the teacher's own literate style and expectations did well at 'sharing time' activities and benefitted from this 'oral preparation for literacy' (1981: 423). But she found that when the child's style and the teacher's expectations diverged teacher–child collaboration was often unsuccessful, and longer-term adverse effects on school performance and evaluation were a danger.

Among the discourse expectations that Michaels found a particular teacher disclosing, in her regulatory reactions to her children's stories, were the following:

1 explicit spatiotemporal grounding of the talk
2 full description and naming of objects involved in a story, even of those in plain sight
3 *minimal* assumptions of shared background knowledge between the teller and his or her addressees; and
4 lexicalization of topic shifts, marking any thematic relatedness that persisted despite change of topic.

In sum, the teacher – 'Mrs Jones' – 'seemed to expect a literate-style, decontextualized account centering on a single topic' (Michaels, 1984: 223).

The problem that Michaels identifies relates to the sharing style of the black children in Mrs Jones's class, a style which turns out to have its own 'systematicness', but is at variance with Mrs Jones's preferred style. While the white children brought to sharing time a discourse style that was already at least embryonically 'topic centered' in the ways outlined above, the black children brought to the task an established 'topic associating' style. In topic associating discourse, the teller presents 'a series of implicitly associated personal anecdotes' (1981: 429), which are actually built around an unstated thematic focus. Information is broken into chunks prosodically, by means of a high sustained pitch on *and*, followed by a pause; no other lexical connectives besides *and* were used to link anecdotes.

> This kind of rhythmically chunked, topic associating discourse is evidently difficult to follow for those who, like the teacher and student teacher, expect the discourse to focus on a single topic and to be prosodically marked with sharp rising contours (signalling 'more to come') or falling contours (signalling full closure). (1982: 430)

The following sharing event sample is slightly abridged from Michaels and Collins (1984: 227). Single and double underlining indicate degrees of increased volume, ellipsis points mark pauses, a colon after a vowel-letter indicates elongation of that vowel, single and double slashes mark tone-group boundaries, and lines above and below the line of text indicate high and low pitch movements respectively: e.g., floor marks a low rise-fall, while one marks a high fall, and so on.

Teacher: Deena/ I want you to share some- one thing/ that's very important// one thing// . . . .

Deena: um . . . in the su:mme:r/ . . . I mean/ . . .w-when um/ I go back to school/ I come back to schoo:l/ in Septe:mber/ . . . I'ma ha:ve a new coat/ and I already got it// . . . and/ . . . it's/ . . .u:m . . . (. . .) got a lot of bro:wn in it// . . a:nd/ . . . when-/ um/ and I got it ye:sterday/ . . . and when . . . I saw it/ my um . . my mother was . . was going some . . where/ when my . . when I saw it/ . . . on the cou:ch/ and I showed my sister/ and I was readin' somethin' out on . . on the ba:g/ and my bi:g sister said⌈(. . .)

Child: ⌊um close the door

Deena: my big sister said/ Deena you have to keep that away/ from Keisha/ 'cause that's my baby sister/ and I said ño//

... and I said the plastic bág/ ... because/ ... um/
... when ... u:m/ ... sh-when the um .. she was
u:m (with me)/ wait a minute/ ... my cou:sin and
⌈her (. . .)

Teacher: ⌊wait a minute// you stick with your coat now// I s-said
you could tell one thing// ... that's fair//

Deena: ⸢this was about my ⌈coat

Teacher: ⌊OK/ [alright/ go on

Deena: [this was- and today/ and
yesterday when I ... got my coat my cou:sin ran
outsi:de/ and he (. . .) ran to tried to get him/ and he/
he he start-/ ... an' when he get in- when he got in
my house/ ... he layed on the floor/ and I told him to
ge:t up because he was cry:in'//   ᴧ

Teacher: mm-what's that have to do with your coat?//

Deena: h-he .. becau- he wanted to go outside// but we ..
couldn't// (exasperated)

Teacher: why?//

Deena: 'cau:se my mo:ther s-wanted us to stay in the house//

Teacher: what does that have to do with your coat?//

Deena: bec- it um ...

Child: (whispers)

Deena: because/ . . . . . . 'I don't know//

Teacher: OK (chuckles)// [thank you very much Deena//

Children: [(talking)

Teacher: OK/ do you understand what I am trying to do?//
Deena?/ I was trying to get her to stick with one/ ...
thing// and she was talking about her . . ./

Children like Deena who used this style had particularly acute
problems with meeting the teacher's requirement that they tell
one thing, of importance: the style itself made it seem (to the
teacher) as if there was no particular topic whatsoever.

'Telling about important things' was, in effect, a *gloss* for topic
centered accounting. It made sense only if one had a topic
centered schema to begin with. (1981: 434)

Subsequently, in order to get a fuller lexicogrammatical description of the differences in the discourse styles (topic-centred *v.*
topic-associating) of such children, Michaels and Collins analyzed
the oral retellings, by four first-graders (two white, two black), of
a short film. To enlarge the comparative exercise, they also looked

at two fourth-graders' narratives, both oral and written, of the same film. They found that

> Of the four first-grade narratives, two use a wide variety of lexical and syntactic devices to signal agent focus, causal connections, old *v.* new distinctions, and coreference relations. We call this a literate discourse style. . . . The other first grade narratives rely more on prosodic cues such as duration and special contouring to signal agent focus, causal connections, and so forth. We call this an oral discourse style because prosodic cues such as duration and contouring, although essential for oral communication, are precisely what is not available in written language. (Michaels and Collins, 1984: 232)

Repeatedly, necessary textual connections are marked lexically in the literate discourse style, but prosodically in the oral discourse style. For example one of the literate-style speakers first introduces one of the main protagonists thus:

there was a man/ . . . that was . . . ˥picking some pears//

Twenty-four lines later she can recycle the relative clause to confirm that here is second mention of the same man:

they walked by the man who gave/ . . . wh-who was picking the˥pears//

By contrast one of the oral-style speakers introduces the same character thus:

it was about/ . . . this mān/ he was um/ . . . um . . . takes some um . . . peāch–/ . . . some . . . pea:rs off the treē/

using two independent clauses. Twenty-five lines later, on second mention of this character, the speaker relies almost entirely on prosody (vowel elongation and high rise-fall contour on mān) to signal old information, subsequent mention:

. . . and when that . . . when he 'pa:ssed/ by that ma:n/ . . . the man . . . the ma:n came out of the treē/

In fact there is some lexical signalling of coreference here: the speaker's use of the deictic word *that* in the phrase 'that ma:n'. But it is reasonable to argue that this is an inadequate lexical marker of the coreference intended.

Another lexis/prosody contrast concerns the marking of an important resultative connection between two narrative events in the story. This is marked in the literate-style speaker's account by the standard written connective, s̶o̶, while in the oral-style speaker's account it is signalled prosodically by a stressed high fall on then̄. In other words when then̄ is prosodically marked in this particular way it is intended to convey casual relation and not merely temporal relation; whether addressees *hear* that meaning-difference or not is precisely the problem at issue.

Similar oral-literature disparities, with attendant handicaps, were found in the oral narratives of the fourth-graders (both of whom were fluent readers and writers 'at the top of their class'); and the potential problems in the oral-discourse speaker's spoken narrative become actual defects when that person constructs his written narrative. For Paul, the literate-discourse speaker, 'learning to write involves enriching a system he already knows and uses effectively in oral discourse'.

> Geoffrey, on the other hand, tends to rely heavily on prosodic cues in speaking; these cues are often the sole indicators of highlighted information, coreference relations, and perspective shifts in his oral narrative. His written narrative is characterized by weakly signalled transitions and ambiguous identity relations. For him, with prosodic options lost, learning to write means learning a new system for signalling thematic cohesion. (Michaels and Collins, 1984: 241)

Children's narrative development 6.4

The previous two sections have chiefly considered some of the ways that emergent narrativity in the social setting of the school seems to be best supported – together with some of the ways in which, despite the best intentions of child and teacher, frustrations may arise. But we also need to know more about just what development does occur typically in children's narrative ability. We are fortunate here to be able to draw on the findings of a recent large-scale study of children's stories, to which I will turn shortly.

One classic study to invoke in any reflections on children's linguistic development is Piaget's pioneering work (1926). Focussing on story-recall ability in 6- to 8-year-olds, Piaget identified a number of failings in the recall productions of his younger subjects, failings which are far less frequent in the older children. The major failings concerned order, causality, and orientation:

the actual order of events in a story was not reproduced in recall, cause-and-effect relations were not properly marked, and egocentric use of pronouns (tending to orient narrative events to the child herself) led to misdirections, in the recall texts, over who was doing what to whom in the narrative. Despite sixty years of critical review, Piaget's basic findings are still widely accepted (with the qualification that children can produce non-egocentric text at a rather earlier age (four) than he claimed). But just what conclusions we should draw from such findings remains a matter of great uncertainty.

Quite recently, children's developing grasp of temporal order and causality in stories, as well as of complex qualities such as that narratives should appear adequately 'completed' and evaluated, have been probed in an invaluable study by Peterson and McCabe (1983). Their study is important not least because it is based on nothing so artificial as recall and comprehension tests, but rather focusses on the ordinary stories that particular children chose to tell them – not quite spontaneously, but in a situation that has every indication of having been relaxed and informal. Peterson and McCabe conducted a three-way analysis of 288 stories, elicited during casual conversation, from a controlled sample of 96 children ranging in age from 4 to 9 years (8 children for each of the 12 age/sex combinations). The study is a three-way analysis in that each story is subjected to analysis according to three methodologies: the Labovian method I outlined in Chapter 5, the psycholinguistic 'story-grammar' approach (mentioned in note 12 of Chapter 2 and referenced briefly in the 'further reading' section of the present chapter), and a third, more syntax-focussed, method, called dependency analysis.

First applying Labovian methods (or what they call 'High Point analysis', referring to the top of the diamond in Labov's famous diagram), they found some interesting shifts in the type of narrative that children tend to produce at different ages.

'Leap-frog' narratives are the commonest single type of story produced by the 4-year-olds Peterson and McCabe observed. A leap-frog narrative arises 'where the child jumps from event to event unsystematically, leaving out important events' (1983: 48), and putting a heavy burden of reconstruction on the listener. These are the commonest type amongst 4-year-olds, and the classic pattern (i.e., the full Labovian diamond, with a clear climax and resolution) is still relatively rare. Within a year, however, the leap-frog pattern itself becomes rare and soon disappears completely, while the classic pattern becomes increasingly common, dominating in the productions of the 7-year-olds and above. But in addition, 'chronological' stories persist, with some decrease in frequency, at all ages. Stories classified as chronological are those where there is temporal sequence of events without adequate point or integratedness to the material, i.e., stories that fulfil the referential function of narrative but not the evaluative one. Narratives that Peterson and McCabe labelled impoverished (too few events, too often repeated) or disoriented (confused, contradictory) also become rare.

But the broad progression, in this corpus at least, seems to consist of two broad phases. The first of these begins as a preference for leap-frog and chronological narratives at age 4, which is followed by a shift to experimentation with end-at-high-point narratives at age 5 (end-at-high-point narratives have most of the attributes of the classic pattern, but terminate abruptly without any resolution). Additionally, in this first phase, there is some growth in use of the classic formula, and continued use of the chronological mode in one story out of four. The second phase runs from age 6 onwards when, presumably more sensitive to the inadequacies of the end-at-high-point mode, a broader and permanent shift in favour of the classic pattern, ultimately at the expense of both temporary rivals (end-at-high-point and chronological), begins to take hold.

Table 1 charts the relative abundance of material realizing the Labovian components of a narrative. Note that in this table a 'narrative unit' denotes a sentence or independent clause of narrative, while by the term 'appendages' Peterson and McCabe refer to abstracts and codas as a single set.

Here we should note both the gradual growth in the extent of resolutions that children supply (not surprising since this matches

Table 1 *Percentage of the total number of narrative units that are of the different types*

Mean age	4	5	6	7	8	9
Orientation	20	22	23	24	23	24
Evaluation	13	14	17	13	16	14
Complicating action	58	56	47	49	47	44
Resolution	6	4	8	10	10	14
Appendages	3	4	5	4	4	4

(modified from Peterson and McCabe, 1983: 52)

the increasing incidence of classic narratives in place of end-at-
high-point ones), and the slight decreases and increases in the
amount of material devoted to complications and orientations
respectively. As Peterson and McCabe summarize, drawing on
other data in addition to that reproduced above:

> Niceties increasingly are present [in children's narratives],
> setting apart the narrative from the conversation. Abstracts tell
> what children are going to talk about; sophisticated codas bring
> the listener up to date about the narrated events. Older children
> have more differentiated as well as more usefully placed orien-
> tation, namely more clustered at the outset. They also use a
> richer variety of evaluations. But all children play a great deal
> of attention to this latter crucial component of narratives and
> place it where it is most useful – around the high point. (1983:
> 62)

When Peterson and McCabe subject the same corpus of stories
to a story-grammatical analysis they uncover an equally developmental picture. Most immediately visible is the steady increase
with age in both the length of narratives produced, and their
structural complexity. A broad and cumulative shift from
production of mere sequences (such as clusters of statements that
report descriptions or actions without any protagonist's motivations linking them up) to production of episodes (where some
sort of purposeful planned behaviour is explicitly asserted, or can
be inferred, from the actions of a protagonist) is also uncovered.
Sequences outnumber episodes in the 4-year-olds' narrative
structures by more than two to one; episodes outnumber
sequences in those of 9-year-olds by four to one.

But one type of sequence persists (often alongside episodes)
in narratives at every age examined: this is the reactive sequence,
in which

> a set of changes . . . automatically cause other changes with
> no planning involved. . . . Something happens that causes
> something else to happen, although there is no evidence of
> goals. (Peterson and McCabe, 1983: 71)

An example is the following, from a 6-year-old boy:

E: What happened in the accident that you saw?
L: Car got burned up.

E: A car got burned up? Tell me about what happened when the car got burned up.

L: There was three kids in there. Everybody got out in, just in time, and, and, and then, my Dad didn't keep his eyes on the road and we were almost *wrecked*.

E: You were almost wrecked?

L: *Yeahhhhh*. I wouldn't want that to happen. I'd be out of school about a *week*.

(Peterson and McCabe, 1983: 73)

Peterson and McCabe note both the increasing tendency for older children to focus on planning and the unexpected persistence of reactive sequences:

> Several investigators . . . have suggested that the goal-directed, problem-solving episode may have psychological reality. It may be an important underlying pattern that is used by people in processing and producing both fictional stories and narratives about actual life experiences. However, the present research suggests that it may not be the only one, since reactive sequences are common at all ages and cannot be described as goal-directed behaviour. It is inevitable that important things occur in the lives of children that are not planned, although they elicit reactions. Reactive sequences seem to be the best way of capturing the sense of these important externally imposed events. (1983: 99)

Another broad trend is the increased elaboration and embedding (roughly akin to coordination and subordination) within older children's narratives: multi-structure narratives, and structures within structures:

> Taken together, the findings suggest that older children pay more attention to psychological causality by specifying goals, and they also encompass more of their experience within a single narrative. When they give an entire episode or reactive sequence as a component of a larger episode, they are pulling away from a simple chronological recapitulation of events. Thus, they give a more fine-grained analysis of their experience. Their characters are more fleshed out and their narratives show more understanding of the roles people play with respect to each other. (1983: 99–100)

In specific response to Piaget's claim that young children have

deficient grasp of causality (a claim which itself is based on
findings of children's deficient mastery of causal connectives),
Peterson and McCabe (1983: 91) note the divergences in experimental research findings, depending on whether or not children's
apparent grasp of the *linguistic* means of marking causality is
treated as criterial:

> Of constrained experiments, then, those that look at children's
> understanding of causality irrespective of linguistic expression
> conclude that children have an incipient understanding of caus-
> ality as early as age 1.6, while those that look at language
> (specifically causal connectives) conclude that children do not
> understand causality until age 7 or beyond.

And, drawing on the evidence of the implicitly causal sequences
produced by even their youngest informants, they conclude:

> Overall, the conclusion that young children have little or no
> notion of causal relationships between events seems unwar-
> ranted, irrespective of their frequently-cited inability to appro-
> priately use causal connectives. In the present analysis, it is
> clear that the majority of the children's structures at all ages
> involve events that are causally linked, although this is increas-
> ingly true with age and these causal links are increasingly found
> within goal-directed episodes. (Peterson and McCabe, 1983:
> 92)

Peterson and McCabe's analyses of the sorts of narratives that
one set of children ranging in age from 4 to 9 actually produced
lend qualified support for both Labovian and story-grammatical
models of narrative structure. The support lies in the fact that,
with age, the children's narratives increasingly commonly match
the Labovian or story-grammatical paradigms; the qualification
lies in that other, non-Labovian, non-episodic structures continue
to be produced – and look coherent, reasonable, in no way
defective or aberrational.

If Peterson and McCabe supply abundant evidence of the
structural development in the narratives of children from age 4
to 9, Umiker-Sebeok (1979) gives us a vivid insight into the
younger child's coming-into-awareness of just what narratives are
and can do as a distinct type of social activity, a distinct field of
discourse. She reports a study of the intraconversational narratives of infants (3- to 5-year-olds) in their nursery schools. One
striking finding was the tendency of the youngest children to

produce narratives about situationally proximate matters, i.e., about events that had just occurred in their immediate environment (not just within the school but even within the same play period). The 3-year-olds did this in 89 per cent of their intraconversational narratives. The 5-year-olds, however, described events that occurred *outside* the preschool environment in 53 per cent of the total narratives – i.e., narratives about 'remote' matters. This looks like a striking example of learning to walk before attempting to run. Furthermore, Umiker-Sebeok found that, besides the development of the structurally fuller classic pattern also reported by others, the older children's narratives were far more interactive in nature than were those of the younger children:

> The narratives of very few 3-year-olds (17%) got any response at all from other children, in contrast to 61% of the 5-year-olds' narratives eliciting a response. Furthermore, the responses of older child listeners are more relevant to the narrative they've just heard. They often ask for information on orientative context, evaluation, and results, suggesting that they too share some notions of how narratives are to be structured, i.e., what elements are to be present. (Peterson and McCabe, 1983: 66)

It is interesting to compare all the above findings with those of Kernan (1977), who undertook a Labovian analysis of a much smaller corpus of narratives from somewhat older children – girls in three age bands: 7- to 8-year-olds, 10- to 11-year-olds, and 13- to 14-year-olds. One of the things Kernan found was that the older girls tended to supply an abstract or introducer (such as 'Well see, this what happen') far more regularly than the youngest group. Why this should have been so is hard to determine however, since some narratives were elicited by an interviewer's question, of a standard ('Were you ever really frightened?') or situated (i.e., arising out of the ongoing conversation) kind. More regular use of an introducer perhaps indicates a growing grasp of narrative organization, or perhaps simply a changing assessment of how much overt 'pointing up' of a narrative's beginning listeners need.

Less problematic however is Kernan's finding that older children, in identifying main characters, almost never supply just a name. Peterson and McCabe found the same trend, and a parallel development with regard to fuller identification of the locations of stories:

In fact, children get much better at answering all of the contextual questions of who, what, when, where, how, and why between 3.6 and 9.6 years of age. (Peterson and McCabe, 1983: 64)

But further to this, Kernan suggests that, as children enter their teens, the kind of background information that children supply is more and more built not so much on full designation of the factual specifics of time, place and characters, but rather on getting across information that will ensure proper 'uptake' of the story. As evidence for this he cites the use and distribution (in the various elements of a narrative) of a cluster of strategies of what may be termed 'reinforcement': the full or nearly-full repetition of a clause, or the supplying of a following clause that gives details, or specifies, or generalizes, relative to one or more previous clauses. These reinforcement techniques are common in each age group examined, but there is a sharp distributional switch: amongst the youngest girls, these strategies mostly occur in narrative clauses (of complication and resolution) and rarely in orientations, while in the oldest group they are rarely found in narrative clauses, but very commonly in clauses of orientation and evaluation.

The older children seem to be more interested in elaborating the background information necessary to a proper interpretation and understanding of the narrative than do the younger children. (Kernan, 1977: 99)

Nor, with regard to the younger children, should we assume that their frequent use of these strategies in the narrative sections of their stories means that those sections were particularly well organized. It seems that repetition, for example, was often used after apparent digression, so as to get the story back on the rails of the main story line. This is a very reasonable mechanism to adopt in such situations, one that persists in adult, conversation-embedded stories that are vulnerable to digression, interruption, or side-sequences:

Anyway, as I was saying, he got out of his car and came towards me. (constructed)

But it hardly functions in the enhancing or reinforcing way that is suggested by the term 'reinforcement' above: we might speculate that the reformulatory strategies cited function chiefly as a kind of repair mechanism in younger children's stories, and chiefly as a reinforcement mechanism in older children's stories.

Also of interest in Kernan's study is evidence of a change in relative frequency of use of two simple sets of clausal connectives: *and, then,* and *and then,* on the one hand (where the clauses so linked are said to be either quite independent of each other, or have only a temporal-sequential interrelation); and *so, so then,* and *and so then,* on the other hand (where the following clause is said to depend on the preceding one in order to be understood properly). Table 2 reproduces Kernan's percentages of total clauses introduced by these connectives.

Table 2 *Percentage of total clauses introduced by clausal connectives*

	Youngest (%)	Middle (%)	Oldest (%)
And, then, and then	55	42	28
So, and so, and so then	6	6	20

Finally, and perhaps most significantly of all, Kernan finds a steady growth, with age, of occurrence of clauses that serve what he calls an expressive function:

> clauses that indicate in some way the feelings of the narrator toward the events he is relating and that are used to attempt to convey that feeling to the audience. (Kernan, 1977: 101)

In Labovian terms, these are the means of evaluation that are external to the narrative clause. All such means (Labov distinguishes five sub-types, which I describe in 5.4) are overt or implicit expressions of the teller's attitude to the events she is recounting. It can be argued that they involve the self-as-teller maintaining a kind of distance from the self-as-protagonist – sufficient distance for that teller to be able to 'take up a position' on the events and protagonist. Viewing these expressivities in this light, it is highly significant that the most orientationally detached of these external devices, framed direct speech:

> I said, I'm getting out of here

is never used by Kernan's youngest age group, but becomes frequent later.

Confirmation of this development of perspectival control, this ability to frame one's own narration, is found in Hickmann's study (forthcoming) of children's ability to transform dialogues into cohesive texts (reported in Romaine, 1985: 91). Hickmann's youngest children (4-year-olds) never used direct or indirect quotation frames to separate the act of reporting from the speech that was reported, but used pitch and intonation signals to distinguish different speakers. Older children (7- to 10-year-olds) did, however, use direct quotation frames. Thus the progression is similar to that noted by Kernan, though Hickmann's tellers are using framed quotations earlier. Romaine comments:

> Hickmann views this age-related change in behaviour in Vygot-skyan terms as a movement from external to internal speech. The older children have acquired control over the metaprag-matic functions of language; that is, they have learned to use language to represent language and to guide non-linguistic actions. (Romaine, 1985: 91)

6.5   Narrative in relation to other registers: the systemic-linguistic approach

If narrative is only one use of language, how does it compare and contrast with others, and what are those others? And with regard to the development of language skills in children, is there perhaps too much attention to narrative style, and insufficient attention to other styles (argumentative, expository, etc.)? The work of James Martin and Joan Rothery, two linguists who adopt Halliday's systemic-linguistic approach, tackles just these questions. They have sought 'to identify some of the distinctive features of different genres and some features of development in [children's] writing' (Rothery and Martin, 1980: preface).

Rothery and Martin's work uses linguistic analysis to uncover how children's language skills develop (or fail to develop adequately). Rothery (1980) begins by noting that while all agree that ability to write effectively in a range of situations is a consider-able aid to the personal and intellectual development of the child on all fronts, many teachers remain unsure as to how best to nurture that ability. She argues that

> An understanding of register is essential if teachers are to plan effective writing situations, identify the distinctive linguistic features of different genres and develop strategies for assisting writers. (7)

By 'register' is meant a habitual pattern of language use in a common or well-recognized context of situation. And by 'context of situation' is meant the particular configuration of activity, topic, mode of communication, relationship between participants, and purpose in communicating. As indicated in 6.1, these major dimensions of situation are addressed, in Halliday's grammar, by the notions of field, mode and tenor. Notice incidentally that, as we should expect of any description of context (as distinct from text), field, mode and tenor are all dimensions strictly outside the text: they would exist even if there were no written or spoken text involved. (We could, for example, describe the field, mode and tenor relations of a wordless interaction where two strangers acknowledge each other as their paths cross on a country walk.)

Where language is involved, however, the extratextual facts of the field, mode and tenor will directly affect the format of the constructed discourse, the choices made in and from the lexico-grammar. In short, there is an infinite number of interactional situations people can find themselves in, and there are countless ways of speaking or writing. But between these infinite domains, there are certain institutionalized combinations of field, mode and tenor (i.e., canonical contexts) associated with equally strong norms for ways of using the language (i.e., registers). This is why Rothery stresses that

> Teachers . . . need to consider language development [in children] not simply in terms of mastery of the language system but in terms of developing texts in different registers. (1980: 37)

On the basis of their analysis of the kinds of writing children actually produce from kindergarten to the age of 18, Rothery and Martin have argued that there is a standard order in which registers (or genres: the two terms are used interchangeably) are mastered. The first genre or register to appear is what they call observation/comment, as in the following production from a 6-year-old:

> My surprise
> Oun day my mum bought me
> o some books. and I falte
> glad.
> (from Christie et al., 1984: 69)

This most basic type of written text, in which some personal experience is recorded together with an evaluative comment, is the foundation from which, it is argued, two major styles of writing develop: a narrative style and an expository style. The narrative style entails temporality and an affective trajectory; the expository style is a-temporal, has no affective trajectory, and is basically a process of describing by means of increasing depth and detail of analytical observation.

Accordingly, two genres appear a year or two after observation/comment in children's writing. Recount represents the first narrative-style genre to be grasped, while report is the first expository-style genre to be mastered. Recounts are a bald kind of narrative – a chronological sequence in Peterson and McCabe's terms: a series of events temporally sequenced, often with 'and then' as conjunctive link, optionally framed by an orientation and, at the close, a reorientation:

> I went to the Zoo. I saw the snake and then I saw the boa constrictor it was big and thick and the colour was green and brown. Then we went to the koala house and the baby koala and then we went down and then we went to see the seals and one fat one did not go in the water. . . . We sang Mr Postman and then the boat then we went to catch the train and we went home. (Christie et al., 1984: 73, from a 7-year-old)

Reports are a more factual and objective description than observation/comments, relatively depersonalized. Below I reproduce the developmental genre typology that Rothery and Martin propose. The two strands of the typology develop from left to right across the page, with the year of school in which a typical child begins to control a particular genre indicated underneath.

	recount narrative narrative personal vicarious	thematic narrative
Observation/ Comment		
	report exposition	literary criticism

Year of school	K	1	2	3	4	5	6	7	8	9	10	11	12
Age in years	5	6	7	8	9	10	11	12	13	14	15	16	17

As the diagram shows, in fourth grade children begin to write personal narratives. This genre, for Rothery and Martin, is distinguishable from recount since in a narrative events do not go smoothly: things that are awkward or unforeseen happen and need sorting out. Unlike recounts, then, narratives have evident complication and resolution sections (with an orientation section also and, sometimes, a coda). The above diagram sketches the broad pattern of written genre-development in the children studied: Rothery and Martin note that many children appear to develop their writing in ways that depart from this standard pattern. But they also, tentatively, report evidence of teachers' preference (as reflected in grading) for writing which includes expression of personal attitude or opinion: report-genre writing is less well received, graded lower. This, they speculate, may be unfortunate since, at secondary-school level, it is precisely the expository strand of writing, that is not personally expressive, that will predominate and be expected by teachers.

Fleshing out the picture of genre-development we can again draw on the notions of field, mode and tenor. As far as story subject-matter is concerned (one aspect of field), children progress from writing stories about personal experiences to writing ones about vicarious experience. In mode we see a shift to relative context-independence (far less reliance on accompanying pictures, less assumption of addressee's shared knowledge, and a growing grasp of the fact that texts *may* address a remote hypothetical audience, and not just the teacher and classmates). In tenor there are transitions from stories disclosing an inflexible spirit of solidarity with, for example, friends of the teller, to stories where there is far greater neutrality of tenor, where evaluations are no longer the stock counters such as 'yuck', 'grreat' and 'lovely'. Growing flexibility in control of tenor is of course part of a developing non-egocentric sense of point of view, of the possibility of writing a story from another's viewpoint.

Martin (1983) provides invaluable insight into the enlarging linguistic repertoire that indicates developing mastery of the register of narrative. His article describes the performance of 90 British schoolchildren of both sexes, of average ability and predominantly working-class, on several story-telling tasks. The population comprised 30 children in each of three age groups: 6- to 7-year-olds, 8- to 9-year-olds, and 10- to 11 year olds. Task 1 presented the child with a pile of cards that – in sequence – told a story about a frog purely by pictorial means. The cards were laid face down on the table; the child was simply asked to turn them over one at a time and tell what was happening in each. Task 2 involved setting aside the cards and retelling the story in his or her own words. Task 3 involved an interviewer reading a version of one of Aesop's fables to each child, and asking them to retell it in their own words. The three tasks clearly probe the child's ability to handle related but different tasks: the target text of the third task (being a fable) is generically somewhat unlike those of the other two tasks, while these differ from each other with regard to contextual dependency. In relation to the linguistic systems of reference and conjunction, in particular, Martin found the youngest group of children producing more context-dependent text, with an impoverished repertoire of conjunctive relations (chiefly just additive), than the older children. Before demonstrating this, a few notes on reference and conjunction are in order.

> Reference is the semantic system whereby participants are identified in English text. It draws a basic distinction between participants that the speaker thinks his listener knows the identity of and those he introduces to the text for the first time. 'Given' participants are realized through demonstratives, the definite article, and pronouns, whereas 'new' participants are presented in indefinite nominal groups (*the man* v. *a man*, for example). (Martin, 1983: 11)

In the chart of reference options below (taken from Martin, 1983:11), the most basic choice between introducing an entity as new or alluding to an entity as given, is labelled as a choice between presenting and presuming.

Within the types of referring that presume the listener can retrieve the information, each terminal label indicates just where

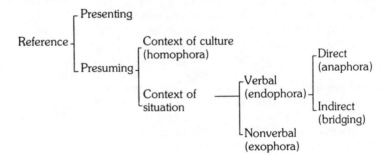

the listener has to go to identify the entity referred to. Thus homophoric reference obtains when, even on first mention of this person, British speakers say 'The Queen looked wonderfully relaxed on telly last night': there is no need to specify *which* queen is being denoted. Similarly homophoric will be references to the moon, the sun, and so on. Presuming reference that involves a co-textual verbal tie may be direct (e.g. by way of pronouns such as *she* and *it*) or indirect, via the bridging links that are discussed in 6.6. Most significant in analysis of children's text production is the reliance, on both first and subsequent mention, on exophoric reference to immediate context, standardly by means of a definite noun phrase (*the frog*) where more mature storytellers would be expected to follow the convention of *presenting* the entity as new on first mention, and drawing an anaphoric means of reference in subsequent mentions. Compare these two retellings (task 2) of the frog story, from a 6- to 7-year old boy and a 10- to 11-year-old girl respectively (exophoric nominal groups are underlined, noun phrases involving bridging inferences are in bold face):

1 Well there was a frog in the jar. The boy was looking it in the jar with the frog. then the boy was in bed and the frog jumped out. then it was morning. the frog then the boy looked in the jar and he saw the frog was gone. then he got dressed no then he looked in the boots his boots. Then it wasn't there. Then he looked out **the window**. The dog got the jar on and then the dog fell out. Then the jar broke. then he called for the frog. Then the then a deer came. He got then he climbed on the uh rock and then a deer came and got the boy on **the antlers**. then he ran and then the deer stopped. Then the boy fell in the river. Then they sat down and then the dog was on the boy's head. Then they looked over the log. Then they saw the family. Then **the little babies** came out. Then the boy walked in the river.

2 Tommy was laying at the bottom of his bed looking at his pet frog with his dog. While he was asleep with the dog on his bed the frog tried to get out of the glass jar. **The next morning** they saw the frog had gone. So they looked out the window and the dog had a glass on his head. The dog fell out the window and smashed the glass and Tommy came out and held the dog and the dog licked his face and they called for him. They went down to **the woods** and there was a swarm

of bees coming out of a bee-hive. He went to the top of a rock and **the next minute** he was on top of a reindeer. The dog went behind the rock and the next thing they knew the reindeer was running after the dog with Tommy on his head. They fell into the water off a cliff top and Tommy saw a hollow tree so they both went over the tree and Tommy told his dog to be quiet and they saw his pet frog and another frog and lots of baby frogs. Tommy took one of the baby frogs home with him. (Martin, 1983: 19–20)

By contrast with the seven exophoric nominals introducing participants in text 1, Martin finds only two in text 2 (arguably the first mention of Tommy is a third). But the generally appropriate management of entity-introduction (appropriate in relation to mainstream storytelling conventions) in text 2 clearly contrasts with inappropriate means in text 1. (And the 'definite reference' introduction of 'Tommy' in text 2 can be defended as a *conforming* to story introduction conventions: we often dispense with the near-redundant 'There was a boy called Tommy'). Again, when we consider the bridging references in the two texts, it is the mainstream norms of appropriacy that highlight 'the little babies' in text 1 as rather awkward. Whether any of the three noun phrases Martin puts in bold face in text 2 really involves a bridging interpretation is questionable: two are more simply temporal connectives, not entities in the story; the third seems predominantly exophoric, but in any event not hard to interpret given the preceding text with its dog and frog. These queries of Martin's labelling highlight the way that whenever a lexico-grammatical descriptive system attempts to capture differences to do with meaning, then different analysts are unlikely to produce identical analyses. This problem is endemic in meaning-oriented language analysis; however, this is no reason for jettisoning the system, but rather for making its categories more explicit: the important point is that, to a substantial extent, my analysis would tally with Martin's.

What is more interesting to realize is that, for example, frequency of noun phrases involving bridging is not in itself an index of maturity: rather it is increasingly appropriate recourse to bridging that we should look for. Nor do the above remarks even broach the question of intention, though that issue is surely important. For example, did the speaker of text 1 *intend* us to bridge between 'the family' and 'the little babies'? One final point to consider would be the ways in which entity introductions that are identical in terms of the system of choices set out above are yet substantially different as regards effective storytelling. Thus first mention of the frog in both texts is by means of presenting, but notice how much more appropriate is the fuller description in text 2, *his pet frog*, than the bald *the frog* in text 1. The special relationship between boy and frog conveyed in text 2 fails to be explicitly recorded in text 1. Similarly contrast the narrative adequacy of 'his pet frog and another frog and lots of baby frogs' in text 2 with the multitudinous possible referents of 'the family', the description that is its counterpart in text 1.

Limits of space preclude extended discussion of conjunction (but see the notes and exercises at the end of this chapter). However, it is worth recording that Martin finds that, on task 3 especially, the older children's texts break free from the narrow dependence on additive conjunctive relations (*and* and *or*) found in the youngest children's versions of the fable. The older children explicitly use (not merely imply) temporal and consequence conjunctions, in addition to additive ones.

Stories for and with children   6.6

Much of the research reported above, on the kinds of stories children produce, would suggest that even at a very early age, even under 2, children have a well-developed sense of what happens in stories and what they can expect in them. They expect one or more characters, human or personified, one of whom they can firmly identify with or emphatically reject. They expect interesting or amusing things to be caused by or to happen to the main character(s), and they expect there to be some difficulty or worry resolved happily by the close. Children's stories rarely have the coda 'And they all lived happily ever after' today, but the sense of a happy outcome remains the norm. But if those are the bare bones of stories for, especially, pre-literate children, it also needs to be stressed that the popularity of particular published stories for children rests on their creative departures from and exploitations of the mainstream norms. This blend of the standard and the unexpected, the given and the new, very probably answers to a child's need for both the reassurance provided by the familiar and the mental stimulation provoked by the unexpected.

Now it might be argued that the requirements of reassurance

and mental disturbance apply to narratives for all ages, but there seems not to be as strong an emphasis on the instructional function of stories for older readers. Accordingly, both traditional and original stories for the young are often marked by their structural similarity to fables, and their 'happy outcome' codas often carry an implicit moral that could be cast as a generic sentence or proverb. Relatedly, fiction for adults permits all sorts of unreliability of narration, and immoralities of thought and action that go uncondemned and unpunished within the narrative. In stories for young children, by contrast, narration is almost invariably – and marvellously – reliable, reliably reporting good conquering evil.

In what follows I want to discuss the text of one or two stories for young children, noting both those elements that confirm and conform to the canonical format and those aspects that are absorbing and entertaining breaches of the norm. I will begin with the text of a very simple story that combines – as do all those I will discuss – text and pictures:

Mooty and Grandma

1 Mooty was a lovely little mouse. He had twinkling eyes and a long curly tail.
2 One day, Mooty fell asleep under Grandma's favourite chair. His long curly tail lay in a coil on the floor. He dreamt of cheese and bread crumbs. He dreamt of sweets and juicy plums.
3 His tail twitched as he dreamt. It curled and it straightened. It straightened and it curled till his dreams stopped. Then it lay quietly in a little gentle curve on the floor.
4 Grandma came into the room. 'Oh, how careless I am,' she thought. 'I've dropped my sewing thread again.' She bent to pick the long strand of thread from the floor.
5 Poor Mooty! Poor Grandma! 'Help!' screamed Mooty as he tried to wiggle free. 'Help!' screamed Grandma as she dropped him on the floor.
6 Mooty ran into his hole as fast as his legs could carry him. Grandma ran into the kitchen as fast as her legs could carry her. They both quivered and shook. Poor Mooty! Poor Grandma!

(Jessie Wee and Kwan Shan Mei, *Mooty and Grandma*, Federal Publications, 1980)

Some observations as to the role played by the illustrations that accompany this text may be in order. The pictures perform many functions: tautologically, we can say they depict, but we should clarify what that in turn involves. First, to depict is to supply visual validation or confirmation of what the text asserts. Thus the first frame depicts a green Mooty, in lovable pose, with huge ears, large bright eyes, and long curling tail, dressed in a red lungi and red slippers. The text's asserted descriptions are thus confirmed, and young listeners in need of reminders of what 'mouse', 'twinkling' and 'curly tail' mean can profit from the kind of **ostensive definition** the picture provides. In addition, for viewers alert to such things, the lungi and slippers, together with his name, identify Mooty as an Asian mouse.

Pictures thus regularly confirm, clarify, explain, and elaborate (for example, the picture of Mooty's dream shows more types of edible goodies than the text lists). At a more abstract level, pictures stimulate the child to grasp that words can represent pictorial scenes even when no scenes are provided in advance. The business of experiencing and understanding the implications of text/scene matching, which all illustrated stories nurture, is a crucial step to the more decontextualized children's story, the one with text alone, where the child is required to produce in her own mind, using her imaginative resources, satisfying mental pictures of what is going on. This important progression is surely one of the clearest cases of Vygotskyan interpersonal capability becoming transformed or enlarged so as to become an intrapersonal one.

Grammatically, we have here several of the characteristic means of supplying an orientation and reporting complicating action. The main character is introduced by means of stative verbs of relation, in which his name, his species, and his most crucial plot-determining attribute (his long tail) are recorded. From these permanent states, caption 2 focusses on a singular occasion of Mooty's sleeping and dreaming, with imaginative depiction of what Warren *et al.* (1979) would call the internal psychological cause for his tail's enthusiastic twitching. Accordingly, the text's elaborate drawing of the reader's attention to the moving tail in caption 3 seems well motivated, even though the tail really needs to be still when Grandma sees it. In reporting the preparatory steps to that encounter, the tail's actions are reported in the expected format: dynamic verbs in past tense and active voice, with the tail as subject, and repetition of the salient feature of setting – 'on the floor' in captions 2 and 3. The most important narrative development prior to Grandma's intervention is reported at the close of caption 3, where the verb *lay*, that is open to both stative and dynamic interpretations, is used. We readers-listeners know that here the stative description is also terminative, a point of rest after all the excitement (of the dream) is spent. For Grandma, however, there is not even a residual impression that what she sees as inert could ever be mobile.

We should also take account of the significant role played by inference and implicit messages, even in such a simple text as this Mooty episode. Notice, for example, that there is no explicit textual confirmation, in caption 4, that what Grandma interprets to be a thread is in fact Mooty's tail. (The accompanying picture manages to avoid clarification: it shows Grandma's reaching hand, and the thread/tail, but not the rest of Mooty's body.) Similarly, although caption 4 ends by reporting that Grandma 'bent to pick the long strand of thread from the floor', there is no direct reporting of Grandma's act of picking it up, nor of her immediate shock of realization. Both of these have to be inferred in the light of the caption and picture that follow. Even in simple stories for the very young, then, it seems that important plot-developing judgments and events may sometimes be left implicit, to be inferred, rather than spelt out. Whether this is a good thing deserves more detailed review. My own impressions of my children's reactions to the Mooty story are that they do make the necessary inferences, and are aware of the logic of cause and effect involved. But we should not dismiss out of hand a very different view, which might argue that in stories for very young children who may not yet have properly grasped the orthodoxies of sequence and consequence we require in narratives, it is ill-judged to have stories that fail to reinforce those orthodoxies as explicitly as they might.

The text above comprises the first of the two episodes that make up the story. In the second episode a flour-blanched Mooty, and Grandma in her white nightclothes again manage to terrify each other, with the same parallel reporting of their ludicrous and reciprocal misapprehensions:

'I've seen a ghost,' they both cried as they pulled their blankets over their heads.

The outcome of these episodes, then, is an interesting variant of the 'happy outcome' norm, heavily mitigated, however, since the child knows that the characters' misery is unjustified, laughable. And behind the laughter lies a clear fable-like message, of how unfortunate inter-species misapprehensions may stem from fear, ignorance, and reliance more on prejudiced impressions than close scrutiny. The clear analogy here with inter-racial and inter-ethnic relations almost certainly should not be spelt out to the child. It is more important that they get the general point that appearances and impressions can be deceptive.

Another story that can be seen creatively blending departures from and conformities to mainstream cultural and textual norms for children's stories is *Burglar Bill* by Janet and Allan Ahlberg. Bill is a decent, hardworking thief who in the course of his work acquires a 'nice big brown box with little holes in it'. Upon returning home he discovers that it contains a baby, and is introduced to the responsibilities of care-giving (as distinct from those of property-taking). That same night Bill himself is burgled, but he catches the intruder – Burglar Betty – redhanded. When these two professionals get into conversation it transpires, in the fine traditions of the eighteenth-century novel, that Betty is the widowed mother of the baby Bill has acquired. This well-matched pair repent their wrongdoings, make literal restitution by taking everything they've stolen back, and begin a new life together (a church wedding, in white). Burglar Bill becomes Baker Bill.

That story summary should indicate fairly clearly how the unorthodoxy of having a burglar as hero becomes only transitional to the final state of rampant nuclear family orthodoxy. But there are textual unorthodoxies here too: there is a jaunty sense of the unusual in the way Bill's life as a burglar is described, very much at odds with the high moral assumptions of the orthodox children's story. Much of the jauntiness of the opening lies simply in the brazen recurrence of the adjective *stolen*, even in cases where we suspect the narrator of dishonest exaggeration:

> Burglar Bill lives by himself in a tall house full of stolen property. Every night he has stolen fish and chips and a cup of stolen tea for supper. Then he swings a big stolen sack over his shoulder and goes off to work, stealing things. Every morning Burglar Bill comes home from work and has stolen toast and marmalade and a cup of stolen coffee for breakfast. Then he goes upstairs and sleeps all day in a comfortable stolen bed.

But the non-standardness extends to speech as well as behaviour: Bill and Betty speak vivid working-class Cockney English.

Together they produce dialogue such as the following, a long way from the 'correct' mainstream speech that dominates children's stories:

> 'Who are you?' says Burglar Bill.
> 'I'm Burglar Betty,' says the lady. 'Who are you?'
> Burglar Bill puts on his own mask.
> 'Oh,' says Burglar Betty, 'I know you – it's Burglar Bill! I seen your picture in the *Police Gazette*.' Then she says, 'Look here, I'm ever so sorry – breaking in like this. If I'd have known . . .'
> 'Don't mention it,' says Burglar Bill. He holds out his hand. 'Pleased to meet you.'
> 'Likewise, I'm sure,' Burglar Betty says.

And with this tenor of discourse established between the pair, there's more than a hint of tolerant mockery of our standard expressions when Bill, repenting, declares:

> I can see the error of my ways . . . I've been a bad man.

The final children's story I will consider is the magnificent *Bear Goes to Town* by Anthony Browne. Bear has a magic pencil, so that whatever he draws comes into existence (itself a subtle exploitation of the requirement of text-to-pictures match discussed earlier). Although his good friend Cat is seized and imprisoned by menacing guards, Bear uses his pencil to free Cat and some other animals, and resettle them in a pastoral setting far from the threats of the town. The core of the plot, then, is slight. What is absorbing however is the extent to which the details over and above the basic plot create a richness of thematic texture. This texturing is achieved more by the messages in the pictures than the words, and it is quite striking just how dependent the story is on the pictures to articulate developments and connections that the text does not spell out. Consequently a rather high degree of inference-making is required in the reader/listener. And it is only when higher levels of theme and analogy are considered that several scenes can be understood as properly motivated parts of the narrative rather than somewhat incidental occurrences in a mere report or sequence. Thus the second frame of the story book depicts Bear, in town, being knocked over by the human traffic that dwarfs him, and the accompanying text reads, in part,

> It was rush hour. Bear was small and people could not see him. They knocked him down.

Strictly irrelevant to the main plot, and evidently an accidental mishap, this incident can nevertheless be treated as presaging the threat to the animals that humans constitute, indicative of how vulnerable animals are to human power. The next frame has a cat's face looking down into Bear's, the latter still lying flat on his back from the fall. The caption simply reads 'Bear saw big yellow eyes looking down at him.' Without any further introduction, Cat becomes a full participant in the story – the text continues:

'What is that?' asked Cat, looking at Bear's pencil.
'It's my magic pencil,' said Bear.
'Then draw me something to eat,' said Cat.

Somehow Cat has immediately understood just how Bear's magic pencil works – and the child reader has to accept that Cat understands. This seems to have less to do with standard inference-making and more to do with this particular story's chosen dynamics of informativeness. In other words, the interpretive leap assumed in Cat, expected in the reader, is just one of many sense-making bridges that the child has to supply when reading this story. And, what is equally important to report, if the experience of my own child and her peers is representative, it seems that these sense-making demands are not baffling, not beyond them, but rather make *Bear Goes to Town* a favourite story, preferred to the bulk of stories for 3-year-olds, which conform to a plodding explicitness of informational links between actions and reactions.

In the course of this chapter I have attempted to show that, behind their seeming simplicity and playfulness, stories for and by children are, on closer consideration, remarkably complex, and an aid to and index of the interactional and cognitive development of the child. Relative to respective ages and quantities of experience, the fact that many adults do cope with Joyce's 'Eveline' (and *Ulysses*) seems a far less impressive achievement than that 3-year-olds manage to cope with *Bear Goes to Town*. When one makes allowances for the age of the child and her limited acquaintance with story processing and story production, one is almost drawn to end on a gloomy note, and remark on how scant is the enlargement of reading and writing skills in many adults. Be that as it may, what should be abundantly clear is that all the key elements of sophisticated narratives, as discussed in the foregoing chapters of this book, seem present in simpler form in children's narratives: causal connectivity of events, temporal

order and reordering, scenic and summarized presentation, focalization, inferred linkage, and so on.

One curious effect in *Bear Goes to Town* seems striking
confirmation that 3- and 4-year-olds are already aware of the
way narrative voice can shift. In the middle of the story, there is
a scene where Bear is absorbed by a shop's window display and
Cat walks on along the street, unaware that a menacing black-
coated figure is lurking in a doorway. In a sudden departure from
the narrative's neutral reportage stance, the text suddenly cries
'Look out, Cat!'. It is fascinating to see just how regularly children
comment on this as they hear the story – especially if they are
hearing it for the first time. 'Who says that?', they ask, or 'Where
did that come from?' Who indeed? – whether this modulation of
voice is best described as one from the impersonal to the
personal, or from the extradiegetic to the intradiegetic, the
important thing is to have recognized – as these infant readers,
astonishingly, clearly do – that a shift in narratorial voice has
occurred.

Further reading

In the area of children's narrative development, the following are
simply a small selection from a very long list: Peterson and
McCabe (1983), Cazden (1981), Applebee (1978), Piaget
(1926), Vygotsky (1962), Christie *et al.* (1984); and, from a
systemic-linguistic perspective, in addition to Rothery and Martin
(1980) and Christie *et al.* (1984), Hasan (1984) is a probing
study of generic possibilities in the structure of nursery tales. On
the use of stories in emergent literacy, see Farr (1985). A special
issue of the *Journal of Education* (1985) looks at the question of
differing storytelling styles from a number of angles; Bennett-
Kastor (1983, 1986) focusses on the growing syntactic complexity
of children's narratives; and Galda and Pellegrini (1985) is a
recent collection with several useful contributions on preschool
narrative 'play'.

Cook-Gumperz and Green (1984) question the assumption
that children's storytelling is based on an adult model of the
narrative form. They suggest that, on the basis of familiarity with
picture story books, the child may develop a model of what a
story consists of as including both pictures and words, so that
when they are asked to tell a story they try to 'tell a book'. Heath's
Ways with Words (1983) is particularly to be recommended: it

is developing 'landmark' status as an exemplary way of doing properly contextualized study of language in use. A long-term participant-observer of the communities she describes, Heath's ethnographical perspective means that careful consideration is given to the numerous bases which, taken together, nurture and validate these different 'ways with words': not just race, but also education, socioeconomic status, employment, religion, family pattern, and cultural practices. As a result her subjects emerge as people, not stereotypes. Romaine (1985) contains brief but interesting and comparable commentary on narrative development in a group of Scottish adolescents.

As the reader may have gathered from allusions in 6.4, an immense body of psycholinguistic research has been undertaken into the questions of whether humans develop mental frameworks specifying the standardly-accepted linear and hierarchical structuring of stories, and which frameworks they can then use as an aid in the comprehension, storage and recall of actual stories. These mental frameworks are termed **story schemas**, and their probable configuration can be represented on the page as a grammar. Hence researchers in this area are often described as story-grammarians. The issue of whether people do have, in their heads, such **default formats** for stories, and unconsciously invoke them in comprehension and recall, remains controversial but fascinating, with numerous implications for studies in other disciplines. I have space here only to direct the reader to some key texts in the literature: Rumelhart (1975; 1977), Mandler and Johnson (1977), and Stein and Glenn (1979). A rather different psycholinguistic approach is advocated by Warren, Nicholas and Trabasso (1979), who attempt to specify the basic types of logical, informational and evaluative inferences that story-processors must use in comprehension. The work of Clark (1977) and his associates is yet another approach to inference theory. A valuable overview of the entire field is contained in Chapter 7 of Brown and Yule (1983); Schank and Abelson (1977) and Johnson-Laird (1981) are rather more advanced treatments.

Notes and exercises

1 The story-grammars mentioned in the 'further reading' section above often adjudge that the simplest stories are about a situation in which some want arises and prompts an action which helps

fulfil the want, or prompts proceeding to some different action. An 'if . . . then . . .' logic is particularly visible in such schemes.

It may be that such simple schemes are themselves most apparent in stories for young children, who are only just beginning to encounter stories in books. Consider the following text, for example, which is taken from a words-and-pictures storybook entitled *Dear Zoo*, by Rod Campbell.

> I wrote to the zoo to send me a pet. They sent me an . . . [flapped picture of an elephant]. He was too big! I sent him back.
> So they sent me a . . . [flapped picture of a giraffe]. He was too tall! I sent him back.
> So they sent me a . . . [flapped picture of a lion]. He was too fierce! I sent him back.
> So they sent me a . . . [flapped picture of a camel]. He was too grumpy! I sent him back.
> So they sent me a . . . [flapped picture of a snake]. He was too scary! I sent him back.
> So they sent me a . . . [flapped picture of a monkey]. He was too naughty! I sent him back.
> So they sent me a . . . [flapped picture of a frog]. He was too jumpy! I sent him back.
> So they thought very hard, and sent me a . . . [flapped picture of a puppy]. He was perfect! I kept him.
> (comments in square brackets are my additions)

The storybook is aimed at children still some way from actual reading, but old enough, and familiar enough with books, to participate while an older person reads the text. At every point in the text where there is ellipsis indicated above, the child has to lift a flap representing one side of a crate or container. And behind the flap, of course, lurks a picture of the animal to be identified and named by the child.

Comment on the sorts of skills and understanding that such a book may nurture in the child. Think especially about the idea of storytelling collaboration mentioned both in 5.10 and 6.2; about appropriate timing of the flap-lifting; about the skills of recognition, recall and naming that are involved; of how the text performs the two fundamental Labovian functions, of reference and evaluation, in a particularly overt way; and of the association of attributes with individuals in the course of characterization, which was discussed in relation to literature in 4.3 and 4.4.

2 Below are reproduced the opening paragraphs of William Faulkner's novel, *The Sound and the Fury*. This first part of the novel is narrated and focalized by Benjy, the 33-year-old youngest son in the Compson family, on his birthday. Benjy is mentally retarded and has the mind of a very young child; he is pathetically attached to his memories of his sister Caddy, who now lives far away. Luster is a black teenager 'minding' Benjy.

> Through the fence, between the curling flower spaces, I could see them hitting. They were coming toward where the flag was and I went along the fence. Luster was hunting in the grass by the flower tree. They took the flag out, and they were hitting. Then they put the flag back and they went to the table, and he hit and the other hit. Then they went on, and I went along the fence. Luster came away from the flower tree and we went along the fence and they stopped and we stopped and I looked through the fence while Luster was hunting in the grass.
>
> 'Here, caddie.' He hit. They went away across the pasture. I held to the fence and watched them going away.
>
> 'Listen at you, now.' Luster said. 'Aint you something, thirty-three years old, going on that way. After I done went all the way to town to buy you that cake. Hush up that moaning. Aint you going to help me find that quarter so I can go to the show tonight.'
>
> They were hitting little, across the pasture. I went back along the fence to where the flag was. It flapped on the bright grass and the trees.
>
> 'Come on.' Luster said. 'We done looked there. They aint no more coming right now. Lets go down to the branch and find that quarter before them niggers finds it.'
>
> It was red, flapping on the pasture. Then there was a bird slanting and tilting on it. Luster threw. The flag flapped on the bright grass and the trees. I held to the fence.

Discuss Benjy's text in relation to

(a) textual signalling of temporality, and causality (or lack of such signals); where there is lack of explicit temporal connectives, how pervasive is an *iconic* conveying of implicit temporal progression (i.e., where the order of clauses matches the order of the events, in actuality, that they report)?

(b) topic-associating *v.* topic-centered discourse: does the style of Benjy's text fit either of these styles?

(c) orientation: it was argued in 6.4 that maintaining an orientation, and signalling a switch in orientation, are things that young children take time to master. To what extent is orientation under control in this text?

(d) episodic structure: it was also argued in 6.4 that children's stories evince a progression from a preponderantly reactive-sequence structure to a goal-directed episodic structure. Is Benjy's text an episode (or series of episodes), or a sequence (or series of sequences), or some mixture of these two?

3 There is a fundamental assumption within Michaels' and others' treatment of the dichotomy between oral-style and literate-style storytelling by infants that needs fuller review. This is the assumption that the two styles, the two ways of narrativizing experience, are 'equal but different'. Similarly, Wolf (1984:71) argues that 'children from different language backgrounds all have systematic repertoires of narrative genres and registers' and that the challenge is for educators to recognize those skills, and use them as a link to literacy. Now that last point I wholeheartedly support: whatever the repertoires – however 'literacy-removed' – a child is identified using, somehow these systems have to be built on, rather than simply ignored or overriden, in the fostering of literate language use, i.e. written language with its reduced integration with immediate situational context but enhanced cotextual articulation.

But the question remains: are the oral and literate styles equally effective ways of making sense of human experience? Can we demonstrate that both ways are equal as representations of logical and cognitive grasp of the events we witness and value? The secondary issue, of whether those two styles are equal in the real world, is one we can address subsequently; but we should first consider whether these two styles are equal as effectively sense-making, suitably interpretive, and successfully message-conveying formats. If they are, then we might wonder whether promoting a rather sharp change of style, as when oral-style users are encouraged to develop a literate 'code', is justified. Why shouldn't such oral-style users continue with their 'equal but different' style in their written language? The self-evident answer to this, that oral-style prosody-based signalling just won't work in written language, should prompt us to ask further why the oral-style will not work.

It is arguable that the question here is not just one of effective and recognizable signalling. Prosodic cohesion could be signalled (and taught). If we can teach literate-style children to write *because* when, in speech, they would say /bɪkəz/, we can also teach children to write *then* when, in speech, they say /ðɛn/. (If someone complains 'But we don't do that in standard writing style' the reply should be 'Exactly!')

The real problem may not be to do with different-style prosody, but different-style topic-treatment. To repeat the earlier question, now just focussing on the divergence between topic-centred and topic-associating styles: can educators and others be confident that narratives that are 'a series of associated segments that may seem anecdotal in character, with implicit links but no explicit statement of an overall theme or point, with numerous shifts of spatiotemporal orientation and focus and the impression [to white middle-class outsiders] of lacking an ordered beginning, middle and end' are really as effective a way of making sense, and communicating that sense, of the world around us?

4   Once there was a dog named Whiskers. He got run over, because he ran in front of a car. He was very sick after. He had to be rushed to hospital by Ambulance and fast. At the end he ended up dieing isn't that 'Sad'
(quoted in Christie et al., 1984: 78)

Analyze the text above in relation to the linguistic features of narrative genre that Rothery and Martin have drawn attention to:

(a) the types of processes the verbs express (on process-types, see 4.7)
(b) the types and variety of lexical items
(c) the consistency or variation of sentential **theme** (see glossary)
(d) the manner of introducing protagonists and making subsequent reference to them
(e) the types of conjunctive relations (additive, temporal, causal, or of comparison) there are between clauses, whether explicitly or only implicitly.

5 Compare and contrast the types of conjunctions used in the following fable retellings. These are taken from Martin (1983: 32), the first coming from a 6- to 7-year-old boy, the second from a 10- to 11-year-old girl.

1 There was a donkey and he had sacks of sugar and they were too heavy. He went in some water and he got out and the sugar wasn't heavy and he had another sack with

sponges and they were too heavy. He went in the water and he drowned.

2 There was a donkey and he was carrying some sacks of sugar on his back and it was a very hot day and the donkey was tired. Soon he came to a stream and to get home he had to cross the stream; but at the bottom of the stream it was very muddy; so when the donkey stepped in he sank; but then he decided to have a little rest and when he got up he found that the sacks were very much lighter than they were before; so that didn't bother him; and that's because all the sugar had melted in the stream; so there was none left. Another time the donkey had some sponges in the sacks and again he had to cross the stream; so he thought last time he went in the stream the sacks got lighter; so he thought he'd do it again on purpose; so he stepped in and when he and after a short while when he got up again he found that the sacks were very heavy and that's because all the sponges collected water and he found that he couldn't walk very well and so that's what happens if you don't know the difference between sponges and sugar.

Under the umbrella term 'conjunction' you should consider here two independent bases of subclassification:

(a) semantic or logical type – the four basic logical types of connective are **additive**, **temporal**, **consequential** (including purpose, cause, condition, and concession), and **comparative** (contrast and similarity)
(b) implicit or explicit – is the conjunctive relation explicitly expressed or simply to be logically inferred? For example, we infer an implicit temporal relation – in addition to the explicit additive one – between the following two clauses in text 1:

He went in some water and he got out.

6 A third basis for subcategorizing conjunctive relations concerns whether those relations are external or internal.

External conjunctive relations make connections between propositions about the real world. *Internal* relations make rhetorical connections between speech acts. (Martin, 1983: 21)

This distinction may be best teased out by way of examples:

1 I'll get some dinner if you'd like some.

2 Dinner's ready if you want some.
3 John went to the shops because I told him to.
4 John was at the shops because I saw him there.

In the subordinate clauses of sentences 1 and 3 we are given a condition and a reason respectively, each denoting a real-world situation that is said to be the prerequisite, or the cause, respectively, of 'making dinner' or 'John's going to the shops'. Notice that the order of clauses in these sentences can be reversed without creating incoherence:

If you like, I'll get some dinner.

This is often possible with external conjunctive relations, rarely so with internal relations as in sentences 2 and 4. Compare:

(??) If you want some, dinner's ready.

Relatedly, contrast the possibility of negating both clauses where the conjunctive relation is external, with the implausible results when this is attempted with internally conjunctive clauses:

I won't get any dinner, if you wouldn't like any.
(??)Dinner isn't ready, if you don't want any.

With internal conjunctive relations, each second clause is some kind of justification for the claim or offer made in the first clause. Hence Martin's emphasis that external relations link proposition to proposition, while internal ones link speech act to speech act. The former feel more like genuine world-disclosing causes, conditions, etc; they allude directly to a world external to the text, while the latter are oriented to adjacent propositions within the text. A final simple test that will often highlight the internal type by contrast with the external is the possibility of inserting 'I say this' immediately before the conjunction in question:

John was at the shops; I say this because I saw him there.
Dinner's ready; I say this if (in case) you want some.
(??)I'll get some dinner; I say this if you'd like some.

Now this lengthy excursus to distinguish internal and external conjunctions is only tangentially relevant to narrative, for in narratives virtually all conjunctive relations tend to be of the external kind. But the important point is that when young writers proceed to other, expository, genres of writing, they find that internal relations are more prominent and need to be mastered. That is to say, writers of analytical essays, reports and literary criticism have to become skilled at explicitly signalling the logical links between their claims, proposals, and questions. Martin sums up some of the broader contrasts between narrative and exposition as follows:

> The schematic structure of a narrative of vicarious experience is basically Orientation ⌃ Complication ⌃ Resolution (cf. Labov and Waletzky, 1967) while that of exposition is Introduction ⌃Argument⌃Conclusion. The thematic development of narrative involves heroes while that of sophisticated exposition involves abstract ideas. Conjunction in narrative is largely external, with temporal relations, particularly successive ones, predominating. In exposition consequential and comparative relations are much more prominent and the texts depend crucially on internal relations of similarity. . . . Finally, lexical cohesion in a story tends to involve concrete words referring to people, places, or things in a real or imagined world while in exposition many lexical strings involve abstractions from this world. These patterns repeat themselves over and over again in narration and exposition in such a way that there can be no doubt that genre exists. Moreover, genre is clearly something students recognize their texts must approximate if they are to succeed in the cultural context in which they are written. Teachers, whether or not they give students models of the genre at stake, by and large demand this approximation. (Martin, 1980: 24)

7 Finally, and in a less strenuous vein than the preceding notes, we might consider more fully the content of young children's spontaneous stories, and also why they are told. My informal impressions are that my daughter's earliest, two-proposition narratives were usually recalls of particularly salient recent experiences that had happened to her or to someone very close to her (her mother, her brother, a friend). And most typically these tellings seemed designed and intended to secure the addressee's active sympathy, rather than to inform, to shock, to entertain, etc. Among older children, judging by the kinds of content Peterson and McCabe encountered, the goals of informing and shocking, by means of stories about disasters, accidents, and fights, involving 'pain, gore and keystone cop style mishaps', seem to predominate. Be alert to the spontaneously-offered stories of any children you encounter, and determine whether

the stories you hear confirm the above general speculations, or run counter to them, and why.

7 Narrative as political action

7.1 The contexts of narratives

In the previous chapter considerable attention was paid to children's growing control of narrative texts as decontextualized. When we say that narrative text is **decontextualized** we mean it is possible – indeed it is a mainstream cultural preference – for story texts to stand on their own, without the need to rely on extra clarifying communications (verbal or gestural) between teller and immediately-present addressee, nor any intense reliance on shared background knowledge of teller and addressee. As Martin and others were shown arguing in Chapter 6, adequate decontextualization only comes when the child-teller has grasped – among other things – how to introduce characters and signal reference and use a range of explicit conjunctive relations in the standard ways, and has become a good judge of whether information increments should be overtly conveyed or can be left to be inferred. Such decontextualization is a development of one's language as a communicative resource that both builds on and departs from the canonical situation of utterance as described in the quotation from Lyons (1977) in 4.13. And it bears repeating that these techniques of decontextualization are matters of language-manipulation and genre- and convention-observance that are not immediately obvious to the novice and have to be learned (Umiker-Sebeok's study, reported in 6.4, highlights this as vividly as any).

Now it may have been apparent to the reader that my enthusiasm in Chapter 6 for the idea of narrative text as decontextualized remained qualified. The qualification chiefly has to do with avoiding giving the impression, which the term 'decontextualization' might do, that narratives are interpretable, can stand on their own, without reference to the background assumptions and values of the community out of which they arise. That is why, in the previous paragraph, I write of decontextualized narratives as texts freed from *intense* reliance on shared background knowledge: I wanted to imply that a more general assumption of shared background knowledge is always relied upon.

Thus a child can learn to decontextualize to the extent of telling us that 'Billy' is his pet budgie, so that the removed addressee can make sense of an otherwise ambiguous or opaque story opening such as 'Billy swore at the cat today'. (Or, worse, 'He swore at the cat today'.) But the more general cultural background, in which budgies are commonly pets, are given human names, mimic (often rude) words, and so on, is simply assumed. There are many cultures around the world where, one is heartened to realize, the story-opening 'I have a pet budgie called Billy. He swore at the cat today', would not translate directly and remain interpretable: the broader cultural context would need to be explained too. The distinction I have drawn here, entailing acknowledgment that narrative text can be decontextualized as far as immediate situation is concerned, but never in so far as the broader cultural framework is concerned, is implicit in the systemic linguistic distinction between **context of situation** and **context of culture**. Notice, relatedly, that these immensely different contexts figure in the diagram of reference types reproduced in 6.5.

With those two types of context clearly distinguished I can assert a thesis central to this chapter: that a narrative is *never* without contexts which both shape and come to be shaped by the story that is told and heard. And I have put contexts in the plural for the obvious but often-neglected reason that the teller and addressees of the very same narrative may assume quite different grounds for that tale being told, and may individually deduce rather different 'points' from the story, grounds for its tellability, and real-world consequences. It is because any narrative inevitably has some effect on its addressees and consequences in the real world (whether or not these effects and consequences are overt or hidden) that we have to recognize that narratives are, among other things, a kind of political action. Narratives, in short, carry political and ideological freight.

In the following sections I have space to present only brief glimpses of the political dimensions of narratives. But by looking particularly at the language of stories in the press, in the legal courtroom, and at the narrative aspect of certain types of cultural commentary, I hope to show that the worlds our narratives represent and make sense of may be politically distinct worlds, with differing and even clashing assumptions.

7.2   Political narratives in the news

To the outsider, journalism has often been presented as a tough, uncompromising, digging up of facts, in the face of all resistance, a purveying of the objective truth of the major incidents relevant to the community. Publishing all the news fit to be printed, struggling to wriggle free of the tentacles of government censorship, stonewalling, repressive libel laws, the disfavour of proprietors, etc., courageous reporters and editors deliver the unvarnished truth. To be fair to the minority, newspaper journalism may sometimes be that heroic. But in general it seems that journalists do not wriggle very hard. The norm, instead, seems to be that censorship, silence, the threat of libel action, the hobbyhorses of proprietors, the need to maintain circulation and sell advertising space, to name only the most obvious factors, are routine contextual pressures shaping what gets told and how it gets told from one newspaper to the next.

Particularly thought-provoking linguistic study of these hidden ideological or interest-group pressures on the press story as it is published has been conducted by Tony Trew (1979) within a tradition of linguistic criticism of text developed by Roger Fowler and others at the University of East Anglia. These analysts apply the Hallidayan system of linguistic description to the texts they study. Since I will be making copious reference to the Hallidayan notion of clause transitivity in the following pages, the reader unfamiliar with this grammar might want to reread 4.7, where I attempt a thumbnail sketch of clause transitivity.

Trew's thesis is that newspapers typically espouse some variant or other of the dominant ideology of the community of potential readers, and have to engage in this espousal (or articulation or legitimation) even in the course of reporting news that is 'awkward' for that ideology. Somehow awkward facts which are a threat to the journal's long-held view of the world (probably explicitly expressed over innumerable editorials) have to be dealt with so that the newspaper's 'background' narrative of how the world is prevails over any local 'incongruities'. (The clash between prosecution and defence 'narratives' in a court of law, discussed below, is in many ways parallel.) In a telling passage Trew writes

Often one can see over a period of days a sequence in which
something happens which is awkward from the point of view
of the newspaper reporting it, and this is followed by a series
of reports and comment over the succeeding days, perhaps
culminating in an editorial comment. By the time the process
is finished, the original story has been quite transformed and
the event appears as something very different from how it
started. (Trew, 1979: 98)

Trew exemplifies his method of analysis in a comparison of two
British newspapers' reporting of a particular incident. Below are
the openings of those stories, from *The Times* and *The Guardian*
respectively:

RIOTING BLACKS SHOT DEAD BY POLICE AS ANC LEADERS MEET

Eleven Africans were shot dead and 15 wounded when Rhode-
sian police opened fire on a rioting crowd of about 2,000 in
the African Highfield township of Salisbury this afternoon.

The shooting was the climax of a day of some violence and
tension during which rival black political factions taunted one
another while the African National Council Executive
committee met in the township to plan its next move in the
settlement issue with the government.

POLICE SHOOT 11 DEAD IN SALISBURY RIOT

Riot police shot and killed 11 African demonstrators and
wounded 15 others here today in the Highfield African township on the outskirts of Salisbury. The number of casualties
was confirmed by the police. Disturbances had broken out
soon after the executive committee of the African National
Council (ANC) met in the township to discuss the ultimatum
by the Prime Minister, Mr. Ian Smith, to the ANC to attend
a constitutional conference with the government in the near
future.

Trew makes two major points about the headlines and opening
sentences of these reports. The first of these concerns their syntax.
Despite similarities of content, *The Times* report is in the passive
voice, while *The Guardian* is active; and while *The Times*'s headline mentions the agent of the killings (*by police*), this agent is
deleted, as passivization commonly allows, in the first clause of the
report, and has to be 'retrieved' by inference from the subordinate

temporal clause. A situation where the causal sequence would have been more explicitly marked by stating 'this happened *because* that happened' is rendered by 'this happened *when* that happened'. (On a cline of causal explicitness, even less explicit would be 'that happened *and* this happened'.) But, Trew argues, even in the passive sentence without agent-deletion, *The Times*'s headline, there is a shifting of attention away from the postposed agent (the police) and onto the syntactic subject, the rioting blacks.

> Looking at this in purely syntactic terms, with the deletion of the agent there is no longer any direct reference to who did the action and there is a separation of the action from whoever did it. This is something that can only happen if the description is in the passive form or some equivalent. (Trew, 1979: 99)

It is worth noting, in addition, that the appended temporal clause of circumstance in *The Times*'s headline, 'as ANC leaders meet', has the effect of implying that some part of the responsibility for the misadventure may be apportioned to the meeting ANC leaders. Deciding whether surrounding circumstances are ever indirect causes is often difficult, and a circumstance that is actually foregrounded in a headline is definitionally no longer neutral background: at the very least, to highlight a circumstance is to suggest that it is rather less tenuously involved in whatever incident has occurred. All of these implications are strengthened by the use of the conjunction 'as', which sometimes expresses a causal connection, at other times merely a temporal relation of simultaneity; readers may attribute a residually causal emphasis here even while seeing that the intended interpretation is temporal.

Trew's second major point concerns the vocabulary used to describe things in these reports. Both papers describe the circumstances of the shooting as a 'riot'. This description – like 'rampage' – legitimizes some kind of firm police intervention (cf. '[peaceful] demonstration', 'gathering'). While not in itself legitimizing the shooting, 'it opens a way to justifying it'. One might also note that *The Times*'s headline's description, 'Rioting blacks', in first position, might be seen as attributing some of the responsibility for the shooting to the blacks: first we are told they were rioting, then we are told they were shot. Actually *The Guardian*'s opening sentence introduces emphases a little at variance with the headline: the descriptor 'riot' is transferred to the police ('police who are trained to deal with riots') from the rather neutral place of the riot in the headline ('Salisbury riot'), while the '11 Dead' of the headline is elaborated, in a relatively sympathetic description, as '11 African demonstrators'.

Now detailed linguistic analyses like that above, focussing on how actual incidents are syntactically and lexically encoded (what kind of process is selected as predicate; who or what is selected as agent of the process, affected, recipient, or merely circumstantial extra; what kind of evaluative categorization is carried in the naming and describing of the people and issues involved; and so on) could proceed so as to develop a sense – even if only through the contrast – of the different background political evaluations of those two newspapers. But Trew focusses instead on the daily revisions to the story of the Salisbury killings in subsequent issues of *The Times*. The next day, for example, the story continues thus:

SPLIT THREATENS ANC AFTER SALISBURY'S RIOTS

After Sunday's riots in which 13 Africans were killed and 28 injured, a serious rift in the ranks of the African National Council became apparent today.

This headline makes no mention of deaths or even killing, the opening sentence only talks of killing rather than shooting, and nowhere here is there reference to the police. The specific manner of death, and the police's agentive role, are quite obscured. Instead, the killings and the ANC rift have happened 'After Salisbury's Riots': if anyone's to blame here, it's the riots.

But riots, we know, certainly have causes as well as being causes. It would hardly do for *The Times*, which prides itself on analytical coverage, simply to conclude that the riots caused these things (i.e., the killings and the rift) regardless of whatever caused the riots. In the story above, with 'Split' as sentential theme in the headline, and 'a serious rift' as sentential subject in the introduction, factionalism within the ANC begins to emerge as the cause responsible for these other undesirable events. This revision, with concomitant presentational reformulations, also begins to emerge in *The Times* editorial of 2 June, which opens in this way:

THE RIOTS IN SALISBURY

The rioting and sad loss of life in Salisbury are warning that tension in that country is rising as decisive moves about its future seem to be in the offing. The leaders of the African National Council have ritually blamed the police, but deplore the factionalism that is really responsible.

The chief point to bear in mind is that *The Times*'s version of events is (a) partial and (b) changing over time. The thrust of this analysis, and of this whole chapter, is that it is naive optimism at best, and alarmingly mistaken at worst, to look to any single teller for the truth. *The Times's* version of events differs somewhat from *The Guardian*'s, which differs from Trew's own comments –

> Police statements and other reports make clear that what sparked 'the riot' was not a conflict between 'rival groups of demonstrators', but conflict between police and demonstrators, especially after police dogs were brought in. (Trew, 1979: 103)

– which differ from the *Tanzanian Daily News* editorial that he quotes:

COMMENT

Rhodesia's white supremacist police had a field day on Sunday when they opened fire and killed thirteen unarmed Africans, in two different actions in Salisbury; and wounded many others. Their pretext was that the men had been rioting.

(Even more starkly, the *Tanzanian Daily News* headline on the incident ran RACISTS MURDER ZIMBABWEANS.)

We have to recognize that although the truth *may* be single, reports of the truth are always plural, mutually inconsistent, partial. Accordingly, for many readers, the collocations 'true account' and 'true story' advertise the incompleteness they attempt to deny. The upshot of this is that, like detectives investigating a crime, we are well advised to inspect a multiplicity of narrative opinions about those incidents that affect our lives directly, so that a range of recapitulations and evaluations are given, in the legal phrase, 'a fair hearing'. But there are very strong impulses in the other direction, made more compelling by the pressures and limitations on our time and energy as life goes on. As a matter of self-protective rationality we have to break off from the potentially endless sifting of evidence in relation to any reported incident. Readers can and must call a halt to this political process of review. Whatever a reader's suspicions about nuclear weapons may be, it may be a rational decision when she decides *not* to read yet another exposé of military conspiracy and negligence in that left-wing magazine, or another measured apology for deterrence in that highbrow cultural journal. *Historiae longae, vita brevis.*

Tony Trew summarizes *The Times*'s ideology-guided steps of reformulation as follows:

> By, first, weakening the linking of the agents with the killing, second, eliminating the agents and their action of killing so that only the effect of what they did is left, third, focussing on 'riots' and putting to one side all questions about what caused them, and finally coupling the abstract nouns 'rioting' and 'loss of life', it becomes possible to move to a new explanation at a higher level of generality or abstraction.
>
> The picture [of deadly factionalism] which *The Times* presents in the end is right in line with the view which has been used to justify white rule in Africa . . . The view of 'African politics' in this ideology is, roughly, that it is the site of factional division determined by tribalism, and based on violence and intimidation, with the whites concerned merely to promote progress, law and order. (Trew, 1979: 105–6)

Below, somewhat modified from Trew (1979: 109), is a charting of some of the subtle stages of linguistic and referential-evaluative shift that occur in press reports and elsewhere. We can see here the operation of **transformational** processes which are transformational in a much broader discoursal sense than that denoted by that term in the phrase 'transformational syntax'. Discoursal transformation is the exploiting of the possibilities of reformulating sentences, lexically and syntactically, so that semantic alteration is effected.

Narrative discourse transformations

1 An initial representation of a key event may use a transitive material process clause, that is to say, a clause containing a verbal process done by one participant to another. Active voice, the normal and simpler ordering, places the agent as subject, followed by the process undergone, followed by the affected entity as object, e.g.

Police shoot Africans

A common variant of this is the complex transitive clause where an attribute or condition of the affected, perhaps arising as a result of the process stated, is also mentioned:

Police shoot Africans dead

2 By passivization the affected participant is brought to the focal subject position in the sequence, and the semantic agent can optionally be deleted:

Africans (are) shot dead (by the police)

With reference to informativeness, the reformulation says less: we no longer have an indication of the cause or agent of the process of shooting.

3 An (agentless) passivized complex- or transitive clause can be supplanted by an intransitive clause (in an older terminology, an intransitive verb) relatively smoothly. Typically, both clauses will have the structure S-P-(A), and while there may have to be a change of lexical verb the new verb choice can be close in meaning to the original:

Africans shot dead (in Salisbury riot)

Africans die (in Salisbury riot)

The affected participant formerly in object position is now the sole stated participant, occupying subject position, and the former description of a causal relation, what x did to y, is now simply a report of what happened to y, or even, of what y 'does'.

4 Finally the sense of 'shooting dead' or 'dying' as experienced processes can be further attenuated in a transformation which recasts the whole process as a noun phrase:

The deaths of 13 Africans

This reformulation distracts the reader's attention even further from reflecting on whether these deaths were killings or not, and if so who the killers were. Nominalization transformations such as this recast an implicit process into the form of a static condition or thing. This nominal condition or thing can now be used as the agent or affected participant or carrier of some *other* process, now become the focus of our attention:

Factionalism caused the deaths of 13 Africans

The deaths of 13 Africans are deeply to be regretted

The deaths of 13 Africans triggered a further wave of violence in Salisbury townships today.

It is arguable that nominalization is one of the linguistic techniques most relied upon in British newspapers. By ingenious use of nominalization, stories can report the actions of people protesting the current situation in ways that suggest that those actions – and not the situation to which they are a response – are the problem. Protesters, strikers, demonstrators, be they never so peaceful, in their demands for change and reform (of pay and conditions, defence policy, or the route of the by-pass), are a threat to the status quo. And by and large the British press, controlled by right-wing proprietors and financed by profit-seeking advertisers, has little sympathy for such disturbing departures from the status quo.

We may find, for example, that in a British right-wing newspaper's treatment of the 1984 miners' strike particular attention was paid to 'picketing' and 'picket-line violence' and 'uneconomic pits', with relatively little careful consideration of just who was picketing whom, and why; and of who judged the pits to be uneconomic, for whom, and by what criteria. Behind such nominalizations – such is the complexity of industrial society – stand other nominalizations (for example, 'international competitiveness') which similarly partially conceal the questions they beg.

But nominalizations are certainly not the preserve of the right: radical and leftist discourse also has its share of awkward facts and events in the world that have to be assimilated and reformulated. We can expect to encounter cosmetic and reorienting nominalizations in leftist discussions of abortion, of terrorist violence on those who really do seem (to me) to be innocent bystanders, of racist practices within trade unions, and so on. Often no better than narratives of the right, these, too, are often characterized by a covert buck-passing, the implicit or explicit transfer of blame. But this is hardly cause for surprise, or regret: varying answers to the question 'Who's to blame?' are the heart and purpose of all political discourse.

The point is not that nominalization is inevitably 'wrong' or undesirable – it seems to be a vital means of textual condensation in, for example, academic and scientific writing. It is simply that it can be used, in barely perceptible ways, to background that which arguably should be in the foreground. In some ways nominalization is more threatening than the ultimate kind of backgrounding, declining to report a story at all: nominalizing reformulations are still a *kind* of reporting of what happened, usually, with most of the main participants noted, and the 'hard' facts (numbers, times, places, etc., involved) recorded correctly. Given that degree of accuracy, busy readers rarely have the energy or inclination to reflect on the lexicogrammatical slantedness of the interpretation.

On the other hand, it needs to be acknowledged that readers are not dummies: they become adept at sniffing out – rather less consciously and laboriously, no doubt, than has been done here – the linguistic and communicative manipulations that newspapers perform. Innumerable readers, whether of the left, the right, or the centre, learn to reinterpret the incidents that their newspapers interpret for them. The important thing to remember is that these nominalizations can never really be simply taken at face value, that an uncritical acceptance of them often involves assumptions about who has caused what in the world, and why, that we wouldn't be happy to endorse. Thus we can and sometimes should 'unpick' such phrases, working back to the underlying process, with its participants and circumstances, so as to see what a particular narrative version of events is tacitly committed to.

Cumulatively, through a lengthy text, and across a series of stories filed over days and weeks on the same issue, and given the likely congruence of a newspaper's treatment of the particular issue with their treatment of a broader grouping of issues, the effect of enforcing and reinforcing a particular view of the world can be almost irresistible. George Orwell's novel *1984* dramatizes these efforts of world-view construction and reconstruction at a tyrannical and conscious extreme. However, as I have argued since the preface of this book, narratives are also enabling props as well as insidious reconstructions. Accordingly, and bearing in mind that ideological perspectivism in language-use is inescapable, we should recognize the good side of stories in the press, be it *The Times* on Rhodesia or the Falklands, *The Daily Telegraph* – or *The Morning Star* – on the miners' strike. This is that readers of such journals are afforded *some* interpretation, some halfway coherent construction of what is past, present and to come in the larger world around them. And obviously these constructions are supplied far more rapidly and presented far more effectively than any individual reader could manage on her own. It makes sense, then, for a certain kind of Conservative-voting middle-class non-feminist reader to be nourished daily by the sense of the world that *The Daily Telegraph* makes, and, *mutatis mutandis*, for certain kinds of leftists to be fed daily by *The Morning Star*.

I have argued that the press narratives that construe and reconstrue newsworthy facts and events (both awkward and convenient) so that these jib with the 'macro-story' of a newspaper's broader view of the world are themselves a sequence of tellings in which changes of emphasis, over time, are very likely. We cannot always safely predict that a particular paper's angle on an issue or story will stay constant – as Trew's very local example shows. But the world has moved on a long way since the Salisbury killings of June 1975 that Trew discusses, and it would be interesting to chart the shifts in *The Times*'s own broader account of 'the Zimbabwe story'. One might take shifts and revisions in the presentation of just one participant, for instance, by way of illumination.

What sort of character, for example, did *The Times* construe Robert Mugabe to be, over the years from 1975 to 1987? My impression is that, along with many other conservative journals, *The Times* first cast Mugabe as a Marxist ideologue presiding over senseless terrorist violence, bent on the annihilation of the white factions in Africa, and impervious to conciliatory dialogue. After the Whitehall conference, however, in which ZANU participated – and especially after the substantially free and fair democratic elections in which, to the surprise of many western commentators, Mugabe emerged a clear victor over Nkomo and Muzorewa – it was, quite literally, a different story. Now Mugabe appeared reasonable after all, educated and religious: his two western degrees were emphasized, as was his devout Catholicism. More recently yet, there has been a very definite cooling towards Mugabe and the new order in Zimbabwe as stories have emerged of inter-tribal persecution and sharp control of political opposition. (Notice my nominalizations of those events that undoubtedly have agents and affecteds: I nominalize since I have neither the time nor the knowledge to offer useful comment on the nexus of causes, inside and outside Zimbabwe, of these phenomena.)

What all those impressions of fluctuating characterization suggest is that either Mugabe has changed his tune rather often or *The Times* has changed its. I suspect the latter. If Mugabe were a character in a novel, we would regard such drastic shifts in presentation as reflecting a grossly unreliable, if not incompetent, narrator, who doesn't seem to know his own story. But this is one major way in which press narratives differ from literary ones.

Unlike a literary narrative, press narratives are never 'finished': there is always tomorrow's edition, which may have to assimilate new and awkard events, even to the extent of revising the newspaper's background construction of events. The conclusion one is tempted to draw is *caveat lector:* let the reader beware. Newspapers – like governments – often do not know what they're talking about; their macro-narratives are interpretations of the past and 'authoritative' predictions about the future, but the future is a foreign country, ill-understood, so that reading newspapers for the truth is in part at least a bit like religious belief – an act of faith.

7.3   The linguistic apparatus of political emphasis: notes on the basic toolkit

A fuller rehearsal of the linguistic features it seems sensible to examine when analyzing the political orientation of a narrative might now be useful. Below is an annotated listing of some of the most important lexicogrammatical systems where choice of formulation, or 'slant', is possible.

1 Following Halliday's account of clause transitivity as the representation of reality (see 4.7), it seems reasonable to look at just which entities are presented as participants in a text's representation of events. Before we consider the tendency of one individual or group to be agentive, and the tendency of other individuals to be the affected, we should first consider who these individuals are that are presented as the major participants. There are many ways, for example, of telling the story of the 1984 Briitsh coalminers' strike. Some versions will have Mr Ian Macgregor (of the National Coal Board) and Mr Arthur Scargill (of the National Union of Mineworkers) as very prominent participants, with little or no mention of the government or of Mrs Thatcher, the then Prime Minister. Those versions are just one partial way of representing things, contestable by other (partial) ways. The point is simply that there may be hidden or neglected participants in events who never get textual mention or attention.

If we attempt to assess just who turns up as a participant, we should do the same for the processes in which they engage: the process choices between material action, mental processing, the expression of relational connection, and of behavioural and verbal process, are highly significant choices. Consider the miners' strike again: was it chiefly a physical battle (as the abundant television coverage of picket-line confrontations would suggest) or a battle of wills? It was a combination of both, of course, for each side: but did one dimension predominate? The media, in their pursuit of exciting copy and a more dramatic portrait of the day's happenings, are surely likely to represent matters in a more material and less mental way than might be the case. The success or failure of various campaigns (military, industrial, terrorist) may have even more to do with winning hearts and minds than we tend to think. Or it may be that the dominant party seeks to reinforce whatever physical/material advantage they have, by their emphasis on that advantage in their statements (= stories) to the press, so that mental (and verbal) opposition is worn down. These are highly speculative comments, but they seem to me to be important issues to do with textual presentation – and they are issues that a Hallidayan anatomy of transitivity enables us to explore.

Finally, we should not neglect circumstantial elements in the clause of narrative. Circumstances can extenuate or incriminate and, as noted earlier, they often have more to do with underlying causes than is first apparent. In the case of the controversial sinking of the *General Belgrano* during the Falklands war, discussed below in the 'notes and exercises' section, a number of surrounding circumstances that might influence one's evaluation of the action were absent or variably presented in initial reports. For example, just where was the *Belgrano* in relation to the British 200-mile exclusion zone; in which direction was it steaming; how close to British ships was it at the time of the attack; how near to it were other Argentine naval vessels (which might have rescued the crew); and how long did it take to sink?

2 Passivization, especially with agent-deletion (discussed in 7.2).

3 Suppletion of agentless passives by intransitive clauses (clauses with the semantic pattern of an affected participant followed by the process that participant has experienced).

4 Nominalization: recasting what is intrinsically a process in the syntactic form of a noun phrase, hence giving the impression that it is simply a thing, a participant in some *other*, more directly relevant, process.

5 Modality and evaluation: modality is to do with the qualifications of, especially, the probability or the obligatoriness of

something being the case or of something happening, using modal verbs and adverbs, and a range of clausal devices (*It is very likely that, It is vital that*). Modality is the most grammatically structured end of teller evaluation, indicating a teller's confidence about, or degree of commitment to, particular propositions (for further discussion see Note 1, on grammatical metaphor, at the end of this chapter). Use of teller-expressive verbs and adjectives are a more pervasive means of narrative evaluation ('My mother unloaded some ghastly perfume someone must have given her onto me for my birthday present last week'). We have seen both modality and adjectival elaboration figuring in Labov's treatment of evaluation in Chapter 5.

6 Namings and descriptions (of participants and processes): in the Salisbury story, were the affected group rioters, demonstrators, or troublemakers; were they a unified group or was there a ruthless, violent minority amongst the majority; were those actually shot representative of the entire group, or innocent bystanders, or ringleaders, or what? Were the police ordinary police or special police, black or white or mixed or both-but-stratified; if special, special in what way? If trained to deal with riots, trained by whom, with what objectives? How many police actually opened fire, or was it just a few young, nervous recruits, or just a few bloodthirsty old stagers? All the foregoing descriptions carry some interpretative and political charge, all are possible descriptions of the incident, and in the most salient areas of political contention in our societies journalists – like the rest of us – have rich inventories of overlapping descriptors to choose from as they sort out which characterization fits their (ideologically contextualized) account of things best.

In every arena of potential political contention and ideological discrimination we will find a rich inventory of standard alternative descriptions: *terrorist, criminal, nationalist, freedom fighter*, etc. Such different ways of describing mean you often end up with startlingly different messages. As Sykes (1985: 85) suggests, even seemingly innocuous differences in lexical treatment as in the sentence below

Black females have the same natural intelligence as white women.

will be understandably heard as demeaning of the black participants so described, despite the proposition's assertion of intellectual equality. Quite often, however, it seems that there are lexical 'gaps' in the vocabulary standardly available for describing events and participants. Take the case of workers going on a one-day strike: how might the strike's proponents best describe their action? One common description, 'day of industrial action', seems particularly ill-advised, a kind of ready-supplied ammunition for critics who, quite reasonably, point out that such occasions are days of industrial *inaction*. Alternatively, nominalizations like 'one-day stoppage' (which gives no kind of purpose to the action) and 'one-day strike' draw some attention to those doing the striking, but fail to implicate any other party or circumstances as the true causes of the stoppage. Some unionists like the emphasis on workers as powerful, as having some control over production, that phrases like 'industrial action' and 'day of protest' suggest. But that in itself may be bad strategy when your narrative is to be taken up by the likes of *The Daily Telegraph* and the BBC. There really does seem to be something of a lexical-descriptive gap here, with no standard pithy expression that would represent the one-day stoppage as a demonstration of desire for reform of, typically, the management's injustice.

To consider lexical gaps is to consider single lexical points in a text. But it is important also to look at the lexis of stories more holistically, and consider what kind or kinds of lexis predominate and recur. Is the lexis abstract or concrete, and in either case, which kind of domain is it standardly used to refer to? Matches and mismatches (intentional or otherwise) between the basic message to be conveyed and the language used to convey it can rapidly be uncovered in this way. There are umpteen texts which argue for peace and reconciliation (between the classes, or the races, or whomever), but do so using networks of lexical items that ordinarily articulate violence and aggression ('We must *smash* through the ignorance that divides class from class, and *mobilize* the *battalions* to *fight* for international harmony', and so on).

In a parallel way, it is quite possible to write up the life story of a physically or mentally handicapped individual with abundant use of lexis ordinarily used with reference to juvenile delinquents, and so give a very slanted account. This is one of the things J. M. Coetzee does at the opening of his magnificent novel, *The Life and Times of Michael K*. Here he is describing the childhood treatment of Michael K, a child born with a hare lip:

Because of his disfigurement and because his mind was not

quick, Michael was taken out of school after a short trial and committed to the protection of Huis Norenius in Faure, where at the expense of the state he spent the rest of his childhood in the company of other variously afflicted and unfortunate children learning the elements of reading, writing, counting, sweeping, scrubbing, bedmaking, dishwashing, basketweaving, woodwork and digging.

This writing – in a tradition once dominated by Dickens – is both savage and ironical, and serves as as good a reminder as any that in our linguistic analyses of ideological sympathies and antipathies we must always be alert to an ironical intent. It *is* possible for *The Morning Star* to publish a report that looks to all intents and purposes an extreme right-wing evaluation of workers as subcriminal layabouts. In the face of such lexical treatment (and given its context of having appeared in *The Morning Star*) we may have to look for much smaller textual clues than trends in lexis or transitivity for confirmation that such a story is not to be taken at face value, and is, rather, a veiled mockery of such right-wing thinking.

7 **Presupposition**: this is the term used to describe a speaker's backgrounding, in his utterance, of certain of his assumptions. This backgrounding is of a rather specific and 'encoded' sort: the background assumptions are directly retrievable from the utterance that is asserted. If I ask:

Is the choir practice on Tusday?

I *presuppose* (and assume my addressee accepts or knows) that there is a choir and there is a choir practice: I just want to know on which day the practice will take place. I treat the claims that there is a choir and there is a choir practice as background knowledge. But this happens to be a rather special kind of background knowledge since it is actually encoded in my utterance. Very importantly, these encoded aspects of background knowledge, or presuppositions, remain presupposed even when the utterance is negated. The utterance

Isn't the choir practice on Tuesday?

still presupposes there is a choir and there is to be a choir practice.

It would be impossible to do justice here to the topic of presupposition use in political narratives. Their most strategic use of this is in the expressing on record (but in the background, as if they were uncontroversial facts known and agreed to by the addressee) of propositions that might be highly controversial. In:

> British industrial relations entered a period of relative quiet in 1985, when mindless disruption of the economy was faced down with the defeat of the miners' strike.

the reader's attention is directed first and foremost to the main proposition here, about industrial 'quiet' in Britain since 1985. Because this main claim is fairly reasonable, it takes a greater effort of critical reading to see that the temporal clause that follows contains a host of highly partial presuppositions: that the miners' strike was 'mindless disruption', that such disruption was 'faced down', and so on.

The above are examples of relatively direct, linguistically-encoded presupposition that conform to the definition I supplied above. But probably even more interesting to explore are the societal presuppositions that we can infer on the basis of the way societally valued or disvalued issues are presented. At the time of writing (June 1987) there is something of a political commotion in Singapore, where the government have invoked powers under their Internal Security Act to imprison sixteen people whom they claim were conspiring towards subversive ends, and using obscure religious publications as a forum for anti-government leftist propaganda. That is the gist of the government's story: no allegations have emerged that this anti-government activity was anything but peaceful.

There are certainly quite different interpretations of this set of incidents, some of which would cast the sixteen arrested, at least, in a far less sinister light. One normal development would be for these variant accounts to be put to the test in a fair trial – whether the Singapore government will go to that trouble in this case remains uncertain. In the meantime, again normally, one might expect some of these alternative accounts to surface in the press but in the present climate in Singapore no domestic journalist or editor is going to risk incurring the kind of treatment now enjoyed by the imprisoned sixteen. All my earlier reminders that events and incidents can be represented in a plurality of lights does not guarantee that such a plurality *will* be entertained: the special powers of governments (not least Internal Security Acts) mean we may never learn all the versions of the story of the Singapore Sixteen, or the sinking of the *Belgrano*, or of umpteen incidents in Northern Ireland in recent years.

In the Singapore case, one pro-government newspaper continues to report the government's position, at length and uncritically, under such blazing headlines as the following:

ARTICLES QUESTIONED VALUE OF NATIONAL
SERVICE
PLANS TO LINK GRASSROOTS GROUPS REVEALED
(*Straits Times*, 29 May 1987: 18, 19)

Such headlines bring me back to the topic of societal presupposition introduced above. Notice that in some communities, such headlines would be dismissed as being intolerably limp, and simply not drawing our attention to newsworthy items. The very fact that the writer of these headlines thinks otherwise alerts us to what he or she believes are societal presuppositions of the newspaper's readership. In the first case, it is societally presupposed that (military) National Service is unquestionably of value, and that to publish opinion to the contrary is newsworthy (newsworthy at best, a criminal offence at worst). In the second case, it is societally presupposed that to plan to link up grassroots groups is in some way a bad thing and, again, at least newsworthy and perhaps even criminal. Or are these presuppositions more the government's than the society's?

The above list of linguistic features to examine in the political assessment of narratives should come with the reminder that these items are not invariably used to construct mystificatory discourse surreptitiously purveying obnoxious ideology. There is a tendency in some analysts of texts to cry 'Conspiracy! Oppression!' on first sighting a nominalization, or a transitive material process clause where the haves are agent and the have-nots are affected. As I have suggested earlier, quite distinct from the possible bad reasons there are very often good reasons for a text to evince heavy nominalization, passivization, modality and lexical elaboration. Scientific discourse, for example, commonly exploits all these resources: not so as to mask and distort and legitimize, but in its own generic context – so as to condense and clarify. But even in cases far less extreme than that of science and its demands on language, it is important to recognize that there will be linguistic complexifications and reformulations that are simply a reasonable way of handling the specialization and complexity of relationships of the world being described and narrated. From such texts we may be able to draw up tables of glaring lexicogrammatical prominences, but they may well not be ideologically interesting: they do not blatantly beg political questions, in the way that *The Times*'s discourse on the Salisbury killings does.

Stories of class and gender   7.4

Besides race, the other two most universal axes along which division, exclusion, and ideologically-motivated discrimination proceeds are gender and class. To put this starkly, the inferiority of women to men, and of the working class to the middle class, has been and continues to be quietly assumed in innumerable narratives, from high literary to low conversational. This is entirely as it should be, it might be argued, since in reality (the reality our narratives represent and make sense of) women and workers have been and continue to be treated as inferior (by agents upper-class and lower-class, male and female, too variegated to mention). On the other hand, since (increasingly?) many members of society are at least uncomfortable with such class and gender hierarchies, those members' narratives may depart, in their treatment of people, from the society's *status quo*. Again using a Hallidayan analysis to specify the choices of process and participant that have been made, we can ask with whom lies the power, in our standard narratives, to do, to cause, and to affect?

To take a specific area as an example, to what extent is the nineteenth-century British fiction still read today a collection of stories of the middle class, by the middle class, for the middle class (or for those aspiring to that status)? Nowhere is this more apparent than in Dickens, with his numerous sketches of the working class, portraits of characters stoical, poignant, and so on. These are 'characters' but hardly individuals, in the way that Dombey or David Copperfield are individuals: the lower orders are essentially the masses, representable via broad stereotypic descriptions – their lives are too mean, brutish and short for matters to be otherwise. Women cannot be quite so sweepingly dismissed, given that a minority of them comprise the middle-class privileged in life and story. These women are conceded (note the agent-deletion) sensibility, depths of feeling and under-standing, but they are rarely conceded power or independence. They are rarely seen to do much, as controlling agents.

Now of course these observations are as perilously sweeping as the generalized stereotyping they allege, but they are at least plausible hypotheses about the norms of nineteenth-century British fictional narrative. It would be interesting to see whether non-canonical fiction of that era (roughly, all the stuff that only literary specialists read today) holds to these postulated norms, or reveals other ones. And as we move on into the twentieth century, 'high' fictions begin to appear that depart quite radically from the above norms: women are presented as strikingly agentive in, for example, Theodore Dreiser's *Sister Carrie*, Kate Chopin's *The Awakening*, Willa Cather's *My Antonia*, and Virginia Woolf's *Mrs Dalloway*. Three of the four novels cited here are written by women, itself reflective of very broad social changes in relation to the enfranchisement of women. That (middle-class) women in the early twentieth century are now permitted to tell stories in mixed company, address written narratives to a wider public (both sexes, all classes), is just part of that enfranchisement.

The general picture then – and I have space only to make such grossly generalized claims – is that even today workers and women are marginalized if not invisible in most written narratives, highbrow and lowbrow. In stark confirmation of this, and of the kind of 'demoralization' that it can bring in train, there are long traditions of stories for the consumption of these marginalized majorities which are all about the exploits of powerful middle-class males. One has only to think of the numerous stories, in the Biggles and Billy Bunter tradition, of public-school boys or ex-public-school men in comics aimed at working-class state-school children; or of the parallel asymmetries of content and readership of Mills & Boon and Harlequin romances.

To the extent that the above generalizations hold, it seems that such narratives simply replicate mainstream reality and mainstream ideology. But there are numerous departures – and ways of departing – from the narrative-ideological norms, whether we are looking at published novels or personal stories embedded in conversation over lunch. All such ideologically non-standard narratives are like 'minority reports' on the way things are (or were, or might be). They express a local sub-group's preferences as being at some degree of variance from the larger society's assumed dominant norms. And although the impression may have been given that such local contestings of the sociopolitical orthodoxies are unusual, it is equally possible to argue that they occur everywhere. But they often fail to be sharply visible because those contestations are themselves heterogeneous syntheses of normative positions on some issues and radical positions on others. Stories can very evidently contest orthodoxies of class and race discrimination and yet remain covertly sex-discriminatory (or patriarchal), and so on: using the list of linguistic features in 7.3 as a guide, it should be possible to identify the aspects of a discourse which represent one position, and those which articulate a perhaps conflicting one.

(Endnote: it is only now as I read over this section that I realize how offensive the conjoined phrase 'women and workers' – as if these were distinct groups rather than heavily overlapping – might be. I used the phrase as a shorter and alliterative alternative to 'women and the working class' – which has its own problems of implied disjunction! I leave this recurring descriptive gaffe in place, as one reminder of just how pervasive, in our ways of thinking and narrating, is a male-oriented 'macro-story'. While composing this section, I struck upon the phrase 'women and workers' and thought 'Yes, that'll do nicely': I can't imagine that, even if the phrase 'men and workers' had come to mind, I would have thought it appropriate or usable for a single moment.)

Prejudice in ethnic narratives   7.5

The sociopolitical partiality of certain types of everyday discourse emerges very vividly in van Dijk's study of ethnic prejudice in cognition and conversation. Van Dijk analyses informal taped conversations with members of the white Dutch majority in Amsterdam, in which those interviewed were prompted to turn their attention to the 'foreigners' in their midst (immigrant workers from Morocco and Turkey, black Dutch citizens originally from Surinam).

> Prejudiced talk is on the one hand taken and analyzed as a prominent form of social interaction and of verbal discrimination by majority group members. On the other hand, it is examined as an observable indication of assumed cognitive representations of ethnic attitudes and of the strategies for the mental and social uses of such 'delicate' beliefs. (van Dijk, 1984: 1)

His study is interesting not least for the way it applies and extends a (chiefly Labovian) structuralist framework while paying attention to important contexts and consequences of these stories: social, personal, and cognitive. The argument, as before, is that the way we tell just what stories we do tell is itself multiply 'telling' or revealing: those choices of manner and matter indicate whom we identify with, whom we distance ourselves from; what we approve of and what we abhor; how confident we are that our listener shares our evaluations (the line between shared knowledge and shared prejudice may be imaginary); and how we wish to update and reinforce, in our minds, our views of the world (what van Dijk calls our 'cognitive representations'). Such stories

> provide other ingroup members with a social 'data base' of subjectively interpreted but socially relevant 'facts' about the outgroup. (van Dijk, 1984: 84)

And those interpreted data operate as models to be drawn upon and elaborated upon by others.

Turning specifically to the stories conversationalists tell about the ethnic minorites, van Dijk first emphasizes that there are rather a lot of them. And this should not be surprising:

> If stories are about people, and especially about those actions and events that complicate or threaten our daily tasks, we can imagine that one type of preferred participant in stories will be those people we consider as threats to our fundamental goals and values. (van Dijk, 1984: 80)

To the prejudiced person, 'foreigners' fit this description precisely: they are seen as culturally and even physically threatening, alien and strange, incomprehensible, irrational, untrustworthy, irreligious and prone to criminality. Such crude and consistent stereotyping means that a Proppian folktale analysis, even without much amendment, fits the negative stories told about minorities:

> The Dutch people are the heroes or the victims, and the outgroup members are the villains. Even the events and the actions involved may be drawn from a limited repertory. Minorities cause us trouble of various kinds: they make noise, cause dirt in the street, take our jobs or houses, or are engaged in crime. Minority stories are becoming a specific genre of the folklore of ingroup prejudice. (van Dijk, 1984: 81)

And as far as the topics of stories about minorities are concerned, just three broad topics, each of which is condemnatory and nega-tive, occur in over half the stories:

(a) aggression, crime (30%)

(b) bother, nuisance (20%)
(c) deviant behaviour (8%)

In general the 133 stories about foreigners (not all of which, be it noted, represent them negatively) have the Labovian components we would expect, with one highly significant exception: a dearth of resolution sections. Typically resolutions supply an answer to the problem or predicament in the complication section, but fully half of these stories lack a solution to the problems raised in the complication.

> And that is precisely how the ingroup storyteller sees the social conflict: minorities cause problems, but we cannot do anything against that. Instead of a heroic success story, we then have a complaint or accusation story. (90)

In fact the lack of resolution, the impossibility of reaching an ordered and sensible conclusion with 'these people', seems often to be the point of such stories. We might go on to speculate that, however well-plotted and well-crafted one's stories against minorities may be, the ultimate point of telling them is not to release tension, to report a resolution, to excite and then dissipate pity or terror or fear or loathing (emotional reactions in general), but rather to use those narratives as *exempla*, underlining or underwriting negative evaluations cast, typically, in generic sentence form.

> They can't be trusted; they eat cats; they send all their money back home; you don't want to go round that area on your own/ at night/ if you can help it; they're not like us; etc. etc.

(Van Dijk does note the frequency of generic sentences in sections of explicative evaluation and of coda/conclusion.) As far as discourse structure is concerned, however, this constitutes a pull away from the particularity and completedness of the trajectory of a narrative, and towards the generality and imperfective ongoingness of a static description or exposition.

Stories in court   7.6

A final arena in which I want to draw attention to the political dimension to assessments of tellers and their stories is that of the law. That, contrary to official assumptions, not all tellers are equal under the law is highlighted in the work of O'Barr and his co-researchers. Lind and O'Barr (1979), for example, report the findings of a detailed analysis (using actual US court transcripts) of the different kinds of language used by witnesses. Their first finding was that

> Many of the most common and important dimensions of variation in court speech seemed to carry information about the power, status, and control of the speakers. (Lind and O'Barr, 1979: 70).

In particular, speakers seemed to divide rather noticeably into two camps: those who used a way of speaking with most or all of the features of what has been called 'women's language' but is better termed 'powerless language', and those who adopted a way of speaking that is socially recognized as 'powerful language'. Powerless language style, first identified in Lakoff (1975), is marked by the following features:

> a high frequency of intensifiers like *so* and *very*; of 'empty' adjectives like *cute* and *charming* and *ghastly*; hyper-correct grammar; polite forms (*would you like to . . .?*); higher frequency of accompanying gestures; more hedges (*well, I guess*); rising (question-type) intonation in declarative sentences; greater pitch range and more rapid pitch changes (heard as more dramatic than the powerful male's drone).

(Powerful language is defined negatively, as speech that is largely devoid of the above features). Correlation of social position with use of powerful *v*. powerless language was unmistakeable: witnesses who were professionals, people in authority, of either sex, tended not to use powerless language features; but low social-prestige witnesses, including the unemployed, did. The researchers now re-recorded actual powerless-speech testimonies in four versions: versions with and without the powerless-speech features, and with male and female actors as speakers. When these versions were presented to judges under controlled conditions, they found that

> For both the male and female witnesses, the power speech produced perceptions that the witness was [markedly] more competent, attractive, trustworthy, dynamic and convincing than did the powerless speech testimony. (72)

The obvious conclusion to draw is that the credibility of testimony may be seriously affected by listeners' (judges, jurors) evaluations of the way that you say what you say.

Lind and O'Barr went on to observe that witnesses' testimony tended to vary in another, immediately evident, way: in the length of a witness's response to a lawyer's question. Some witnesses supplied (and were allowed to supply) lengthy narrative answers to relatively few lawyer questions, while others produced fragmentary testimony – brief answers to numerous lawyer questions. Both intuition and courtroom manuals (which advise lawyers to have their own witnesses give them narrative answers but to restrict opposition witnesses to fragmentary ones) suggest that narrative answers imply trust in a witness. That trust and evaluation is of course the lawyer's, but there seems to be plentiful evidence that subjects in the role of jurors will to some extent accept and adopt a lawyer's assumed evaluation of a witness.

As before, four versions of an actual testimony were produced, varying in sex of witness and use of narrative *v.* fragmented style. These versions were presented to two sets of informants, some law students and some non-law undergraduates, who were asked to rate them in terms of the competence and social dynamism of the witness each heard:

> For undergraduates hearing the male witness and for law students hearing the female witness the narrative testimony produced higher ratings on each dimension than did the fragmentary testimony. (1979: 76)

If the undegraduates' response (ranking narrative above fragmentary, and male above female) simply matches social norms and stereotypes, the law students' positive rating of female-witness narrative is more intriguing. Lind and O'Barr's explanation is that in the 'marked' situation of a female witness permitted narrative testimony mode by the lawyer, certain stereotypes and norms have been overridden:

> Only this unexpected combination of stereotypes and speech behaviour would be viewed as particularly indicative of the lawyer's impressions of the witness, in this case suggesting that the lawyer held high evaluations of the female witness when she was permitted to deliver narrative testimony. (Lind and O'Barr, 1979: 79)

The provocative conclusion of these and other findings is that the manner in which witnesses and attorneys speak in the presentation of testimony – the manner and format of narratives in court – can affect social evaluations of them by those who hear the testimony (and are to pass judgment).

It is possible to treat courtroom hearings as situations in which two pre-eminent tellers, the counsels for the prosecution and the defence, are the architects of two extended and partially conflicting narratives. Each of those narratives is a collaborative effort, with attempts at validation and corroboration from perhaps a number of witnesses, and each is also a fragile and threatened narrative, in that witnesses' assertions may be challenged and probed under cross-examination. The upshot of hearing both the case for the prosecution and that for the defence is that judge and jury are presented with two clashing narratives, possibly with partially divergent sequences of events, and contrasting claimed motivations, resolutions, and evaluations. Judge and jury have to attempt a sifting of those two narratives, a merging which may involve rejecting very many of one party's assertions regarding the events, characters, setting, and motivations. The particular goal that will delimit these activities of sifting and merging is that of upholding or rejecting a specific charge that certain individuals are guilty of criminal wrongdoing.

One interesting feature to notice is the way witnesses are required to state only those things they know to be the case, and to avoid airing opinions or judgments (except when specifically asked to do so, as in, for example, 'Did the accused appear troubled or anxious at that time?'). In other words, judicial procedure attempts a separation of what Labov has distinguished as the referential and the evaluative: witnesses are to provide unevaluated referential reports; lawyers incorporate these in their submission of evaluated, point-laden narratives; and judge and/ or jury decide whether to accept those narratives, in part or in whole.

So the persuasive but inherently suspect narratives (suspect given that, as everyone is aware, they can't *both* be true) that lawyers weave are always constructed with the end in view of compelling acceptance 'beyond reasonable doubt' that the alleged illegal action has or has not occurred. Permeating these narratives are complex attributions of blame, responsibility, and negligence.

What applies to courtroom narratives applies to a large degree to coroner's inquiries and legal tribunals as well. The work of Atkinson and Drew (1979) shows how subtle can be the negotiations of description, evaluation, and inferable intention during cross-examination of tribunal witnesses. One interactionally-achieved feature of tribunals and trials that Atkinson and Drew examine in detail is the construction of accusations (by lawyers, of witnesses). Their close analysis of courtroom dialogue confirms that

> Questions may be designed to build up the facts *progressively* – and get the witness's agreement to those facts – which form the basis for the accusation.

They stress that

> The counsel's *selection and use of descriptions* [is] with an eye to their interactional (i.e. accusatory) purpose, rather than to their descriptive adequacy. (Atkinson and Drew, 1979: 106, original emphases)

Like the analyses of O'Barr and his co-researchers, those of Ruth Wodak address the question of the varying consequences, for example, in terms of sentence, that different strategies of self- and testimony-presentation may have. In Wodak (1985) she summarizes the findings of her analyses of 15 Viennese court-room trials of motorists who had been involved in severe car accidents in which pedestrians had been injured. Courtroom interaction here centred on dialogue between the judge and the motorist defendant.

> The central hypothesis claims that, due to different modes of class- and sex-specific socialization, some defendants will be more able to cope with the authority situation at court than others (e.g., middle-class defendants know the role expectations better than the working-class defendants). (Wodak, 1985: 184)

Wodak notes that the defendant's own version of the accident is one of the most crucial stages of the trial:

> The strategies used in 'storytelling' create a good or a bad image for the defendants. Does the story fit the facts? Is it obviously memorized, or does the defendant succeed in convincing the court that he or she is telling the truth? Does the defendant use technical vocabulary? Is the story consistent and coherent? How does the defendant evaluate the situation? (Wodak, 1985: 185)

Many other factors are also relevant, but Wodak emphasizes that

> It was important, finally, for the defendant to combine the role of a guilty person and, simultaneously, the role of a socially acceptable, humble person. (Wodak, 1985: 185)

Below are Wodak's transcriptions (1985: 186–8) of two highly contrasting actual 'storytellings' – the first from a highly-educated middle-class man, the second from a working-class woman with only basic education:

1 Judge: . . . Now what happened?
  Def.:   Yes, I was in the center lane, because there were cars parked on the right side and about at the place where the accident later occurred, the row of parked cars ended on the right side, and therefore I wanted to change lanes because the right lane was then clear and also I looked into the mirror and suddenly I see in front of me, or rather, left of me, a figure, and my first thought was that it's completely impossible and I was really shocked that this could be possible at all, that now in front of me something to my left, a human being appears, and before I could start braking, the collision happened and somehow I had also realized that the vehicle behind me skidded. With this I had realized that woman was thrown towards the curb and there this was my thought: no further accident, if behind me cars crash into me and therefore – eh – I went to the left. After this, upon later consideration, this had to be explained that due to the deformation of the fenders on the right side, braking occurred. I already wanted to steer the car to the right in order to stop it in this way against the curb, therefore I had the impression that the car was going to the left. I then could orient myself and braked and stopped right at the curb.
           . . . . [after sentence has been passed]
  Def.:   Yes, I wish to thank you for the conduct of the trial and especially for the mild sentence, and I accept the sentence.
  Judge: Hopefully it will go all right in June. Then you will become a professor. . . . Will you earn more then?

Def.:   Professorship? Yes, one can live on that quite
        well. . . .
Judge: O.K. Thank you.

2 Judge: Yes, and what else?
Def.:   Yes, I was near the crossing, suddenly the car came
         from the right, I saw it, but I couldn't manage to
         brake anymore. So –
Judge: You couldn't brake, couldn't you try to swerve
         somehow?
Def.:   No.
Judge: Do you know what that is?
Def.:   No.
Judge: No again. You can't answer this question either?
Def.:   Yes – to steer somewhere else did you mean? Or?
Judge: Yes – every vehicle has a steering wheel. If one turns
         it around, the direction changes, doesn't it? If it's not
         broken. If one turns this thing, it is called swerving
         – to put it briefly. Understood? Yes?

While the defendant's account in 1 is a fluent and comprehensive
story, a coherent application, that in 2 is almost no story at all:

> A scene is described, but no metacommunicative frame, no
> orientation, no evaluation, and no explanation are given. The
> event itself is pointed to, the minute of the crash and the panic
> felt, but no other parts of the story are told. . . . Statistical
> results show that this text type is very common for the working
> class and for women. . . . The outcome of these two trials is
> not surprising: the first defendant had to pay a nominal fine,
> although he was guilty of manslaughter. The second defendant
> received a 3-month jail sentence, although she was less guilty.
> (Wodak, 1985: 189)

Further reading

An excellent place to begin further reading is in the collection of
essays on language, power and control (Fowler *et al.*, 1979)
which includes the work by Trew that I have discussed. For
an excellent wideranging examination of language's powers of
manipulation (in both narrative and non-narrative situations),
Bolinger (1980) is essential reading, while Burton (forthcoming)
promises to be an invaluable source of ideas and analytical

methods exploring 'the sociolinguistic construction of reality'. An interview with the British cultural analyst Stuart Hall, on 'the narrative construction of reality', published in *Southern Review* (Adelaide), vol. 17, no. 1, (1984), 3–17, is a readable rehearsal of the problems the British government strove to minimize – and of unforeseen problems that their strivings sometimes engendered – by its careful and often delayed 'feeding' to the media of its version of the Falklands war. Vol. 40 (1983) of *International Journal of the Sociology of Language* is a special issue on 'Language and Mass Media' (ed. G. Leitner). The systematic and critical analysis of the ideological biases in television news reporting received new impetus in recent years from the work of the Glasgow Media Group (1976; 1980), although this work has itself been accused of distortion. A recent contribution in this area is Schlesinger (1987). On the political aspects of ethnic stories, see van Dijk (1984), and on the political consequences of courtroom discourse see Lind and O'Barr (1979), O'Barr (1982), Atkinson and Drew (1979), and Wodak (1981; 1985). A new journal entitled *Textual Practice* (ed. T. Hawkes) is only one of many that is likely to devote some attention to the overtly political in our narratives (written or otherwise).

Notes and exercises

1 Halliday (1985) argues that nominalization (as presented in 7.2) is only part of a larger, language-renewing phenomenon which he calls **grammatical metaphor**. This is an immensely rich topic for linguistic study and application to texts, and I can only offer the briefest sketch of it here. Grammatical metaphors are widespread in our encodings of both transitivity (see 4.7) and modality (outlined below). Examples of grammatical metaphor in transitivity are the recasting of actions standardly expressed as material processes *as if* they were participants in a relational process:

The guests ate supper and then swam gently.

becomes

The guests' supper was followed by a gentle swim.

Similarly,

Instead of *Mary saw something wonderful*, I may choose to

say *Mary came upon a wonderful sight,* where the process has been represented as a material process *came upon* and the perception has been turned into a 'participant' *a sight.* (Halliday, 1985: 322)

Modality, for Halliday, principally concerns a speaker's assessment of

(a) how probable, or obligatory, or frequently-occurring the asserted event or state is; or
(b) the clause-subject's intent that the event or state should come to pass.

If we consider just the encoding of obligations, we find that there are first the standard ways of expressing such speaker assessments, through modal verbs and adverbs within the clause:

Germany must devalue its currency.
Germany should definitely devalue its currency.

However, alongside these there are metaphorical ways of expressing substantially the same message, but now overlaid with either an enhanced impression of dispassionate objectivity:

It is essential that Germany devalues its currency.

or of impassioned subjectivity:

I insist that you come to my party.

Concerning probability metaphors Halliday writes:

The speaker's opinion regarding the probability that his observation is valid is coded not as a modal element within the clause, which could be its congruent [standard] realization, but as a separate, projecting clause in a hypotactic clause complex. To the congruent form *it probably is so* corresponds the metaphorical variant *I think it is so.* . . . The reason for regarding this as a metaphorical variant is that the proposition is not, in fact, 'I think'; the proposition is 'it is so'. (Halliday, 1985: 332–3)

Analyses of texts probing the multiple ways of resorting to transitivity and modality metaphors have hardly begun, but there is considerable promise of gaining new insights on the construction of, for example, the potted stories of press editorials, or of the journalistic style made famous by *Time* and *Newsweek.* Compare and contrast the transitivity and modality choices in an editorial from a tabloid and a quality newspaper. In what ways do the differences you uncover suggest that the two newspapers assume and inhabit rather different worlds; each paper assuming its own rather distinct relationship with the reader?

2 Working with the descriptive categories discussed in item 1 of the checklist (7.3), Hodge (1979) offers an analysis of the processes and participants that appear in the headlines of *The Times*'s foreign news coverage on just one day. His conclusions are a provocative assessment of the implicit 'general picture of the world' that these headlines assume. The trends that emerge include a broad tendency for prestigious public persons, individually named, to be reported as participants in verbal processes (as opposed to material ones). By contrast the verbal and mental processes of the ordinary layperson as a named individual are almost never reported in such foreign news pages. Hodge summarizes the trends in the following way:

1 Public persons say and tell, they do not otherwise act and are not acted on.
2 Private persons only exist if they are the subject of violent action, but what they say or feel does not exist as news.
3 The world outside Britain is unrelievedly a world of conflict, usually between states, or within states, or between governments and subversive forces, such as traitors, guerillas, anarchists, or (purged) radicals. The conflict is sometimes resolved, temporarily at least, but is more usually the motive for the reported action.
4 Since they are mediated through public persons, conflicts exist mainly through statements and attitudes.
5 Since public figures predominate over private, words and feelings predominate over actions.
(Hodge, 1979: 161–2)

Extract the headlines of the foreign news stories of any newspaper you have to hand. Analyze these headlines, in terms of their transitivity (see 4.7), and draw up lists of the agents and affecteds in material processes, the sayers and processors in clauses of verbal or mental process, and so on. To what extent do you find Hodge's claims confirmed? Attempt a similar analytical exercise on the same newspaper's headlines for (a sample of) its domestic news stories. Which – if any – of Hodge's generalizations needs amending if they are to apply to this rather different sample? Do any amendments have to do with domestic journalism's greater attention to 'human interest' stories – whether of the plebeian or patrician kind? In fact, can we use a Hallidayan transitivity analysis to uncover some of the basic ingredients of what newspapers count as a story with human interest?

3 In 7.2 I suggested that, in British political discourse at least, varying answers to the question 'Who's to blame?' are the very rationale of the enterprise. But upon reflection it might strike us that as far as the broad activity of people causing things to happen is concerned, only the bad outcomes merit blame. There are assuredly threads of British political discourse that are are praise-oriented, political parties and pressure groups telling stories of all the good things they've achieved. The danger in such discourse, however, which I take to be the reason why such narratives are less relied upon in Britain, is that it risks rejection as complacent self-congratulatory tub-thumping.

In general, then, is British political discourse as I allege: gloom-mongering, contentious, recriminatory – in short, excessively blame-oriented? Compare and contrast the manifestoes of two or more of the political parties in the recent general election, or the campaign leaflets of those parties' candidates in one constituency. To what extent are these texts centred on attributions of blame? Is it possible that a different kind of text, which identifies various problems (what is wrong with Britain today) and proposes various solutions, without devoting attention to the sources and causes of those identified problems, might be a more effective political strategy? The question is in part one of which style of political narrative may be more persuasive to the undecided voter. For that reason, it would be useful to test out the reactions of a number of informants to these contrasting styles of political text (using real or constructed examples).

4 The attack on the Argentine cruiser *General Belgrano* was first reported by the London *Times* on Monday, 3 May 1982, as part of a summary of the main news from the Falklands, in a short passage in bolder face, and immediately below the front page headline:

**Argentine cruiser hit
by torpedoes from
Royal Navy submarine**

The Argentine cruiser General Belgrano was hit last night by torpedoes fired from a British submarine, the Ministry of Defence said early today. The cruiser was believed to be severely damaged; the submarine was undamaged and had resumed patrol. The cruiser had posed a significant threat to the British task force the ministry said. The action, at about 8 pm British time, was said to be fully in accordance with the instructions given to the task force commander based upon the right of self defence under Article 51 of the United Nations Charter. The General Belgrano is a 13,644-ton cruiser carrying helicopters and Seacat missiles. It was commissioned in 1939.

Analyze this crucial first representation of events, using the checklist of topics in 7.3, and perhaps considering especially the degree to which the various human agents and affecteds involved do or do not get directly mentioned. If you feel the above report (which is all there was on the incident in *The Times* on that first day) is incomplete, specify the additional material you would ideally want to see in a fuller report. (You might wish to subcategorize the material according to the Labovian narrative elements – orientation, evaluation, and so on.)

Compare the text above, and your analysis of it, with the text below (which you may also want to analyze). This report appeared in the (Penang) *Star* in Malaysia, on page 14 (sic) of the edition for Wednesday 5 May.

WARSHIP SINKING
123 RESCUED

Buenos Aires, Tues.
Argentine Navy ships say they have rescued 123 men from the torpedoed cruiser General Belgrano and are still searching icy Antarctic seas for more of the ship's 1,042 crew.

The 13,645-tonne cruiser, Argentina's second largest warship, was sunk by a British submarine on Sunday outside a blockade zone declared by Britain around the Falkland (Malvinas) Islands, the Foreign Ministry said last night.

It condemned the sinking as a treacherous act of aggression by Britain in violation of the United Nations charter.

The loss of the cruiser has hardened Argentina's stand in its conflict with Britain over ownership of the bleak archipelago. The islands were ruled by Britain for 149 years before Argentine forces seized them on April 2.

5 As emphasized in this chapter, one major means of varying our representation of what has happened is variation of naming and description. Thus every stage of the Falklands War can be redescribed in different terms, with a sharply different political or ideological charge. To start with, do we call the disputed territory the Falklands or the Malvinas; was the Argentinian action repossession, even liberation, or assault; was the British response the protection of British territory and citizens, or a reversion to imperial gunboat diplomacy? Wherever there are situations of contention, there can be contrasting descriptions of actors and events. Some sets of variant description are particularly familiar, and often contain noticeably positive or negative evaluation: cf. terrorist *v*. freedom fighter; question *v*. allegation; reply *v*. rebuttal; answer *v*. refute; opinion *v*. allegation; opinion *v*. fact; answer *v*. justification; national interest *v*. governing party's interest.

Examine any newspaper report on some issue that is evidently a matter of ideological contention, and rewrite it from an ideological orientation sharply differing from that which you impute to the original writer. You might first like to work through the text simply replacing the original descriptions with your radically divergent ones. But you might subsequently want to retell the story in its entirety, changing the emphases on various factors in the story, backgrounding this element of the orientation, foregrounding that explicative evaluation, and so on.

6 The following sentences come at the beginning of a column written by Peregrine Worsthorne and published in *The Sunday Telegraph* of 14 August 1983. The column argues for a new Anglo-Irish unity, with Ireland 'reintegrated' within a new United Kingdom federation. Specify and discuss some of the more important linguistic and cultural presuppositions (item 6 in the checklist in 7.3) you can find here:

Backward is way ahead for Ireland

Even young Indians quite often tell visitors from Britain how much better off they were under the Raj before their country began, literally, to fall apart again. Throughout formerly British Africa the same nostalgic sentiments are also often expressed by blacks disillusioned by the years of so-called freedom.

Needless to say, in the case of Africa and India there can never be any question of Britain once again taking up the white man's burden, however beneficial such an imperial replay might be for the hungry and misgoverned masses of those two benighted continents. But at least, at long last, recriminations about imperial exploitation are being replaced by a new sense of debt owed to the mother country. For in the light of what has been happening since independence, Britain's achievements are beginning to seem comparatively impressive and deserving of much more credit than an earlier generation was prepared to concede.

Glossary

context and **co-text:** the context of an utterance or text is the non-verbal, extra-linguistic environment of that utterance, which may be of crucial help to us as we try to make sense of the text. Context includes the people involved in a particular text, e.g., as speaker and addressee(s), the purpose of the speech or writing, the proximity or otherwise of the participants, and so on. (See, in addition, 6.1.) By co-text is meant the verbal or linguistic environment of any particular utterance or fragment of text (i.e., the text that precedes and follows), which again may be of crucial help in text-comprehension.

deep structure: native-speakers have strong intuitions that pairs of sentences such as the following are identical in meaning and structurally related:

John fed the cat.
The cat was fed by John.

Generative syntactic theorists have therefore suggested that beneath or behind the apparent 'superficial' differences between such pairs of sentences, there is an underlying structural identity: the two surface structures differ, but these are minor rearrangements of a single deep structure. More generally, deep structure has come to mean the underlying and core format of one or more texts (or other cultural product), according to which, with enrichments and transformations that do not change that deep format, particular texts are produced.

deictic/deixis: deixis is the linguistic term for all those elements of a language that have a specifically orientational function. In English, such orientational words include *this, that, here, there, now, then, I, you, tomorrow, yesterday* (also temporally orientational is tense). Notice that none of these words can be properly interpreted without attention to the spatiotemporal location – the orientation – of the speaker. Compare

It's wonderfully hot here today.

which you cannot properly interpret without knowing where and when the speaker is speaking, and:

Friday 26 June 1987 was wonderfully hot in Seattle.

hypotaxis: the chaining together of words, or phrases, or clauses of unequal syntactic status: in each case, one item in the combination is the head or superordinate item (hence hypotaxis is synonymous with 'subordination'). Below are examples of hypotaxis at word, phrase and clause level, with the superordinate parts in italics:

ripe *apples*
the man in the street
They went for a picnic because it was sunny.

Here, only the superordinate material can integrate grammatically with adjacent text. The subordinate material cannot: it is directly dependent on that superordinate material. Cf.:

Apples are delicious
*Ripe are delicious

intensive: intensive verbs include *be, seem, become, appear,* etc., where the description immediately following the verb is to be applied to the subject of the verb. E.g.:

Bill seemed angry.
Helen became a chartered accountant.

Semantically, in such intensive clauses, there is a kind of loopback so that we attach the attribute or description following the verb back to the subject. By contrast, in extensive verbs, no such loopback of interpretation is involved. Instead, what follows the verb (if anything) is semantically distinct from the subject:

John laughed (at the singing dog).
John congratulated the chartered accountant.

nominalization: an invaluable grammatical resource, this is the condensed reformulation of an entire clause (with a verbal process and various participants) as a noun phrase (often just one word). A process is represented as a thing. E.g.:

The mechanic tuned up the car; [for this he charged $30].

becomes

The tune-up [cost $30].

ontological status: the status of an entity as a part of reality, and especially the question of whether or not a thing really exists. With reference to character, the issue seems to hinge on what kind of existence we claim a fictional character has. Does Jane Austen's Emma Woodhouse have a fuller existence, in the minds of some readers, than Jane Austen herself, although we know that Emma is only words?

paradigmatic: a paradigm – in linguistics – is a set or class of words, or other linguistic elements, that are especially related to each other and are possible alternatives at particular points in the continuum of speech or text. The paradigmatic axis of language is the vertical axis cutting across the chain of speech or writing, and calling to mind all the other members of the set or paradigm that might have been used at a particular point in the chain. Look at the opening of 'Eveline':

She sat at the window watching the evening invade the avenue.

The first word might call to mind two paradigms of elements all of which are alternatives to the item chosen. The smaller paradigm would be that of the subject pronouns (I, *you, he, it, we, they*) which could all fit this slot in the sequence; the larger paradigm would be that of all the noun phrases – an infinite set – that could also fit this subject slot.

The **syntagmatic** axis of language is the horizontal one, and concerns all our possible syntactic options in chaining words or phrases together. In the sentence above, after *window*, there is the option to end the sentence, or continue with a relative clause, or a coordinate clause, or – as Joyce chose – an adverbial clause.

parataxis: the chaining together of words, or phrases, or clauses that are of equal syntactic status (the term is synonymous with 'coordination'). Thus any one of the items so chained (there may be more than two) can stand, grammatically, independently of the other(s). The following are paratactic at the level of word, phrase, and clause respectively:

salt, pepper, mustard, vinegar.
the preservation of life, and liberty, and the pursuit of happiness.

The Lord giveth and the Lord taketh away.

stative: English verbs can be divided into two broad classes, the stative and the dynamic. Stative verbs describe states of affairs, or unconscious processes of cognition or perception (e.g., *be, seem, see, know*). Syntactically, they resist progressivization:

(?) I am being very angry with you.
(?) He was knowing Paris intimately.

Dynamic verbs depict events and active processes, and even mental processes where these imply some degree of conscious involvement on the part of the processor (e.g., *run, smile, watch, learn*). Syntactically, they accept progressivization:

He was learning French very rapidly.

synecdoche(ic): synecdoche is the rhetorical term that denotes the use of a phrase that refers only to some significant component part of an entity, when reference to the larger whole is to be understood. Thus two common ways of synecdochically referring to a car are by using the phrases 'wheels' or 'motor'. Other examples are 'hands' (for manual labourers or sailors), and 'have a bite' (for eat a meal).

syntagmatic see **paradigmatic**

teleological: the teleology of a thesis of philosophy, or argument, is its goal or ultimate purpose – the intellectual or moral destination to which the text wishes to bring the reader. More broadly, we typically assume that a narrative will have a concluding point or message, and look for material dispersed through the narrative that is designed to confirm and sustain that point or teleology.

theme: in traditional grammar, the theme of a sentence is the first major constituent (e.g. subject, object, predicate, adverbial) to appear. In unmarked ('normal') declarative sentences, theme and subject will coincide:

The dog bit the vicar on the finger.

although other constituents can be brought to the front, or 'thematized', for special attention:

The vicar, the dog bit on the finger.
On the finger, the dog bit the vicar.

Theme is often important because it is the constituent that the writer or speaker has chosen to make the starting-point of the message, a topic to be commented on.

transitivity: in traditional grammar this concerns the relations that particular verbs enter into with following elements such as direct and indirect objects. Some verbs have no inherent post-verbal partners, and so are labelled intransitive: *breathe, laugh, stroll,* etc. Many verbs take a direct object and are therefore labelled (mono)transitive: *eat, see,* etc. A few verbs always imply both a direct and an indirect object, and so are labelled ditransitive: *put, give.*

He put the record on the shelf.

(On Hallidayan transitivity, see 4.7.)

vraisemblance: this may denote the means adopted in a text to convince the reader that the text is a true and faithful representation of reality. Vraisemblance also often refers to the interpretive manoeuvres readers adopt so as to make sense of disturbing texts in accordance with the orthodoxies of common sense and 'normal assumptions'.

Bibliography

Ahlberg, J. and Ahlberg, A., (1979), *Burglar Bill*, London, William Collins.

Applebee, A. N. (1978), *The Child's Concept of Story*, Chicago, Chicago University Press.

Armstrong, P. (1983), 'The conflict of interpretations and the limits of pluralism', *PMLA*, 98, 341–52.

Atkinson, M. and Drew, P. (1979), *Order in Court*, Atlantic Highfields, N.J., Humanities Press.

Austin, J. L. (1962), *How To Do Things With Words*, Oxford, Clarendon Press.

Bakhtin, M. M. (1981), *The Dialogic Imagination: Four Essays*, ed. M. Holquist, Austin, University of Texas Press.

Bal, M. (1985), *Narratology: Introduction to the Theory of Narrative*, Toronto, University of Toronto Press.

Bally, C. (1912), 'Le style indirecte libre en français moderne', *Germanisch-Romanisch Monatsschrift*, 4, 549–56, 597–606.

Banfield, A. (1982), *Unspeakable Sentences*, New York, Routledge & Kegan Paul.

Barthes, R. (1970), *S/Z*, Paris, Seuil.

Barthes, R. (1977), 'Introduction to the structural analysis of narratives', *Image-Music-Text*, London, Fontana.

Bauman, R. (1986), *Story, Performance, and Event: Contextual Studies of Oral Narrative*, Cambridge, Cambridge University Press.

Bayley, J. (1963), *The Character of Love: A Study in the Literature of Personality*, New York, Collier Books.

Beaman, K. (1984), 'Coordination and subordination revisited', in D. Tannen (ed.) *Coherence in Spoken and Written Discourse*, Norwood, N.J., Ablex, 45–80.

Bedient, C. (1969), '*Middlemarch*: touching down', *Hudson Review*, 22.

Bennett, G. (1983), ' "Rocky the police dog" and other tales', *Lore and Language* 3, 8, 1–19.

Bennett-Kastor, T. (1983), 'Noun phrases and coherence in child narratives', *Journal of Child Language*, 10, 135–49.

Bennett-Kastor, T. (1986), 'Cohesion and predication in child narratives', *Journal of Child Language*, 13, 353–70.

Benveniste, E. (1966), *Problèmes de linguistique générale*, Paris, Gallimard.

Berendson, M. (1981), 'Formal criteria of narrative embedding', *Journal of Literary Semantics*, 10, 79–94.

Berendson, M. (1984), 'The teller and the observer: narration and focalization in narrative texts', *Style*, 18, 140–58.

Bhaya, R., Carter, R. and Toolan, M., forthcoming, 'Metaphor as locally-determined risk-taking', *Journal of Literary Semantics* xvii/2.

Bickerton, D. (1967), 'Modes of interior monologue: a formal definition', *Modern Language Quarterly*, 28, 2, 229–39.

Bissex, G. (1981), *Gnys at Work: A Child Learns to Write and Read*, Cambridge, Mass., Harvard University Press.

Bolinger, D. (1980), *Language, the Loaded Weapon*, London, Longman.

Bolinger, D. (1981), *Aspects of Language*, New York, Harcourt Brace Jovanovich.

Booth, W. (1961), *The Rhetoric of Fiction*, Chicago, University of Chicago Press.

Bronzwaer, W. J. M. (1970), *Tense in the Novel*, Groningen, Wolters Noordhoff.

Brown, G. and Yule, G. (1983), *Discourse Analysis*, Cambridge, Cambridge University Press.

Brown, P. and Levinson, S. (1978), 'Universals in language usage: politeness phenomena', in E. N. Goody (ed.), *Questions and Politeness*, Cambridge, Cambridge University Press.

Browne, A. (1983), *Bear Goes to Town*, London, Arrow Books.

Bruner, E., ed. (1984), *Text, Play and Story: The Construction and Reconstruction of Self and Society*, Washington DC, American Ethnological Society.

Burton, D. (1980), *Dialogue and Discourse: A Sociolinguistic Approach to Modern Drama Dialogue and Naturally Occurring Conversation*, London, Routledge & Kegan Paul.

Burton, D. (1982), 'Through glass darkly: through dark glasses', in R. Carter (ed.) *Language and Literature*, London, Allen & Unwin, 195–214.

Burton, D., forthcoming, *Eccentric Propositions: The Sociolinguistic Construction of Reality*.

Carter, R. (1985), 'Narrative Analysis and Hemingway's "Cat in the Rain"', in D. Birch, ed., *Style, Structure and Criticism* (special issue of the *Indian Journal of Linguistics*, vol. 10, nos 1–2).

Carter, R. and Simpson, P. (1982), 'The sociolinguistic analysis of narrative', *Belfast Working Papers in Linguistics*, 6, 123–52.

Cazden, C. (1981), *Language in Early Childhood Education*, Washington DC, National Association for the Education of Young Children.

Chatman, S (1969), 'New ways of analysing narrative structures', *Language and Style*, 2, 3–36.

Chatman, S. (1978), *Story and Discourse*, Ithaca, Cornell University Press.

Chomsky, N. (1957), *Syntactic Structures*, The Hague, Mouton.

Chomsky, N. (1965), *Aspects of the Theory of Syntax*, Cambridge, Mass., MIT Press.

Christie, F., *et al.* (1984), *Children's Writing: Reader*, Victoria, Deakin University Press.

Clark, H. (1977), 'Inferences in comprehension', in D. Laberge and S. J. Samuels (eds), *Basic Processes in Reading*, Hillsdale, N. J., Erlbaum.

Cohn, D. (1978), *Transparent Minds: Narrative Modes for Presenting Consciousness in Fiction*, Princeton: Princeton University Press.

Colby, B. (1970), 'The description of narrative structures', in P. Garvin (ed.), *Cognition: A Multiple View*, New York, Spartan Books.

Cook-Gumperz, J. and Green, J. (1984), 'A sense of story: influences on children's storytelling ability', in D. Tannen (ed.), *Coherence in Spoken and Written Discourse*, Norwood, N.J., Ablex, 201–18.

Culler, J. (1975a), *Structuralist Poetics*, London, Routledge & Kegan Paul.

Culler, J. (1975b), 'Defining narrative units', in R. Fowler (ed.) *Style and Structure in Literature*, Oxford, Blackwell.

Culler, J. (1981), *The Pursuit of Signs*, London, Routledge & Kegan Paul.

Dijk, T. van (1984), *Prejudice in Discourse: An Analysis of Ethnic Prejudice in Cognition*, Amsterdam, John Benjamins.

Dillon, G. and Kirchnoff, F. (1976), 'On the form and function of free indirect style', *Poetics and Theory of Literature*, 1, 3, 431–40.

Dundes, A. (1968), Introduction to Propp (1968).

Eagleton, T. (1983), *Literary Theory: An Introduction*, Oxford, Blackwell.

Farr, M. ed. (1985), *Children's Early Writing Development*, Norwood, N. J., Ablex.

Faulkner, W. (1942), *Go Down, Moses*, New York, Random House.

Faulkner, W. (1950), *Collected Stories of William Faulkner*, New York, Random House.

Fillmore, C. (1974), 'Pragmatics and the description of discourse', *Berkeley Studies in Syntax and Semantics*, 1, Chapter 5.

Fish, S. (1980), *Is there a Text in this Class?*, Harvard, Harvard University Press.

Fowler, R., ed. (1975), *Style and Structure in Literature*, Oxford, Blackwell.

Fowler, R. (1977), *Linguistics and the Novel*, London, Methuen.

Fowler, R. (1981), *Literature as Social Discourse*, London, Batsford.

Fowler, R. (1986), *Linguistic Criticism*, Oxford, Oxford University Press.

Fowler, R., *et al.* (1979), *Language and Control*, London, Routledge & Kegan Paul.

Fromkin, V. and Rodman, R. (1978), *An Introduction to Language*, New York, Holt, Rinehart & Winston.

Frow, J. (1986), 'Spectacle binding: on character', *Poetics Today*, 7, 2, 227–50.

Galda, L. and Pellegrini, A. (1985), *Play, Language and Stories: The Development of Children's Literate Behavior*, Norwood, N. J., Ablex.

Genette, G. (1980), *Narrative Discourse*, trans. J. Lewin, Ithaca, Cornell University Press.

Ginsberg, M. P., ed. (1982), 'Free indirect discourse: a reconsideration', *Language and Style*, 15, 2, 133–49.

Glasgow University Media Group (1976), *Bad News*, London, Routledge & Kegan Paul.

Glasgow Media Group (1980), *More Bad News*, London, Routledge & Kegan Paul.

Greimas, A. (1966), *Sémantique Structurale*, Paris, Larousse.

Grice, H. P. (1975), 'Logic and conversation', in P. Cole and J. Morgan (eds), *Syntax and Semantics 3: Speech Acts*, New York, Academic Press, 41–58.

Halliday, M. A. K. (1971), 'Linguistic function and literary style', in S. Chatman (ed.), *Literary Style: A Symposium*, London, Oxford University Press, 330–65.

Halliday, M. A. K. (1978), *Language as Social Semiotic*, London, Edward Arnold.

Halliday, M. A. K. (1985), *An Introduction to Functional Grammar*, London, Edward Arnold.

Halliday, M. A. K., and Hasan, R. (1976), *Cohesion in English*, London, Longman.

Halliday, M. A. K., and Hasan, R. (1985), *Spoken and Written Language*, Victoria, Deakin University Press.

Harris, R. (1981), *The Language Myth*, London, Duckworth.

Harvey, W. J. (1965), *Character and the Novel*, Ithaca, Cornell University Press.

Hasan, R. (1984), 'The nursery tale as a genre', *Nottingham Linguistic Circular*, 13.

Hawkes, T. (1977), *Structuralism and Semiotics*, London, Methuen.

Hawthorn, J., ed. (1985), *Narrative: From Malory to Motion Pictures*, London, Edward Arnold.

Heath, S. B. (1982), 'What no bedtime story means: narrative skills at home and school', *Language in Society*, 11, 49–76.

Heath, S. B. (1983), *Ways with Words*, Cambridge, Cambridge University Press.

Hernadi, P. (1972), 'Free indirect discourse and related techniques', appendix to *Beyond Genre*, Ithaca, Cornell University Press, 187–205.

Hickmann, M., forthcoming, 'Metapragmatics in child language', in E.

Mertz and R. J. Parmentier (eds), *Signs in Society: Psychological and Socioculutral Studies*.

Hodge, R. (1979), 'Newspapers and communities', in R. Fowler et al., *Language and Control*, London, Routledge & Kegan Paul, 157–74.

Hymes, D. (1972), 'Models of the interaction of language and social life', in J. Gumperz and D. Hymes (eds), *Directions in Sociolinguistics*, New York, Holt, Rinehart & Winston.

James, H. (1963 [1884]), 'The art of fiction', in M. Shapira, (ed.), *Henry James: Selected Literary Criticism*, Harmondsworth, Penguin.

James, H. (1966 [1888]), *The Portrait of a Lady*, Harmondsworth, Penguin.

Jameson, F. (1970), 'Metacommentary', *PMLA*, 86, 9–18.

Jameson, F. (1972), *The Prison-House of Language*, New York, Princeton University Press.

Jefferson, A. (1981), 'The place of free indirect discourse in the poetics of fiction: with examples from Joyce's 'Eveline', *Essays in Poetics*, 5, 1, 36–47.

Jefferson, G. (1978), 'Sequential aspects of story-telling in conversation', in J. Schenkein (ed.), *Studies in the Organization of Conversational Interaction*, New York, Academic Press.

Johnson-Laird, P. (1981), *Mental Models*, Cambridge, Cambridge University Press.

Jones, C. (1968), 'Varieties of speech presentation in Conrad's *The Secret Agent*', *Lingua*, 20, 162–76.

Joyce, J. (1956, [1914]), *Dubliners*, Harmondsworth, Penguin.

Joyce, J. (1960 [1916]), *A Portrait of the Artist as a Young Man*, Harmondsworth, Penguin.

Kennedy, C. (1982), 'Systemic grammar and its use in literary analysis', in R. Carter (ed.), *Language and Literature*, London, Allen & Unwin, 83–99.

Kernan, K. (1977), 'Semantic and expressive elaboration in children's narratives', in S. Ervin-Tripp and C. Mitchell-Kernan (eds), *Child Discourse*, New York, Academic Press.

Labov, W. (1972), *Language in the Inner City*, Philadelphia, University of Pennsylvania Press.

Labov, W. (1981), 'Speech Actions and Reactions in Personal Narrative', *Georgetown University Round Table on Languages and Linguistics*, 219–47.

Labov, W. and Waletzky, J. (1967), 'Narrative analysis: oral versions of personal experience', in J. Helms (ed.) *Essays on the Verbal and Visual Arts*, Seattle, University of Washington Press.

Lakoff, R. (1975), *Language and Woman's Place*, New York, Harper Colophon.

Lakoff, R. (1982), 'Some of my favorite writers are literate', in D. Tannen (ed.), *Spoken and Written Language*, Norwood, N.J.: Ablex, 239–60.

Lanser, S. (1981), *The Narrative Act: Point of View in Prose Fiction*, Princeton, Princeton University Press.

Leech, G. and Short, M. (1981), *Style in Fiction*, London, Longman.

Levi-Strauss, C. (1968), *Structural Anthropology*, New York, Doubleday Anchor.

Lind, E. and O'Barr, W. (1979), 'The social significance of speech in the courtroom', in H. Giles and R. St Clair (eds), *Language and Social Psychology*, Oxford, Blackwell, 66–87.

Lodge, D. (1977), *The Modes of Modern Writing*, London, Edward Arnold.

Lodge, D. (1981), *Working with Structuralism*, London, Routledge & Kegan Paul.

Lyons, J. (1977), *Semantics*, 2 vols., Cambridge, Cambridge University Press.

McHale, B. (1978), 'Free indirect discourse: a survey of recent accounts', *Poetics and Theory of Literature*, 3, 249–87.

McHale, B. (1983), 'Linguistics and poetics revisited', *Poetics Today*, 4, 1, 17–45.

McHale, B. (1985), 'Speaking as a child in *U.S.A.*', *Language and Style* 17, 351–70.

McKay, J. H. (1978), 'Some problems in the analysis of point of view in reported discourse', *Centrum*, 6, 1, 5–26.

McKay, J. H. (1982), *Narration and Discourse in American Realistic Fiction*, Philadelphia, University of Pennsylvania Press.

Mandler, J. and Johnson, N. (1977), 'Remembrance of things parsed: story structure and recall', *Cognitive Psychology*, 9, 111–51.

Mansfield, K. (1981), *The Collected Short Stories*, Harmondsworth, Penguin.

Martin, J. (1983), 'The development of register', in J. Fine and R. Freedle (eds), *Developmental Issues in Discourse*, Norwood, N. J., Albex, 1–40.

Michaels, S. (1981), ' "Sharing time": children's narrative styles and differential access to literacy', *Language in Society*, 10, 423–42.

Michaels, S. and Collins, J. (1984), 'Oral discourse styles: classroom interaction and the acquisition of literacy', in D. Tannen (ed.), *Coherence in Spoken and Written Discourse*, Norwood, N. J., Ablex, 219–24.

Michaels, S. (1985), 'Hearing the connections in children's oral and written discourse', *Journal of Education*, 167, 1, 36–56.

Nabokov, V. (1957), *Pnin*, Harmondsworth, Penguin.

Nelles, W. (1984), 'Problems for narrative theory: *The French Lieutenant's Woman*', *Style*, 18, 2, 207–17.

O'Barr, W. (1982), *Linguistic Evidence: Language, Power, and Strategy in the Courtroom*, New York, Academic Books.

Ochs, E. (1979), 'Transcription as theory', in E. Ochs and B. Schieffelin (eds), *Developmental Pragmatics*, New York, Academic Press, 43–72.

Ong, W. J. (1975), *Orality and Literacy*, London, Methuen.

O'Toole, L. M. (1975), 'Approaches to narrative structure', in R. Fowler (ed.), *Style and Structure in Literature*, Oxford, Blackwell.

Pascal, R. (1977), *The Dual Voice*, Manchester, Manchester University Press.

Peterson, C. and McCabe, A. (1983), *Developmental Psycholinguistics: Three Ways of Looking at Child's Narrative*, New York, Plenum Press.

Piaget, J. (1959 [1926]), *The Language and Thought of the Child*, London, Routledge & Kegan Paul.

Polanyi, L. (1978), *The American story: Cultural constraints on the structure and meaning of stories in conversation*, unpublished doctoral dissertation, University of Michigan.

Polanyi, L. (1981), 'Telling the same story twice', *Text*, 1, 315–36

Polanyi, L. (1982), 'The nature of meaning of stories in conversation', *Studies in Twentieth-Century Literature*, 6, 1–2, 51–65.

Polanyi, L. (1985), *Telling the American Story: From the Structure of Linguistic Texts to the Grammar of a Culture*, Norwood, N.J., Ablex.

Pratt, M. L. (1977), *Toward a Speech-Act Theory of Literary Discourse*, Bloomington, Indiana University Press.

Price, M. (1968), 'The other self: thoughts about character in the novel', in M. Mack and I. Gregor (eds), *Imagined Worlds*, London: Methuen, 279–99.

Prince, G. (1973), *A Grammar of Stories*, The Hague, Mouton.

Prince, G. (1982), *Narratology: The Form and Function of Narrative*, The Hague, Mouton.

Propp, V. (1968 [1928]), *The Morphology of the Folktale*, Austin, University of Texas Press.

Rifelj, C. (1979), 'Time in Agatha Christie's novels', *Language and Style*, 11, 4, 213–27.

Riffaterre, M. (1973), 'Interpretation and descriptive poetry', *New Literary History*, reprinted in Young (ed.), (1981).

Rimmon-Kenan, S. (1983), *Narrative Fiction: Contemporary Poetics*, London, Methuen.

Romaine, S. (1985), 'Children's narratives', *Linguistics*, 23, 83–104.

Rothery, J. and Martin, J. (1980), *Writing Project, Papers 1 (Narrative: Vicarious Experience) and 2 (Exposition: Literary Criticism)*, Sydney, Department of Linguistics, University of Sydney.

Rumelhart, D. (1975), 'Notes on a schema for stories', in D. Bobrow and A. Collins (eds), *Representation and Understanding*, New York, Academic Press.

Rumelhart, D. (1977), 'Understanding and summarizing brief stories', in D. Laberge and S. J. Samuels (eds), *Basic Processes in Reading*, Hillsdale, N. J., Erlbaum.

Ryan, M.-L. (1981), 'The pragmatics of personal and impersonal fiction', *Poetics*, 10, 517–39.

Said, E. (1982), *The World, the Text, and the Critic*, London, Faber.

Saussure, F. (1983), *Course in General Linguistics*, trans. R. Harris, London, Duckworth.

Schank, R. and Abelson, R. P. (1977), *Scripts, Plans, Goals, and Understanding*, Hillsdale, N. J., Erlbaum.

Schlesinger, P. (1987), *Putting 'Reality' Together: BBC News*, London, Methuen.

Schiffrin, D. (1981), 'Tense variation in narrative', *Language*, 57, 1, 45–62.

Scholes, R. and Kellogg, R. (1966), *The Nature of Narrative*, New York, Oxford University Press.

Scholes, R. and Litz, A. W. (1969), *Joyce's Dubliners: A Critical Edition*, New York, Viking.

Silva-Corvalan, C. (1983), 'Tense and aspect in oral Spanish narrative: context and meaning', *Language*, 59, 4, 760–80.

Sinclair, J. McH., and Coulthard, M. (1975), *Towards An Analysis of Discourse*, London, Oxford University Press.

Smith, B. H. (1978), *On the Margins of Discourse*, Chicago, Chicago University Press.

Stanzel, F. (1971), *Narrative Situations in the Novel*, Bloomington, Indiana, Indiana University Press.

Stanzel, F. (1981), 'Teller-characters and reflector-characters in narrative theory', *Poetics Today*, 2, 2, 5–15.

Stanzel, F. (1984), *Theory of Narrative*, trans. C. Goedsche, Cambridge, Cambridge University Press.

Stein, N. and Glenn, C. (1979), 'An analysis of story comprehension in elementary school children', in R. Freedle (ed.), *New Directions in Discourse Processing*, Hillsdale, N. J., Ablex.

Sternberg, M. (1982), 'Point of view and the indirections of direct speech', *Language and Style*, 15, 2, 67–117.

Sterne, L. (1967 [1760]), *Tristram Shandy*, Harmondsworth, Penguin.

Stubbs, M. (1983), *Discourse Analysis*, Oxford, Blackwell.

Sykes, M. (1985), 'Discrimination in discourse', in T. van Dijk (ed.), *Handbook in Discourse Analysis: volume 4*, London, Academic Press, 83–101.

Tannen, D. (1979), 'What's in a frame?', in R. Freedle (ed.), *New Directions in Discourse Processing*, Norwood, N.J., Ablex, 137–81.

Tannen, D., ed. (1982), *Spoken and Written Language: Exploring Orality and Literacy*, Norwood, N.J., Ablex.

Taylor, T. J. (1981), *Linguistic Theory and Structural Stylistics*, Oxford, Pergamon.

Todorov, T. (1977), *The Poetics of Prose*, Oxford, Blackwell.

Toolan, M. (1985), 'Analyzing fictional discourse', *Language and Communication*, 5, 3, 193–206.

Toolan, M. (1988), 'Analyzing conversation in fiction', *Poetics Today*, 9, 2, forthcoming.

Traugott, E. and Pratt, M. L. (1980), *Linguistics for Students of Literature*, New York, Harcourt Brace Jovanovich.

Trew, T. (1979), 'Theory and ideology at work', in R. Fowler *et al.*, *Language and Control*, London, Routledge & Kegan Paul, 94–116.

Umiker-Sebeok, J. D. (1979) 'Preschool children's intraconversational narratives', *Journal of Child Language*, 6, 91–110.

Uppal, G. (1984), 'Narratives in Conversation', unpublished MA thesis, National University of Singapore.

Uspensky, B. (1973), *A Poetics of Composition*, Berkeley, University of California Press.

Vestergaard, T. and Schroder, N. (1985), *The Language of Advertising*, Oxford, Blackwell.

Voloshinov, V. N. (1973), *Marxism and the Philosophy of Language*, trans. L. Matejka and I. R. Titunik, New York, Seminar Press.

Vygotsky, L. A. (1962 [1978]), *Thought and Language*, Cambridge, Mass., MIT Press.

Warhol, R. (1986), 'Toward a theory of the engaging narrator', *PMLA*, 101, 811–18.

Warren, W. H., Nicholas, D. W. and Trabasso, T. (1979), 'Event chains and inferences in understanding narratives', in R. Freedle (ed), *New Directions in Discourse Processing*, Hillsdale, N.J., Ablex, 23–52.

Watts, R. J. (1984), 'Narration as role-complimentary interaction', *Studia Anglia Posnaniensia*, 17, 157–64.

Weinsheimer, J. (1979), 'Theory of character: *Emma*', *Poetics Today*, 1, 185–211.

Wodak, R. (1981), 'Discourse analysis and courtroom interaction', *Discourse Processes*, 3, 369–80.

Wodak, R. (1985), 'The interaction between judge and defendant', in T. van Dijk, (ed.), *Handbook of Discourse Analysis: volume 4*, London, Academic Press, 181–91.

Wolf, D. (1984), 'Ways of telling: text repertoires in elementary school children', *Journal of Education*, 167, 1, 71–87.

Wolfson, N. (1976), 'Speech events and natural speech', *Language in Society*, 5, 189–209.

Wolfson, N. (1978), 'A feature of performed narrative: the conversational historical present', *Language in Society*, 7, 215–37.

Wolfson, N. (1979), 'The conversational historical present alternation', *Language*, 55, 1, 168–82.

Wolfson, N. (1981), 'Tense-switching in narrative', *Language and Style*, 14, 226–30.

Wolfson, N. (1982), *CHP, The Conversational Historical Present in American English Narrative*, Cinnarminson, N.J., Foris Publications.

Young, R., ed. (1981), *Untying the Text: A Post-Structuralist Reader*, London, Routledge & Kegan Paul.

Index